A Blueprint for Equity-Driven Community College Leadership

A Blueprint for Equity-Driven Community College Leadership

PAMELA L. EDDY
KIM E. VANDERLINDEN

HARVARD EDUCATION PRESS
CAMBRIDGE, MASSACHUSETTS

Paperback ISBN 9781682539255

Library of Congress Cataloging-in-Publication Data is on file.

Published by Harvard Education Press,
an imprint of the Harvard Education Publishing Group

Harvard Education Press
8 Story Street
Cambridge, MA 02138

Cover Design: Patrick Ciano
Cover Image: Govindanmarudhai via Getty Images

The typefaces in this book are Adobe Garamond Pro and Myriad Pro.

To all the community college leaders doing the work of equity every day.

Contents

INTRODUCTION

A tipping point occurred in 2020 that brought mounting issues of social justice and equity to the forefront of public attention. In the United States, the global COVID-19 pandemic spurred a lockdown of schools, colleges, and typical everyday routines—and it exposed and exacerbated existing inequities. Women left the workforce in greater numbers than men, racially and ethnically minoritized individuals became ill and died at higher rates than white people, and job loss affected women and people of color more than others.[1] The murder of George Floyd in May 2020 triggered protests, brought attention to police brutality and the need for social justice, and negatively affected people's mental health. Hate crimes increased during the pandemic, in particular those targeting Asian Americans. At a time when other forms of hate crimes decreased, hate crimes against Asian Americans in sixteen large cities in the United States increased by 149 percent.[2] During the COVID-19 pandemic and ensuing period of crisis, colleges and universities began a focused internal look into their own practices to support equity and their contributions to the larger public good. In response, leaders of institutions of higher education promised widespread change through the investigation of policies, processes, and practices that were reinforcing inequity. In the years since 2020, citizens and students have demanded the implementation of and accountability for social justice in higher education, both as a vehicle for change and to create opportunities for all students to be successful.

Social justice work requires a commitment to understanding where inequities occur, as well as the factors that have led to the creation and persistence of such conditions. Various definitions and uses of the terms *social justice* and *equity* have emerged over time; here, we use Maurianne Adams and Lee Anne Bell's description of social justice as both the goal and the actions required to achieve the goal.[3] When everyone can fully participate in society and is valued for their contributions, they are affirmed and able to have their needs met. Participation, however, depends on an individual's starting point, and when the playing field is not the same for everyone, equal opportunities do not exist. Supporting equity requires providing individuals with what they need to achieve success, applying distributive justice, and changing systems that reinforce privilege and power.[4] Institutions of higher education play a role in not only improving equity but also, simultaneously, perpetuating inequitable and unjust structures. In particular, community colleges occupy a significant position within the higher education landscape and provide a linchpin to achieving social justice. These institutions serve many populations of students through various means, including dual-enrollment courses that engage high school students, basic education courses for adults, and programs that prepare students for transfer to four-year institutions. Community colleges also educate the majority of nonwhite college students, and they provide critical workforce development for local communities.[5] Long heralded as "democracy colleges," community colleges have a tradition of open access and enrolling students who would otherwise have limited formal educational opportunities. The open-access mission is often pointed to as evidence that, of course, community colleges are equitable and support social justice, not only on campus but also in the broader community. What is needed for sustainable change, however, is a move beyond a mere valuing of access to higher education to a focus on how these institutions and their leaders can work to cultivate collective practices that advance equity and social justice. This book is designed to develop equity-driven leaders who will advance the influence and impact of community colleges on individuals, communities, and society.

THE HISTORICAL ROLE AND VALUE OF COMMUNITY COLLEGES

The story of the founding of community colleges, circa 1901, often centers on how these institutions started as extensions of high schools, how they provided a means to prepare students for four-year college and university settings, and how they served as a vehicle to address community needs.[6] The first junior colleges established a new on-ramp into higher education, casting a narrative of these schools as occupying the lowest rung of the higher education hierarchy. Some states with central system offices that coordinate and oversee policies, funding, and regulations for all their institutions of higher education often codified this position. For example, California's 1960 Master Plan for Higher Education set rigid lanes of operations for junior colleges, state colleges, and state universities that began to change only at the turn of the new millennium. The shadow of power of elite institutions of higher education remains fully present today.

Community colleges have also long been tasked with providing increased access to higher education. This goal was prompted by the 1947 Truman Commission Report, which sought to employ two-year colleges as a mechanism to deal with the enrollment demands of veterans returning from World War II who were taking advantage of the 1944 Servicemen's Readjustment Act (commonly known as the GI Bill).[7] Between 1945 and 1960, the number of community colleges in the United States grew by 23 percent, and in the 1960s the number of colleges doubled. The 1960s ushered in a period of mass education, and community college growth exploded, with the number of students increasing from around half a million in 1960 to 2.4 million in 1970, 4.3 million in 1980, 5.6 million in 2000, and to an all-time high of 7.2 million in 2010. In their seminal work, *The American Community College*, Arthur Cohen and colleagues pointed to the fact that this period of expansion in the 1960s saw a new community college opening every two weeks. Along with increased access came the need for community colleges to meet the needs of the masses.[8]

The long-standing tripartite mission of the community college—academics, transfer, and community development—established the narrative of community colleges as being "all things to all people." These institutions were seen as offering a flexibility that their four-year counterparts did not, which gave them the ability to adjust to new employer demands, curricular needs, and alterations in four-year transfer degree programs. Yet strains on the ability of community colleges to achieve their mission have been constant given their low funding levels. On average, community colleges receive $8,700 per full-time equivalent student annually, compared to the $17,500 per student allotted to four-year colleges and universities.[9] Of total revenue, 38 percent ($6,550) of the annual support comes from state appropriations for four-year colleges compared to 33 percent ($2,874) from state appropriations and 23 percent ($2,016) from local appropriations for community colleges. True, community colleges are lauded for their efficiency and ability to do a lot with little money. However, student success has often suffered as a result. The accountability movement in higher education centers on traditional student outcomes and student success measures (e.g., retention and graduation rates), which leaves absent some of the success measures at community colleges, such as serving part-time students and the community. The accountability movement is not built on the inclusion of equity in institutional strategic goals.

Community colleges provide millions of students with second chances (for some, their only chance) and enroll students with different profiles from those of four-year colleges and universities, prompting the need for targeted and expansive support for learners. Further, community colleges enroll the most nonwhite students in higher education. In 2021, a majority of public two-year students (52 percent) were nonwhite in comparison to 40 percent at all public colleges and universities. This statistic is notable because four-year public universities enroll almost three times more students than public community colleges.[10] Such enrollment patterns result in many community colleges receiving designation as minority-serving institutions. This designation requires either student designations from particular racial or ethnic populations or an enrollment of nonwhite students of at least 25 percent. Of the nation's one thousand public community colleges, approximately 22 percent are minority serving.[11] Community college leaders should note these trends, especially within the larger national context as the population base of the United States continues to shift, with people identifying as white expected to become the minority by 2040.[12] An increase in Black and Latinx student enrollment will require meaningful support and representation for these students within community colleges, a fact that leaders have been grappling with since the vast majority of faculty (80 percent) and administrators (70 percent) are white and thus do not represent their student bodies.[13]

Community colleges have been and continue to be positioned as sites of opportunity to educate citizens and improve communities. The significant role community colleges have in social mobility for students provides a path toward financial and economic justice, though the larger achievement of justice cannot be assured by financial gains alone. In the following section, we consider what evidence exists that community colleges have advanced justice.

WHAT IS THE ROLE OF COMMUNITY COLLEGES IN SOCIAL JUSTICE?

Despite the open-access nature of community colleges, researchers and practitioners alike have highlighted that significant achievement gaps exist for students of color relative to white students in retention, completion, and transfer. These findings require leaders to shift from thinking solely about access and the "open door" of community colleges to thinking with an equity lens in relation to student success. In response to the challenges presented by equity gaps, colleges have placed diversity, equity, and inclusion (DEI) at the forefront of their institutional personas by creating positions and centers dedicated to DEI, offering a myriad of DEI programming, and including DEI efforts in mission-critical plans and documents. However, despite these efforts, evidence of advancing equity is less apparent in community college operations, initiatives, and contexts. While campus constituents and stakeholders (e.g., administrators, staff, faculty, and board members) may purport to support equity, few have moved beyond the rhetoric to address inequities on their campuses and within their communities. Inaction is especially problematic for achieving justice when considering the mission of and the students served by community colleges. Ultimately, advocacy for social justice without action will continue to perpetuate a system of injustice, socially and economically.

However, college leaders may face many challenges in their efforts to achieve equity and social justice goals. For instance, even though the benefits of a college education for individuals and communities alike are well documented, public perceptions of higher education are at a low, with public confidence in the value of higher education falling. The COVID-19 pandemic and the increasing divide of citizens along extreme political lines has also raised questions about the value of higher education. According to Gallup, from 2015 to 2023, a dramatic shift in confidence in higher education occurred. In 2015, 57 percent of survey respondents indicated they had "quite a lot" or a "great deal" of confidence in higher education. By 2023, that percentage had shrunk to 36 percent. Importantly in this time span, the percentage of those with "very little" confidence grew from 9 percent to 22 percent.[14] Among the challenges facing community college leaders is the need to articulate a compelling value proposition for both the individual and the community about the benefit of enrolling in a community college and persisting to earn a credential or degree.

Community colleges have also historically been viewed differently by the public relative to other institutions of higher education because of their strong links to the community and contributions to local economies. Yet the decline in community college enrollments in the last decade and their lack of recovery following the pandemic highlight that these institutions are not immune to external pressures and that leaders must contemplate what it is that today's students want in a college experience. One factor contributing to the issue is that a disconnect has occurred between focusing on individual student needs and making changes to inherently oppressive systems that make change difficult.

Declines in enrollment and graduation rates also demand leaders' attention. College outcomes often run counter to national goals that focus on increasing the number of skilled graduates. Nationally, we have seen pressures on colleges because of ambitious state and national campaigns and calls. In 2009, President Barack Obama urged an increase in the number of certificates and degrees held by US citizens to help meet employer and community needs through the American Graduation Initiative. The target set was an additional five million credentialed adults to be added to the workforce by 2020.[15] And in 2008, the Lumina Foundation set a goal to increase the percentage of Americans with high-quality degrees and credentials to 60 percent by 2025. The early success of these efforts is evident: Lumina reported that the number of adults in the United States with some form of postsecondary education rose from 37.9 percent in 2008 to 53.8 percent in 2021.[16]

Achieving ambitious completion goals requires improvement in community college persistence and graduation rates, especially among marginalized students who have had lower rates of success than those who have not experienced marginalization. The demand for change in institutions of higher education is grounded in a period of transformation in the sector, which requires changing long-standing structures and policies that create barriers to student success and perpetuate inequities. The comprehensive reform of community colleges is incredibly important given the role of these institutions in improving college completion rates and training a skilled workforce. Central to all reform efforts are leaders who understand, center, and are committed to implementing and sustaining the transformative change needed to support equity and justice in community colleges.

THE CURRENT STATE OF AFFAIRS

Colleges are significantly affected by the ever-changing and dynamic ecosystems in which they and their communities exist. Current leaders face a markedly different context from that of the pre-2020 days of operation. The COVID-19 pandemic hit community colleges particularly hard, as evidenced by a 2023 *Associated Press* article entitled "Community Colleges Are Reeling. 'The Reckoning Is Here.' "[17] The increase in higher education enrollments historically seen during economic downturns did not happen during or immediately after the pandemic. Since the 2010 all-time high in enrollment, community colleges have experienced a trend of declining enrollments, with enrollments decreasing by 38 percent between 2010 and 2022. During the pandemic, enrollments at community colleges plummeted more than at their four-year counterparts, particularly among Black and Latinx students.[18]

The reasons for the enrollment decrease during and following the pandemic are clear. Students needed to work to support their families; they expressed a loss of confidence in the value of a college degree; and they could not afford childcare or the other expenses incurred when attending college. Concurrently, in 2020, the country was reeling from social unrest and calls for social justice triggered by the murders of George Floyd, Breonna Taylor, Daniel Prude, and many other innocent victims. These events, in combination with decades of persistent and mounting inequities, necessitate a rethinking of what it means to be a community college leader in modern times and how leaders should be prepared, through graduate education and ongoing professional development, to address the pressing social justice needs facing community colleges. Building from these needs, we may ask, *How can leaders balance economic demands, academic goals, and social justice issues effectively in practice to create equity-driven campuses?*

In an attempt to respond to this question, community college leaders have written DEI plans and included equity goals in their larger strategic plans to bring attention to the needs of students and the larger community. In doing so, however, a backlash of epic proportions has begun. In the scant years since the period of racial reckoning triggered in 2020, a full-scale assault has been waged on DEI. A snapshot of anti-DEI legislation in July 2023 compiled by the *Chronicle of Higher Education* showed twenty-two states engaged in various types of legislative action. The *Chronicle* categorized the legislation into four primary categories: (1) limiting or restricting DEI offices and staff; (2) prohibiting mandatory DEI language; (3) prohibiting diversity statements; and (4) prohibiting identity-based preferences for hiring and administration. In the next section, we take a closer look at the fourth category.

PROHIBITING IDENTITY-BASED PREFERENCES FOR HIRING AND ADMINISTRATION

The DEI backlash has been so great that the *Chronicle of Higher Education* has instituted a "DEI Legislation Tracker" website that is updated on a regular basis. The site describes, state-by-state, where DEI is under attack.[19] Among the forty-three anti-DEI bills introduced across the United States as of July 2023, seven received final legislative approval, and seven had become law. Another twenty-nine were tabled, failed to pass, or were vetoed. At the time of writing, it remains unclear how community college leaders will respond to the new laws. Of concern, however, was the initial reaction in Florida. Leaders in the Florida College System (previously the Florida Community College System) issued a statement in support of and alignment with the governor's path for higher education that included a dismantling of DEI-related efforts.[20]

The evolving language used to support social justice efforts and equity has become weaponized, and community college leaders need tools to achieve their objectives in the current environment. What remains unknown is how community college leaders will "thread the needle" of complying with legislation *while* enacting programs and supports to address racial inequities and support student success. Of particular importance, what happens when a core mission of community colleges is under attack?

Given the ever-present barriers to overcome, leaders may wonder why they should care about social justice in their institutions. To start, college completion rates show an uneven pipeline to graduation that suggests a need for an equity agenda that focuses on the root causes of injustice. Data demonstrate that outcomes for Black, Latinx, and Native American students are not on par with those of their white peers.[21] These opportunity gaps threaten a widening workforce shortfall given employer demands for a skilled workforce. But more than economic justice is required when seeking social justice. John Rawls presented two principles of justice for institutions:

- Each person is to have an equal right to the most extensive total system of equal basic liberties compatible with a similar system of liberty for all.
- Social and economic inequalities are to be arranged so that they are both:
    - to the greatest benefit of the least advantaged, consistent with the just saving principle, and
    - attached to offices and positions open to all under conditions of fair equality of opportunity.

The essence of Rawls's perspective is that unequal distribution should occur when it is to advantage the least favored. However, this perspective stands in contrast to the basic understanding of what is fair in the creation of an equal playing field.[22]

Community college leaders have the opportunity to advance a leadership approach that builds more effective pathways for students through college and into a career. Community college faculty and staff, who traditionally may not have applied the term *leader* to their roles and responsibilities, can also take part by engaging deeply with the work of those with the traditional senior leadership titles of president, vice president, and dean. The reform of higher education in general requires new conceptions of leadership, changes in mind-set, and changes to inequitable campus cultures.

SETTING THE STAGE FOR EQUITY-MINDED AND SOCIALLY JUST LEADERSHIP

We advocate that community colleges need leaders—across all positions and titles—to be focused squarely on organizational-level change to embed equity and social justice in policies, practices, and structures to improve opportunities and outcomes for students. As with most broad, sweeping statements like this one, it is easier said than done. Developing an equity mind-set, assessing situations with a social justice lens, and becoming an advocate are each big tasks. And these tasks are not necessarily things that sitting or aspiring leaders have had formal training or guidance on.

Historically, leadership development programs have been short in duration and have failed to recognize both the complexity and the slow pace of building campus environments conducive to change. A scan of current professional development opportunities and resources related to equity and social justice reveals a focus on mastering particular tasks, such as managing a budget, working with the board of trustees, dealing with difficult employees, and using effective communication strategies. True, these sessions often include topics around building a culture supportive of DEI. Yet a focus on diversity alone is not enough and may involve merely expanding representation versus assessing the underlying ways in which structures and power impede the achievement of social justice. Encouragingly, the Aspen Institute has established a program entitled Leading for Community College Excellence, which identifies equity as one of four measures of excellence for leaders to pursue.[23]

Books and other resources on higher education leadership often take a management slant with a focus on planning, budgets, and managing others. Leaders do need to understand how to manage operations; however, focusing on the taken-for-granted systems and processes that privilege some over others does not advance equity and ignores the root of the problem. Focusing on the unseen forces at work is critical to achieving a social justice agenda.

Community college leaders are positioned to advance equity-driven policies and practices, even with the challenges outlined here. As such, this book provides an understanding of what it means to be a leader that centers equity in the ethos of the college and how that equity focus can be reflected in mind-sets, actions, policies, and practices. Our discussion in this text is informed by data from a 2016 national survey of approximately one thousand community college leaders and a 2021 national survey of about seven hundred community college leaders; respondents to both surveys included midlevel and senior leaders. We also conducted twenty-five interviews with respondents to the 2021 survey to dig more deeply into the survey findings. Appendix A describes the data collection process for the two surveys, and appendix B describes the methodology of the interviews. From both the quantitative and qualitative data, we were able to glean leaders' perspectives and better understand how they are addressing the challenges facing their institutions. Various data points are interspersed throughout the chapters, and it is from these rich data sources that we were able to put the pieces together to create a blueprint for equity-driven leadership.

THE TIME FOR CHANGE IS NOW

Colleges and their leaders must transform in order to continuously serve communities and our modern society. The basic bones of a college education have changed little since the founding of Harvard in 1636. Even so, change can occur. For example, while faculty have expertise in a field or discipline and impart knowledge to students, a clarion for change to make classrooms more student centered began to result in changes to the teaching approach many faculty took. Robert Barr and John Tagg first presented a new paradigm for undergraduate teaching in 1995 that shifted the emphasis from teaching to a focus on student learning.[24] A move to students' active engagement in learning and applied learning experiences put students in the center of classroom experiences. We also see, contemporarily, that the COVID-19 pandemic has highlighted equity gaps among students, faculty, and staff and has presented a transformed context that community college leaders are navigating in a way that is indeed creating change. However, widespread, broad-based change has not yet occurred in the structure of higher education. What remains elusive is how to move from talking about change and thinking of equity and social justice as abstract concepts to actually changing organizations to meet the challenges required to address society's needs and the associated vexing problems it faces.

What is needed is transformative change that reconceives current structures and power dynamics, that builds networked leadership throughout the college to tap the talents of all campus members, and that centers learning more directly in the hands of students. Critically, however, there exist persistent and institutionalized equity gaps built on power differentials, implicit biases, and outdated practices designed to benefit those from dominant cultures. The establishment of community colleges as open-access institutions and as "democracy colleges" provides a strong foundation to counter this narrative. But community colleges also have a conflicted past that has "cooled out" baccalaureate aspirations and "diverted dreams."[25] *How can community colleges that have long been heralded as institutions of innovation and flexibility now assume a leadership role in establishing what it means to be an equity-driven campus?* In the remaining chapters, we hope to answer that question by taking a critical approach to the practice of leadership that supports equity and social justice on community college campuses.

Chapter 1 outlines a framework to develop equity-driven leaders. We argue that traditional approaches to leadership development lack a focus on equity and social justice, and we advocate for community college leaders to take on the characteristics of transformative leadership. With this as a backdrop, we present strategies for developing an equity mind-set in chapter 2. We propose several strategies to help develop this mind-set, including defining one's positionality, understanding intersections of power and privilege, recognizing and combating implicit bias, developing critical consciousness, growing one's humility, abandoning a deficit mind-set, and being comfortable with productive discomfort.

Chapter 3 discusses the importance of building contextual competency with a deep understanding of the internal and external forces acting upon the community college. The essence of developing contextual competence is recognizing the interrelated aspects of the community college by attending to people, places (or spaces on campus), events (both internal and external to the college), and the many systems embedded in and pressing upon the community college. Once an equity mind-set is nurtured and contextual competency is developed, a leader is well situated to move toward critical action. Chapter 4 provides strategies for moving from the rhetoric and performance of equity to the implementation of change on campus that will support a culture of equity. We present a host of action-oriented strategies and ideas that leaders can use to achieve more equity in their community colleges.

In the final chapter, we offer a blueprint for how equity-driven leaders can move to larger organizational change that will outlast individual leaders, propel teams of leaders, and retain hard-won changes that have been fully integrated into the organizational culture. Chapter 5 brings together the ideas presented throughout the text, describing the development of a transformative leadership identity that leverages contextual competency, practice, and ultimately critical action. Cultivating an equity-driven community of practice on campus is a final action step. Communities of practice consist of individuals who share similar values, experiences, and perspectives, and we argue that an equity-driven community of practice builds on a campus culture that centers equity in decision-making and action. For an equity-driven community of practice to be effective, space must be open to different perspectives and constructive dialogue. Building bridges across differences and in the face of challenges is critical to the success of this type of community of practice. The blueprint to develop equity-driven leaders described in this chapter is designed to support larger organizational change using the talents, strengths, and skills of everyone on campus.

CHAPTER 1

A Current Snapshot and Critique of Leadership Development

Leadership has been a focus of study in higher education for decades. The historical conceptions of a singular model of leadership have given way over time to more collaborative approaches. Yet the bureaucratic structure of higher education makes it difficult for newer ideas about leadership to become implemented in practice, especially when interrogating policies and processes that perpetuate privilege for some and exclusion for others. There exists a stubborn reliance on hierarchical leadership models that grant power to a few and leave unexamined (sometimes intentionally) the inequities embedded in policies and processes. To change the vision of traditional leadership vested in heroes coming in to "save the day" to one of leaders driving equity alongside others, who previously may not have viewed themselves as leaders, requires new models for leadership development. Understanding the state of contemporary leadership development requires a look back over time, as history always plays a role in current practices.

Community colleges are often lauded for their efforts to diversify their leadership ranks; however, it is important to question what is happening in practice and the context behind the numbers. On one hand, a portrait of community college leaders highlights a cohort progressively ahead of other institutional types in terms of representation. Community colleges have more women in senior leadership positions (44 percent) and more leaders of color (31 percent) compared to other types of institutions. For example, in doctoral universities, women account for 29 percent of senior leaders. And people of color make up just 17 percent of leaders at doctoral universities.[1] Despite these statistics, community college leaders do not mirror the demographics of their students. Most senior community college leaders in 2022 were still white or men, whereas 60 percent of community college students were women, and students of color comprised 53 percent of the student body.[2]

Moving the Needle

Recognizing the slow progress of women attaining the presidency in higher education institutions, the American Council on Education (ACE) launched its ambitious "Moving the Needle: Advancing Women in Higher Education Leadership" initiative in 2014. The initiative aims to achieve gender parity (i.e., 50 percent of higher education presidents identifying as women) by 2030 by achieving four goals: (1) generating a national sense of urgency in the need to advance women into higher education leadership positions; (2) encouraging governing boards and other decision- and policy-making bodies to consider practices for recruiting and hiring women to chief executive offices; (3) achieving women's advancement to midlevel and senior positions in higher education administration by building capacities in women and institutions; and (4) suggesting practices and models that recognize success in advancing women in higher education. To achieve these goals by collaborating with institutional leaders, ACE asked sitting senior leaders to sign a pledge to do the following:

- nominate and promote qualified women to the highest positions of leadership wherever and whenever possible
- provide opportunities for emerging women leaders to gain access to the skills and experiences necessary to advance
- educate others, including but not limited to members of the board, faculty, and administrators, on the benefits of gender-diversified leadership
- empower teams in their own institution to sponsor women leaders[3]

While more than nine hundred leaders signed the pledge after the launch of "Moving the Needle," the advancement of women into the position of president has been slow, making it unlikely that the initiative's goal will be reached by 2030.

A complicating factor for community college leadership is the shorter tenure of presidents than in the past. In 2022, ACE found that, on average, presidents had been in their positions for 5.9 years—2.6 years less than in 2006.[4] A short tenure affects leadership development, succession planning, and the sustainability of equity-related efforts. ACE also reported that half of current presidents planned to step down in the next five years and that 60 percent of those stepping down would be retiring.[5] The recent period of crisis leadership beginning in 2020 may be spurring leader retirements given the heightened demands of a global pandemic. Lingering post-pandemic pressures include significant enrollment declines and the associated financial crunch, which has led to a relatively large number of two- and four-year institutions operating with severe financial deficits and, in some instances, has resulted in colleges and universities shutting their doors.[6] The churn of leaders in senior-level positions requires the attention of boards of trustees as they prepare to hire the next generation of college presidents.

Of the community college leaders who responded to the 2021 National Survey of Community College Leadership for Social Justice (detailed in appendix A), 21 percent were sixty-one years of age or older, suggesting that a large percentage of leaders may be considering retirement. When asked about their career plans, across all positions and ages of respondents, 29 percent indicated that they anticipate stepping down from their current position in the next one or two years. Of the group that anticipated stepping down in the near future, one-third anticipated retirement from full-time employment rather than seeking out promotions, lateral moves, or positions outside of higher education. Presidents were slightly less likely to indicate planning to step down in the next one to two years in comparison to other senior and midlevel leaders. Approximately one out of four (24 percent) sitting presidents anticipated stepping down in the next one to two years versus 30 percent of vice presidents, 29 percent of deans, and 33 percent of directors. The retirement of midlevel leaders affects the career pipeline to top-level positions drastically, leaving fewer leaders in the pipeline to tap for senior positions. This gap "in the middle" also affects the implementation of policies and practices when these typically longer-term employees with institutional knowledge retire and leave the college.

As leaders age, retire, or choose to exit higher education, who takes their place is critically important given the transformations occurring in the sector and the need to focus on building more socially just institutions. Although it may be difficult for some leaders to acknowledge or admit, traditional leaders typically tolerate advances toward gender and racial inclusion only as long as those advances are not too severe and do not disrupt the status quo.[7] Thus, acts of individual commitment, such as signing a pledge to achieve the goal of gender parity set forth by ACE, seldom result in radical or impactful organizational change and may qualify merely as doing the bare minimum. In the remaining sections of chapter 1, we critically unpack the state of leadership development, the history of leadership in community colleges, and the existing rhetoric around leadership competencies to advance the premise that a new approach to leadership is needed to create equity-driven community colleges.

TRADITIONAL DEFINITIONS AND VIEWS OF LEADERSHIP

Definitions of leadership and leadership development programming provide the foundational elements that will prepare the next generation of leaders. Our review suggests that emerging leadership theories are not being widely adopted; rather, a reliance on leader-centric theories that dominated the second half of the twentieth century continues. For example, transformational leadership, one of the more widely known approaches to leadership put forth in the 1970s, involves inspiring others to work toward shared goals using four strategies: (1) individualized consideration; (2) inspirational motivation; (3) idealized influence by modeling ethical behavior; and (4) intellectual stimulation.[8] On one hand, espousing transformational leadership supports ideals centered on moral purpose and implementing the collective will of community members. On the other, transformational leadership is a leader-centric approach and thus requires top-level leaders to initiate change, set the vision, and execute the plan. As a case in point, the 2016 National Survey of Community College Leaders (detailed in appendix A) asked sitting leaders for their definition of leadership. Most respondents relied on a leader-centric definition: the leader is the person who orchestrates change, motivates others, and gets things done.

Data Spotlight: Definitions of Leadership

The 2016 National Survey of Community College Leaders asked respondents to share their perspectives on leadership, and more than seven hundred community college administrators did so. Content analysis of their open-ended responses revealed that 48 percent used language that aligned with leader-focused transformational leadership rather than with some of the emergent theories of leadership. Their definitions were marked by phrases such as "influencing others," "having the necessary skills and abilities to lead," "leading by example," and "setting the vision for others to follow." The attributes, behaviors, and actions described in the responses coded as "leader focused" were suggestive of those belonging to individual positional leaders rather than those they were leading.

A small percentage (12 percent) of leadership definitions focused on serving others. Phrases that occurred throughout the responses coded as "other focused" included "developing," "serving," "supporting," and "mentoring" others so that they can be successful. Many respondents conveyed definitions with elements of a focus on both the leader and others. The language used was suggestive of a shared partnership between leader and follower whereby leaders and followers are equally responsible for success. For example, one community college president offered that leadership is "the ability to mobilize a collective group around a shared vision and to bring the tools and resources together for implementation and sustaining of the implementation."[9]

Several authors have provided summaries of leadership theories and point out the alignment of favored theories based on the context of colleges and universities.[10] For example, the early founding presidents of community colleges exhibited more autocratic approaches to leadership that were "take charge" as the colleges were starting out. And as community colleges expanded to have more branches and colleges connected within a district, leadership approaches adjusted to become more relational and distributed. Typically, the historical evolution of our theoretical understanding of leadership starts with the "great man" theory in which leaders are purported to be born as leaders who then ascend to leadership positions.[11] Building on this thinking, trait theories of leadership emerged that sought to identify the specific attributes of great leaders to help develop these traits in others.[12] In the mid-twentieth century, behavioral theories of leadership shifted thinking from leadership characteristics and traits to the actions leaders took.[13] Next, leadership theorists considered how actions were linked to specific situations. Here, the focus shifted from the individual leader to the influence of the context, looking at how leaders had to adjust their approach based on the needs of the scenario.[14] After "the situation" was included in contingency theories, attention moved to the behaviors of followers. Transactional leadership theories highlight the importance of the transactions between leaders and employees. The theory suggests that subordinates (followers) are motivated based on extrinsic rewards.[15] The focus on extrinsic motivation is central to transactional forms of leadership and assumes less agency among employees. Transformational leadership theory, in contrast, turned attention to the role of the leader's charisma in building intrinsic motivation among followers. Transformational leaders seek to establish a moral purpose that followers can rally around for the good of the whole and focus less on individual benefits.[16] More recently, in the early 2000s, networked leadership emerged, a theory focusing on the power of collaboration and distributed leadership.[17] Tapping into leadership capacity throughout the institution, rather than relying on the original "great man," may hold more promise for change to occur at multiple levels.

Even though each of these leadership theories is often presented as a discrete approach (e.g., a separate chapter in a book on leadership), all exist concurrently in our educational settings. Take, for example, trait theory. Despite research showing that this approach has limitations, individuals and organizations consistently turn to a "list" that supports leadership development. As will be discussed in detail later in this chapter, the American Association of Community Colleges (AACC) established its first leadership competencies framework in 2005, with updates in 2013, 2018, and 2022. Over time, reliance on a list of competencies remained at the core of this initiative, with changes only in terms of expanding the list and including a wider application of leaders (e.g., midlevel leaders and faculty, with competencies added based on career stage).[18] Likewise, the Aspen Institute, a prominent organization that facilitates professional development to advance college excellence, created a "toolkit" that identifies the qualities of effective leaders.[19] As with any list, the downside is assuming that if you do not check off the "requirements," you should not think of becoming a leader, or, if you do, you may not be successful.

Invisible Checklists

The idea of a checklist of qualities that differentiates effective leaders from those who are not as effective is particularly problematic when considering the "invisible" checklists that leaders are evaluated against when they do not adhere to the norm of what leaders have looked like in the past. Ashley Gray identified the "invisible checklist" that women of color face as they seek to advance into senior leadership positions and that makes visible the expectations for how a leader should look and act.[20] Anything or anyone outside these performative norms is often deemed unacceptable to assume the position of leader. The checklist includes attributes such as age, appearance, name, accent, whether a person has any white allies (and whether any of those white allies are in competition for the position), and other perceptions of organizational "fit." As Gray explained, the existence, albeit invisible, of a checklist for women of color has resulted in a need to be overqualified and overprepared when navigating the intersections of racism and sexism.[21]

Increasing attention specific to community college leaders occurred in parallel with the overarching emergence of leadership theory over time. Even though community colleges have existed for more than a century, the more modern form of these colleges emerged in the 1960s during a period of mass expansion of higher education. The founding years of community colleges from 1900 to 1930 mirrored the overall "great man" model of leadership. The early-era presidents had a take-charge attitude as they worked to establish and grow the first junior colleges. The 1940s and 1950s were an era during which community colleges began to form their own identity as the Truman Commission advocated for an expansion of higher education to include two additional years of education following high school, thus beginning the transformation from junior colleges to community colleges.[22] The 1960s and 1970s were a period of great expansion for community colleges, and the leaders of this era held traits of strength and dominance. George Vaughan's seminal leadership book, *The Community College Presidency*, offered a profile of leadership during this time of expansion. Vaughan's description of the expansion-era presidents identified qualities of courage, connection to community, integrity, and judgment (albeit based on the perspectives of the white men who were presidents at the time).[23] The end of the twentieth century saw community college leaders borrowing from business strategies, and the turn of the millennium witnessed a turn toward the idea of *leaders as learners* as the idea of Terry O'Banion's "learning colleges" took hold.[24]

A watershed moment for the study of community college leadership occurred in 2001 with Christopher Shults introducing the concept of a leadership crisis in community colleges.[25] Later in 2001, the AACC published *Leadership 2020: Recruitment, Preparation, and Support*, a report that in part described the AACC's establishment of a task force to study the topic and propose solutions and signaled the commitment of the AACC to help to solve the impending crisis. Although the mass exodus of community college presidents did not occur as predicted, the COVID-19 pandemic, pressures on presidents, and the aging of presidents likely demonstrate that the crisis was merely delayed by some twenty years.

In 2009, Adrianna Kezar and Rozana Carducci argued that a revolutionary progression of academic leadership was underway that would move from the leader-centric reliance on position to a vision in which leadership is process centered, collective, context bound, nonhierarchical, and focused on processes of mutual power and influence.[26] As with the leadership crisis, it is evident that this "revolution" has not yet occurred; indeed, the challenges of the pandemic and declining enrollment have only further entrenched the power of top-level leaders as campuses look for direction and quick decision-making during periods of crisis. By 2020, attention to the influence of the racialized organizational practices in community colleges underscored the need to think differently about community college leadership development as the traditional theories of leadership did not incorporate a focus on equity.[27] Leadership for equity and social justice challenges historical approaches to leadership and offers alternatives for change.

THE CHANGING DEMOGRAPHICS OF LEADERS

The current community college context creates opportunities for leaders who differ from the leader-centric or "great man" persona. As discussed, the study of community college leadership historically relied on male norms of leading, with writing only recently, over the past couple of decades, expanding to include more women leaders and leaders of color.[28] Research has found that women engage in more connected and collaborative forms of leadership that do not align with traditional leadership definitions. Further, community colleges may be more welcoming to these nontraditional leadership approaches than all other institutional types, yet this may be more accidental than intentional.[29] Some might argue that it is the low prestige (in comparison to doctoral institutions, for example) of community colleges that has allowed an expansion of leadership to include more women and people of color. A counterargument is that more participatory leadership is valued and is needed in order to achieve the mission of the community college.[30]

When examining representation simply through percentages across various leadership positions, women and people of color have seemingly made great strides. For example, more than one out of three community college presidents are now women. After a period of relatively stagnant growth in the percentage of female presidents at community colleges, the ACE American College President Study reported that as of 2023, 44 percent of community college presidents are women, a figure that represents the first substantial growth in the representation of women in a generation.[31] However, women still face significant barriers to attaining leadership positions. Indeed, Amy Diehl and Leanne Dzubinski identified twenty-seven barriers, which they separated into those that exist at the macro- (societal), meso- (organizational), and micro- (interpersonal) levels. At the macro-level, gender stereotyping, cultural norms, and the silencing of women's voices all affect their ascension into leadership positions. The list of barriers at the meso-level is expansive. The devaluing of women's ways of leading, the lack of mentoring, exclusion from informal networks, the gender pay gap, and the "queen bee effect" (occurring when women in high-ranking positions treat other women poorly) are just a few of the many meso-level barriers. At the micro-level, women may face challenges in terms of their communication style, and they may be the target of microaggressions (a topic further explored in chapter 4). Interestingly, the authors point out that women sometimes personalize the problems they experience in the workplace. Women may see that the men around them do not have certain challenges and therefore assume that the problems they encounter are because of something about them personally.[32]

The barriers described here are often magnified for Black women leaders. In addition to the challenges that women of all races and ethnicities face, Black women leaders in higher education also face what has been termed the "Black tax": the additional duties that Black and African American faculty, staff, and administrators must assume by virtue of their skin color.[33] These additional duties include the extra work of being on multiple committees to ensure the presence of a voice of color, mentoring students of color, and navigating diversity, equity, and inclusion (DEI) issues for the entire campus. These contributions are often marginalized and "not counted" in advancement processes such as those for tenure and promotion. The existence and burden of the Black tax may help to explain the lack of representation of nonwhite leaders in colleges and universities. We echo the sentiments of many others who have examined the lack of progress among those who do not adhere to the "great man" model of leadership: the collective findings of the research implore that sitting leaders in higher education must revisit policies and practices to ensure they do not serve as barriers to women and people of color who aspire to reach the upper echelons of the organization.

Data Spotlight: Gender Differences in Team Leadership

The 2016 National Survey of Community College Leaders lent insight into how participants' gender influenced how they used the construct of "team" in defining leadership. The analysis found that just under half of the sitting leaders surveyed (49 percent of women and 42 percent of men) defined leadership through some reference to involving people other than the leader. Despite this evidence, participants did not specifically use the term "team," nor did they describe components of effective team leadership that have been outlined in the literature.[34] Even though a large percentage of the leaders surveyed indicated involving others when leading, there were nuances in their responses as to what was meant by *inclusion* (e.g., the leader led the team via the hierarchy of position versus actual shared roles in decision-making).

Gendered language was also evident in the definitions of survey respondents. Of the respondents, 41 percent of women, versus only 32 percent of men, discussed empowering or advocating for others. One male respondent stated that leadership meant "motivating individuals to perform their best within the mission of the department/institution," whereas a female respondent said that leadership was the "ability to inspire others, individually and collectively, to act in new ways to improve the quality of work/life." A focus on institutional outcomes versus personal agency marked the basis for some of the gender differences. Of note, women leaders used the word *team* in their definitions more often than men (19 percent of women versus 8 percent of men), and the meanings provided by the two groups were distinctly different. Compare the example of a man's response—"A leader is able to draw the best out of his team"—with a woman's: "I utilize data-driven decision-making and lots of committee-based analysis of data. I then require my teams to look for a variety of solutions to overcome problems and then we review those solutions and look for pitfalls prior to implementing them." Overall, female respondents were much more likely to use inclusive language and qualifiers than male respondents. Despite the differences found in how women and men viewed team leadership, however, it is critical to note that the female respondents who provided more participatory definitions of leadership represented a minority voice. Leader-focused definitions still dominated, and language about "others" or teams was nonexistent in most responses.[35]

Providing leadership development programs focused on women and people of color offers one means to address the lack of representation in leadership for these populations; however, such programs may do little to change organizational culture. Adjusting institutional policies, developing equity-driven leadership development opportunities, particularly for midlevel leaders, and continuing to question models of the ideal leader are what is needed to open the door for the adoption of leadership practices that promote equity and social justice.

LEADERS IN THE MIDDLE

Recently, and perhaps because of the "churn" of senior leaders in community colleges, midlevel leaders have garnered more discussion in the scholarly literature. Throughout this book, we highlight data from the 2016 National Survey of Community College Leaders and the 2021 National Survey of Community

College Leadership for Social Justice, paying particular attention to the distinctions among midlevel leaders (e.g., deans, directors, and officers) relative to senior-level leaders (e.g., vice presidents, and presidents, and chancellors). An overarching conclusion from the data analysis is that based on position, title, and associated responsibilities, differences in perceptions are noteworthy. And the group of leaders "in the middle" warrants substantial attention as we consider the future of community colleges.

Discussions about the role of midlevel leaders have traditionally focused on how such roles prepared individuals for the top-level positions of chief academic officer, president, or chancellor. For example, Regina Garza Mitchell and Marilyn Amey argued that outdated conceptions of midlevel leaders as managers rather than leaders limits the leverage individuals in these roles can have in community colleges.[36] Leadership "in the middle" may look different from traditional leadership as a result of distinctive organizational positioning; thus, midlevel leaders have a unique role to play in creating equity-driven campuses.

Specifically, midlevel leaders may play the role of a networked boundary spanner as they must interact with campus community members from across the college. Further, midlevel leaders may function as "sense-makers," helping others to make sense of change on campus. Elaborating on these ideas, Marilyn Amey and Pamela Eddy proposed a way to envision midlevel leadership.[37] First, they highlighted the central role midlevel leaders have in interactions with staff, faculty, and top-level leaders, thus making them central to networked leadership. This vision of leadership highlights how the individual agency of midlevel leaders can connect to the larger organizational structures in place. Second, when midlevel leaders can see themselves as leaders, they can leverage the strong relationships they have in the college, gain social capital, and acquire different types of power beyond position. Finally, how leaders are identified and developed can affect institutional outcomes. Valuing the voice of midlevel leaders helps move beyond an emphasis on individual performance and leverages collective responsibilities.

Data Spotlight: Midlevel Leadership

The 2016 National Survey of Community College Leaders highlights subtle differences between midlevel and senior leaders in how they define leadership. Both types of leaders in the study relied on leader-focused definitions of leadership. The definitions provided by 50 percent of midlevel leaders versus 45 percent of senior leaders were coded as leader-centric. Even though this difference is not statistically significant, we did note differences in the language used by the two groups. For example, midlevel leaders relied on management skills and accomplishing goals. Consider one dean who offered that leadership involved "being able to manage conflicts and putting out fires . . . being able to effectively plan and communicate goals, strategies and resources needed to complete projects by said deadline." The essence of leadership as offered by midlevel respondents was a focus on getting things done and following through on direction set by top-level leaders. While senior leaders' definitions also relied on outcomes, the definitions focused more on the ability to make things happen. Consider a female president who stated that leadership is "the ability to set the vision and road map and to persuade others to join you in the pursuit of that vision." Even though midlevel leaders most often defined leadership as leader focused, as did top-level leaders, their focus was solidly on managing others and following through on plans versus trying to influence others.

LEADERSHIP FOR EQUITY AND SOCIAL JUSTICE

In this book, we are advocating for a type of leadership squarely focused on equity and social justice rather than the traditional leadership approaches that have dominated in community colleges for the last century. It is therefore necessary to define and summarize our understanding of social justice. The concept of social justice is interrelated with diversity but also significantly different from how we define diversity in that it requires the interrogation of the systems of oppression that exist in education. In his 1971 book, *A Theory of Justice*, John Rawls likened social justice to distributive justice or the equal distribution of goods and services to all.[38] Rawls's conceptualization of distributive justice, however, fails to address the systemic and institutional structures that determine the distribution of resources. Thus, the various definitions of social justice advanced by scholars have evolved considerably in the twenty-first century as social problems have grown exponentially.

Our definition of *social justice* is that put forth by Maurianne Adams and Lee Anne Bell in the third edition of their book *Teaching for Diversity and Social Justice*, namely that social justice is both a goal and a process.[39] The goal of social justice is the full and equitable participation of people from all social identity groups in a society mutually shaped by all groups to meet their needs. The process of attaining this goal is democratic and participatory, respectful of human diversity and group differences, and inclusive and affirming of human agency. Those engaging in the process of social justice must have the capacity to work collaboratively with others to create change. While all campus constituents have a role to play in social justice work, we argue that college leaders are instrumental in articulating the goal and shaping the process. Further, we argue that leaders must not only lead for social justice but also become advocates for social justice in intentional, clear, and pervasive ways.

Many scholars have advanced definitions of what it means to be a leader for social justice. For example, Derald Wing Sue and colleagues explained that leadership for social justice equates to having the mind-set and taking the necessary steps to end the oppression, discrimination, and racism that have been embedded in educational institutions since their inception.[40] In a similar vein, Eleanor Drago-Severson and Jessica Blum-DeStefano explained that leadership for social justice is achieved through actions and behaviors, as well as internal mind-sets, beliefs, and understandings that align with diverse communities, interrupt systemic inequities, confront biases and prejudices, and work toward more inclusive and just outcomes.[41] And it is through those actions, as well as the actions, behaviors, and mind-sets that leaders inspire in others, that a leader takes on the role of social justice advocate.

Social justice advocacy includes actions aimed at the realization of a just society that respects and protects human rights, is inclusive of a plurality of interests, and is responsive to the most marginalized members of a society. In the case of education, advocacy for social justice can be conceptualized as existing at three levels: advocacy for individuals, such as for an individual student; advocacy at the institutional (college) level; and advocacy at the societal level. Advocacy by leaders must keep an eye on all levels simultaneously, taking action in a manner that engages in a systems thinking perspective to track the influence of each action on each level. Here, using a Janusian perspective is useful given its ability to hold contradictory perspectives at once. We explore the idea of becoming an equity-minded advocate further in chapter 4.

Recently, Adrianna Kezar and Julie Posselt tackled the question of leadership for social justice in higher education administration.[42] These scholars argued that the day-to-day operations of colleges can inadvertently serve to reinforce inequities and that critical leadership is required to build institutions that are more just. Using an equity mind-set shifts focus in decision-making to being attentive to practices that exclude or marginalize individuals because of embedded power differentials. In Kezar and Posselt's edited volume, however, only one chapter deals specifically with community colleges. The chapter provides a practitioner perspective of equity-minded leadership in community colleges. The author, Luca Lewis, used his role as vice president for student services to ground theory in practice and his positionality to point out how structures systematically produce barriers to equity. In particular, Lewis highlighted that the quest for neoliberal outcomes and a focus on the "bottom line" challenge equity objectives. He provided specific recommendations for individual leaders to develop an equity mind-set, including examining assumptions; defining and operationalizing equity, diversity, and inclusion; developing identity sharing and storytelling practices; and providing direct and clear feedback.[43] This attention to social justice in community college leadership is an important first step but neglects the inequities inherent in structures, policies, and culture. Our work advances a blueprint to move individual change to the institutional level by critically examining how sitting leaders understand social justice and engage in equity-minded advocacy on their campuses.

Data Spotlight: Social Justice Leadership

A question in the 2021 National Survey of Community College Leadership for Social Justice asked participants how they consider themselves to be a leader of social justice. A continuum of responses resulted from this prompt. At one end, respondents did not think they were leaders in this arena. Here, a common response was similar to this quote: "I don't. My staff and I do what is fair, which is not necessarily equal." Those who did not see themselves leading social justice on campus were able to identify pathways forward, however. Examples include "I do not consider myself a leader for social justice. But using the college values and our new strategic plan starting next year, I will be supporting our DEI efforts," and "I am still learning, but I make every attempt in all aspects of my life to speak out against inequity." Central to movement along the continuum of becoming a leader of social justice was a commitment to learning, dialogue with others, and reflection.

At the other end of the continuum were leaders actively leading the way for social justice in their colleges and communities. For these leaders, terms and phrases like "advocate," "anti-racist," "participating in uncomfortable conversations," and "challenge traditionalistic views and practice" showcase the action-oriented ways they were leading for social justice. Individuals who served as chief diversity officers noted that social justice work was a core responsibility for them and that one person could not do this work alone. Individuals working on DEI efforts developed partnerships with others on campus and in the community to do the work. Several participants noted the role of data in calling out areas of inequity and reported describing DEI efforts on their colleges' websites and including DEI issues on the agenda for boards of trustees to keep the issue of justice front of mind. Learning about social justice and equity occurred through personal reading and participating on task forces, in professional development sessions, and in the development of college DEI plans.

ACE's work on shared-equity leadership provides one means to think about leadership for social justice. The essence of this work builds on engaging individuals throughout the college to bring various perspectives and types of background knowledge to the vexing problem of campus inequities. Kezar and colleagues have proposed four models to move institutions forward and created a toolkit to help individuals and campuses achieve their desired outcomes.[44] The overarching information from ACE is useful, yet it lacks a contextual context grounded in community colleges. The central mission of community colleges and their origin story connected to community needs can leverage a tighter connection between social justice and the mission of community colleges.

The leaders surveyed in our 2021 National Survey of Community College Leadership for Social Justice provided a wide range of perspectives on their ability to be social justice leaders. Community college leaders, particularly midlevel leaders, are well positioned to increase the attention paid to equity and social justice needed to move the institutions forward and to fulfill their mission. This movement requires a new approach to leadership, one that follows the tenets of transformative leadership.

TRANSFORMATIVE LEADERSHIP

Community college leadership in the 2020s is influenced by the decades of existing scholarship on this topic while also being affected by the drastic changes that have confronted community colleges in recent years. Leadership and leadership development have been researched in depth since the start of the Industrial Revolution and the expansion of organizational structures that moved beyond simple family business structures. Over time, the type of leader presented as ideal has shifted from autocratic to a focus on human potential and leveraging collaboration. Recently, the concepts of shared leadership, networked leadership, multidimensional leadership, and matrix leadership have gained traction as an expansion of singular top-level, autocratic leadership. However, Daniel Tarker has warned about the construct proliferation occurring in writing on community college leadership. He has argued that focusing on transformational leadership and refining the major frameworks created by the AACC, as described in its *Competencies for Community College Leaders* report, and by the Aspen Institute and Achieving the Dream, as described in their *Crisis and Opportunity* report, would be useful in avoiding the confusion that emerges when too many authors propose too many labels and names for leadership frameworks.[45] Transformational leadership, however, relies on *a* leader (singular) being inspirational and influential rather than more collective forms of leadership.

We argue instead that thinking of *transformative*, as opposed to transformational, leadership theory provides expanded conceptions of leadership and squarely includes a focus on equity and social justice. While often applied as the theoretical backdrop in K–12 research, transformative leadership is not widely discussed in the literature on community college leadership. Transformative leaders differ from reform-minded transformational leaders owing to their focus on changing systems that create or perpetuate inequity and injustice. According to Carolyn Shields, transformative leadership begins with critical reflection and analysis and moves through enlightened understanding to action.[46] Action redresses wrongs to ensure that all members of an organization experience an equitable and just environment. A premise of transformative leadership is that when organizational participants feel disrespected, excluded, or marginalized, they are unable to work to their full potential and to fully participate in the organization. Conversely, when organizational members are encouraged and enabled to fully participate, the organization is strengthened in ways that promote equity and justice. This conceptualization serves as foundational to the remaining chapters in this book, which describe how community college leaders can apply a transformative leadership approach to create an equity-driven campus.

Shields outlines eight tenets of transformative leadership that assist leaders in moving toward just, inclusive, and equitable organizations.[47] Transformative leaders:

- have a desire and mandate to effect deep and equitable change
- deconstruct knowledge frameworks that perpetuate inequity and injustice and reconstructs those frameworks in equitable ways
- address the inequitable distribution of power
- emphasize both the private and public good
- focus on democracy, emancipation, equity, and justice
- recognize and emphasize the interconnectedness and interdependence of individuals and systems
- balance critique with promise
- exhibit moral courage

Living these tenets allows leaders to critique inequitable practices. And this approach offers a promise of not only greater individual achievement but also a better life lived in common with others.[48] A first step for leaders wishing to embrace the concept of transformative leadership is to better understand what differentiates transformative leadership from other leadership approaches. Table 1.1 highlights the different leadership features of transformative leadership, transformational leadership, and shared or team leadership.

Transformational and transformative leadership perspectives are not antithetical to each other; however, they can be in tension. Even though both leadership approaches seek change as an ultimate outcome and are concerned with end values, such as liberty, justice, and equality, transformational leadership still relies on a hierarchy in which the leader works to influence and inspire others,

TABLE 1.1 Comparison of leadership approaches

	Transformative leadership	*Transformational leadership*	*Shared or team leadership*
Values	Equity Social justice	Goal attainment Productivity	Inclusion Diverse perspectives
Leader's role	Advocate Partner	Visionary Charismatic Inspirational	Facilitator Empowers
Process and goals	Examine root causes of inequities Question assumptions of who has power	Create processes to improve and be more efficient Inspire followers to change	Autonomy Shared purpose Interdependence
Beliefs about organizational change	Organizations change by questioning who benefits from policies Building new structures based on equity will create change	Organizations change by motivating followers Moral compass, collective will, and leader vision support change	Organizations change through relationship building Shared cognition, fairness of rewards, and accountability structures support change

whereas transformative leadership relies on critique, structural reconstruction, and dialectical relationships.

When attempting to distinguish between leadership approaches, it is sometimes helpful to examine an applied example, such as one from developmental education. The topic of developmental education can provide a rich case study of equity in community colleges because it spotlights the cumulative impact of an education system that results in inequitable outcomes. A research brief on developmental education for policy makers presented data on the progression of students who started their college education in developmental classes and identified several challenges in developmental education.[49] The brief provided the following suggestions for policy makers:

- Improve the accuracy of assessment and placement.
- Consider strategies to minimize attrition and accelerate students' progress into college-level courses.
- Provide more structured, coherent paths through developmental requirements and making them relevant to programs of study.

- For students with significant needs, consider a sustained and intensive approach with wraparound supports.
- Pair developmental education reforms with comprehensive institutional reforms.

This approach to developmental education aligns with transformational leadership in its intent to change outcomes for students starting college with academic gaps. What the list ignores, however, is a critique of how those gaps exist because of inequities in K–12 systems that privilege some but not others. The interdependence central to transformative leadership would approach reforms to developmental education differently: with emphasis on the influence of pre-college education on students' educational pathways, recognizing and valuing students' funds of knowledge, and engaging students in decisions about developmental programming. A burgeoning base of empirical research exists on transformative leadership in K–12 settings, which is helping move theory into practice. Leaders of community colleges can learn from their K–12 counterparts who have more experience in this area.

Borrowing from K–12 examples of transformative leadership in practice and applying this model of transformative leadership to higher education contexts, we propose leaders can leverage the ethos of community colleges (e.g., open access, democratic) into hubs for social change. Translating Shields's model of transformative leadership into a higher education context involves modifying various factors in her model. First, it is important to acknowledge the external environment in higher education, which increasingly includes neoliberal pressures that commodify education, the continued defunding of higher education (often based on the logic of higher education as more of a private than public good), and the need to address racialized organizational structures and policies. Second, we propose expanding Shields's focus on moral courage and commitment to equitable change by including liberation strategies in leadership. Edward Bush and colleagues argue, "Liberatory or Pro-Black, Indigenous, [and] Latinx education differs from an anti-racist approach in that it asserts that the goal of racial equity is not the achievement of a particular educational outcome but rather that students of color should be able to maintain, learn, and value their own cultural identity in order to build self-sustaining and sovereign communities."[50]

Similarly, Kezar and colleagues argued that focusing on liberation and social justice requires a different set of values and practices (i.e., "love, vulnerability, courage, experimentation"), and they advocate that a shared-equity leadership approach helps achieve these aims.[51]

Finally, transformative leaders must focus on individual learning to address power differentials, reimagine organizational frameworks, and change cultures of inequity. Equity-driven community college leaders are capable of drawing on mind-sets that center equity in all decision-making. When leaders question underlying assumptions of behaviors and practices that prevent deep change from occurring and keep a systems-thinking perspective to foresee and understand how actions are interwoven with contexts outside of the college, they become leaders of change.

LEADERSHIP COMPETENCIES

In advocating for more transformative leadership approaches focused on equity and social justice, it is necessary to juxtapose a transformative approach with the widely known competencies put forth by the prominent organizations that cater to community colleges and then to establish agreed-upon leadership standards. Scholars in higher education administration have long debated the skills, knowledge, and competencies needed to lead college and universities. The result of these debates is that national associations and leadership preparation programs offer an array of lists of competencies that mirror the traditional images of leaders at the "helm of the ship" during a storm rather than the tenets of transformative leadership. For example, a recent report from the Association of Governing Boards of Universities and Colleges emphasized the importance of leadership capabilities by stating, "The effectiveness—and, in a growing number of cases, the very survival—of a college or university requires leaders who make a clear-eyed appraisal of their institution's competitive position in the market for higher education services, bring an entrepreneurial spirit to their work, and possess the talent to advance the enterprise in the face of often conflicting demands."[52]

A focus on equity is missing from many answers to the question of what makes for an effective leader, as is attention to the assumption that college structures effectively serve *all* students, faculty, and staff. The acceptance of the ways colleges operate, which are based on organizational norms and practices, must be interrogated by transformative leaders. Certainly, several national leadership development programs exist to help prepare leaders to become community college presidents. While equity, diversity, or social justice may get a mention in the lists of competencies promoted by associations and leadership development programs, there is no consensus on the skills, knowledge, and competencies needed to be an equity-driven leader.

The clarion of a leadership crisis in 2001 spurred the AACC to convene a series of summits to determine what competencies were required for aspiring presidents. In 2005, the association published *Competencies for Community College Leaders*. This report identified a set of six competencies as critical for community college presidents, namely organizational strategies, resource management skills, communication skills, a willingness to collaborate, advocacy skills, and professionalism. The report further laid out how aspiring leaders could acquire or enhance these competencies. Of note, in this initial list, there is no mention of working toward equity on campus. Since the first AACC competency list was generated in the 2005 report, three updates have published. The first revision, in 2013, expanded leadership roles to include those at various career stages (i.e., emerging leaders, CEOs in the first three years of their positions, CEOs in their positions for more than three years). The updated competencies were organizational strategy; institutional finance, research, fundraising, and resource management; communication; collaboration; and community college advocacy. The calling out of fundraising highlights the need for leaders to respond to external fiscal challenges of community college funding. As with the 2005 competencies, the 2013 competencies made no mention of equity.

The third edition of the AACC's competencies report, published in 2018, was a departure from the first two. Here, guiding principles included a focus on student success (to address the importance of eradicating attainment gaps associated with income, race, ethnicity, and gender) and institutional transformation, as well as guidelines for career progression. A recognition of career pathways resulted in the inclusion of advice for faculty members, midlevel leaders, senior leaders, aspiring CEOs, new CEOs, and long-standing CEOs. The list of competencies was expanded to ten, and for each, examples of representative behaviors were provided. A category entitled "Personal Traits and Abilities" was also added to describe further areas needing attention. Of note, the 2018 report stated, "While diversity and equity are not expressly outlined as a separate competency, AACC understands the importance of creating an environment that embraces diversity."[53] Here, an assumption could be that equity was an element of each competency, but the lack of specific attention to equity gaps in student success points to a shortcoming in the guidance the AACC is providing to sitting and aspiring leaders. The literature is replete with the equity gaps facing community college students in persistence, completion, and transfer. Thus, leadership development programming relying exclusively on the AACC competencies will fall short in achieving equity on campus.

Even though the 2018 AACC competencies report acknowledged that it is important for community colleges to embrace diversity, instead of naming equity or social justice as a sought-out objective, the AACC relied on the ethos of the community college culture, positing that "community colleges by mission strive to create an inclusive environment where all students regardless of the basis of race, color, religion (creed), gender, gender expression, age, national origin (ancestry), disability, marital status, sexual orientation, or military status feel welcome and can achieve their educational goals."[54]

The predominant assumption is that access alone addresses issues of equity – an assumption that ignores the larger organizational issues community college leaders face that impede their ability to advance equity for all students. The fourth edition of the AACC competencies report, released in 2022, shifted perspective, specifically calling out the work needed to be done to support DEI and defining each of these terms. Consider the difference in the following statement from the 2022 report relative to the one presented earlier from the 2018 report: "Many colleges have heightened focus on the equity agenda, which means that community colleges, and by extension, their employees, must work to eliminate visible and invisible barriers to the student's educational journey, which includes policies and processes that disproportionately negatively impact Black, Latina/o/x, Indigenous and other students whose communities are marginalized, excluded, discriminated against, and minoritized by the status quo."[55]

Importantly, the fourth edition of the competencies report also pointed out the role of faculty members in leading efforts on equity within the classroom and for students. For all leadership levels, the competency of "institutional and cultural awareness" advocates that leaders actively focus on ways to eliminate structural bias in the institution's design so that all students, regardless of their personal circumstances, have the resources needed to achieve their educational goals.

In the 2022 report, efforts to support DEI show up in a range of competencies that differ based on role. The report lists the DEI-related competencies, followed in parentheses by the overarching area to which they apply: equity mind-set, cultural self-awareness, cultural competence, community culture (institutional and cultural awareness), equity agenda (governance and local, state, and federal policy), cultural awareness (student access and success), understanding micro-aggressions, sensitivity to cultural issues, website/belonging (communication), combating stereotypes, building a diverse team, diversity, equity and inclusion, tokenism (leadership), and cultural competence for trustees (advocacy).[56] The most common competencies across all roles (i.e., faculty, entry-level, manager, executive, CEO) were developing an equity mind-set and supporting an equity agenda. The 2022 AACC competencies for community college leaders have greatly increased awareness of the importance of equity.

Another prominent organization serving community college leaders is the Aspen Institute, which began recognizing exemplary community colleges in 2011 with the launch of the Aspen Prize for Community College Excellence, which is awarded every two years and is accompanied by a prize of $1 million. The Aspen Institute defines college excellence as "providing students with strong and equitable access to a high quality, continuously improving education; an education that motivates and inspires students to excel, and in the end, equips them with the skills and knowledge they will need to succeed in work and life."[57]

The four domains initially used to measure excellence among applicants for the Aspen Prize were completion outcomes, learning outcomes, labor market outcomes, and equitable outcomes. This early attention to equity in community college outcomes emphasized the importance of success for all students. In 2023, the Aspen Institute updated its definition of community college excellence, with the prize now aiming to celebrate exceptional colleges; advance a comprehensive definition of excellence and equity in student success; and stimulate replication of effective, scalable, and systemic reforms.[58]

In 2016, Aspen established its presidential fellowship leadership development program for new community college presidents; in 2023, the institute both recast and expanded its leadership development offerings. Aspen now offers two programming options: one for aspiring, rising leaders and one for community college presidents who have led campuses for at least three years. More broadly, Aspen provides an open-access set of curricular resources covering a variety of areas. Currently, there are eight modules arrayed across three broad themes: foundational leadership practices, core student success strategies, and evidence-based reforms. Equity leadership, within the category of foundational leadership practices, and more information on guided pathways, within the category of evidence-based reforms, are currently listed on Aspen's website as "coming soon."[59]

The work of the Aspen Institute centers on transformational leadership rather than transformative leadership or other emerging theories. Inherent in transformational leadership is a focus on how the leader works to change systems and set vision. What is typically missing in this perspective, however, is a questioning of the underlying assumptions and systems of inequity perpetuated by current practices and policies. In a module entitled "Defining Qualities of Transformational Leadership," the Aspen curriculum presents the qualities of exceptional community college leaders:

- a deep commitment to student access and success
- a willingness to take significant risks to advance student success
- having the ability to create lasting change
- having a strong, broad, strategic vision for the college and its students that is reflected in external partnerships
- raising and allocating resources in ways aligned to student success[60]

While a leader certainly cannot achieve college excellence alone, when lists such as these are examined in isolation, the broad qualities appear to be very individualistic and based on theories that give scant attention to equity and social justice.

While little explicit attention is evident among the national organizations serving community colleges, competencies related to equity and social justice have been articulated, developed, and measured in other fields and disciplines. Danah Barazanji, for example, defined the following as social justice advocacy competencies for K–12 teachers: an awareness of injustices occurring in the school and other social contexts in which students exist; a knowledge of unique needs and risks associated with specific vulnerable student populations; empowering students to also question social injustices and to become change agents themselves; a commitment or sense of responsibility for ensuring equal rights for all students and empowering students in the school and other social contexts in which they exist; a committed effort to representing underprivileged students where their voice might not otherwise be heard; and taking action within the school context to create changes in school climate that will enhance vulnerable students' ability to succeed.[61]

In the field of social work, the Council on Social Work Education provides competencies for social workers that guide the profession. Two competencies specifically reference social justice: "Advance Human Rights and Social, Racial, Economic, and Environmental Justice" and "Engage Anti-Racism, Diversity, Equity, and Inclusion (ADEI) in Practice."[62] In her book *Just Practice: A Social Justice Approach to Social Work,* Janet Finn delves into the links between social justice and social work and provides a roadmap for how social workers can develop these skills, which assumes that leaders in this disciplinary work have dispositions well grounded in social justice issues.[63] In many instances, community colleges and leadership development programs can turn to examples from other disciplines, like social work, to recast standards and priorities for the creation of equity-driven leaders.

AN EQUITY-DRIVEN LEADERSHIP DEVELOPMENT MODEL

Moving toward a model to support the development of equity-driven leaders in community colleges builds on the core of transformative leadership tenets. The lack of content specific to social justice in existing leadership development frameworks means that these frameworks do not address the perpetuation of injustice within organizational structures or the lack of parity for women and people of color among community colleges leaders. The stark reality is that community college leaders must center equity in new ways with new approaches.

A new approach requires new opportunities for leadership development. It requires moving away from a checklist mentality toward ways to support leaders in achieving an equity mind-set that results in critical reflection and critical action. Our examples and suggestions throughout this book are informed by an analysis of the research and literature, as well as the perceptions and experiences of hundreds of leaders who participated in two national leadership surveys and twenty-five leaders who took part in in-depth interviews.

The data from the 2021 National Survey of Community College Leadership for Social Justice suggest that many community college leaders already have an equity mind-set, but for those who are unsure where to begin, self-awareness provides a critical first step to advancing equity and social justice, particularly for those working from a place of privilege, be it gender, sexuality, race, or economic. Importantly, the national surveys collected data on the educational backgrounds of leaders, most of whom completed their terminal degrees before the emergence of curricular topics such as equity, systemic racism, and social justice. Therefore, a large portion of leaders surveyed may have had little to no formal education on these topics and may not have dedicated much time to contemplating them.

Although we do not see equity-driven leadership as an individual endeavor among those surveyed, for leaders to make sense of equity and social justice in their organizational contexts, they must first make sense of it themselves. According to Homer Johnson, what separates successful leaders from unsuccessful ones is their mental models or meaning structures, not their knowledge, information, training, or experience.[64] Thus, we begin the next chapter with a focus on those mental models, or what we and many others refer to as a mind-set. Developing an equity mind-set requires reflecting on and questioning long-held assumptions, as well as recognizing implicit biases and understanding personal accountability. Reflection is important in increasing leaders' critical consciousness, which is a necessary first step in creating an equity mind-set with the potential to help create an equity-driven campus. Changing one's mind-set is hard work, time consuming, and an ongoing process that never ends because our contexts and organizational environments are also in a state of constant flux. To this end, after fully exploring how leaders can develop an equity mind-set in chapter 2, we turn our attention to the importance of leaders developing contextual competence as they move toward taking action and giving voice as transformative leaders.

CHAPTER 2

Developing an Equity Mind-Set

Chapter 1 introduced the key principles of transformative leadership and proposed that this type of leadership has the potential to create equity-driven leaders in community colleges. Transformative leaders approach situations and relationships with critical reflection, critical analysis, and critical action to disrupt and dismantle inequitable and unjust practices.[1] Each aspect of transformative leadership requires extensive examination if this approach is to be fully embraced by community college leaders. In this chapter, we examine how leaders engage in critical reflection to advance an equity mind-set. In chapter 3, we discuss how those critical reflections are analyzed and situated within institutional contexts and complex systems, and in chapter 4 we discuss how transformative leaders can take critical action.

A foundational premise of this book is that the work of equity and social justice in higher education is often reduced to performance and merely talking about equity rather than engaging in real change.[2] This premise may be difficult to digest given the many efforts underway and attention being given to these topics. If this premise were false, though, we assert that community college campuses would have made significant advances in achieving equity in the areas of student outcomes, representation in leadership positions, and perceptions of campus culture. But this is not the case.

The 2021 National Survey of Community College Leadership for Social Justice asked leaders whether they perceived their colleges as inclusive, diverse, and equitable. Of note, one-third of survey respondents did not see their colleges as diverse, and half saw their colleges as only somewhat inclusive and equitable.

Moreover, women and people of color were less likely to describe their colleges as equitable. When asked the extent to which their college was equitable, only 18 percent of female respondents said "very much," compared to 30 percent of men; with regard to race and ethnicity, just 16 percent of people of color said "very much," versus 26 percent of white respondents. These results suggest that there is significant work to be done around perceptions of inclusivity, diversity, and equity.

To "move the needle" beyond the incremental change that can be achieved by simply talking about equity, community college leaders across the organization must first engage in individual-level work to grow their equity mind-set. As with many individual attributes, an equity mind-set exists on a continuum. Some leaders, through their unique life experiences, have highly developed equity mind-sets, whereas for others, the concepts presented here may provide new insights and considerations. Our intent is not to be prescriptive or to provide linear, step-by-step directions on developing an equity mind-set. Nor are we suggesting that current leaders are not already driven by an equity mind-set. Rather, we provide definitions, strategies, and examples of leaders deeply engaged in individual efforts to develop an equity mind-set, which then translates to deep and pervasive organizational change. Committing to continuous learning helps develop a mind-set primed to advance equity.

ENGAGING IN CONTINUOUS LEARNING

Inherent in becoming an equity-driven leader is continuous learning, especially when operating from an adaptive leadership approach that capitalizes on agility and the ability to pivot direction.[3] A recent literature review of learning-oriented leadership studies found statistically significant relationships between different types of leadership and learning at the individual, group, and organizational levels.[4] Yet little is known about what mediates learning at various levels. This chapter focuses on the learning that occurs at the individual level; in subsequent chapters, we look at taking action to embrace an equity mind-set at the group and organizational levels.

Workplace Learning

Learning at the individual level draws in part from learning that occurs in the workplace. Stephen Billet highlighted that learning at work occurs by engaging in job activities, listening and observing actions in the workplace, and being in the workplace context. The outcome of workplace learning results in changes to how individuals think and act. Learning at work occurs through both formal and informal activities. Critical to this type of learning are interactions with others at work. Situated learning theory illustrates how individual learning is influenced by interactions with others. Here, individual learning is advanced when employees learn about new ideas (e.g., training on implicit bias) and then have opportunities to put them into practice at work. As individuals learn new concepts, their learning is influenced by how they see their actions resulting in change at work and how they understand what they have learned by engaging in conversations with others in the workplace. Learning-oriented leadership in the workplace occurs when leaders facilitate learning for others, and how people learn at work varies depending on the leader and their approach to leadership.

The interviews we conducted with midlevel leaders showed the variety of ways many had been learning about social justice and equity. One commented, "I was in the room for a lot of things that allowed me to understand more." Thus, merely being in the workplace and witnessing discussions can help leaders learn. Others said they relied on their networks for learning opportunities, and some stated that the process of trial and error had helped them learn new things.

Campus initiatives often provide opportunities for leaders to continue their learning about equity gaps that exist among student outcomes. As one senior leader commented, "Our deep data dives that we do where we're looking at data and providing professional development and learning to identify racial equity gaps in the classroom [help] deans understand how to look at that data and then provide actionable items for solutions . . . to work with their program directors and instructors on developing more racial equity." This quote highlights that formal workplace learning via professional development helps leaders learn about racial equity and that this learning can then be shared with others. Formal learning programs provide campus members with the skills required in their positions to help change systems. Leaders we surveyed who lacked opportunities for professional development on campus sought learning opportunities at conferences, used online learning platforms like LinkedIn Learning, or relied on their professional networks. This type of inquiry can highlight why individuals must focus on the underlying issues behind equity gaps and the root causes of injustices. As will be discussed later in the chapter, less than one-fourth of respondents to the 2021 National Survey of Community College Leadership for Social Justice indicated that senior leaders were focused on root causes of injustices.

As adult learners, leaders approach new learning experiences differently from children. Adults want to direct their own learning, build on their life experiences, tie their learning to their work and roles, and seek opportunities for immediate application to current problems, and they are intrinsically, rather than extrinsically, motivated to learn.[5] In developing into equity-driven leaders, individuals must bring a level of inquiry to their learning. In 2008, Lorna Earl and Helen Timperley argued, "Leaders with an inquiry habit of mind do not presume an outcome; instead they allow for a range of outcomes and keep searching for increased understanding and clarity. Inquiry mindedness demands engagement in questioning, reflecting and decision-making."[6]

As with raising critical consciousness, leaders must continually ask questions about current practices, question their underlying assumptions about how colleges work, and engage in deep thinking. One midlevel leader commented, "In doing my own work on my own journey of learning and discovery [about equity], it slowly started to creep into the work that I was doing, in the types of research that I was doing, and that's where equity really developed meaning for me over time." Reflection and past experience help leaders in their continuous learning. For example, one midlevel leader noted that his K–12 school experience occurred within a diverse community. He stated, "You were all in there together and we got a chance to learn about each other, we were in a sense in a crucible that forced us together, and that helped forge friendships that have lasted a lifetime." Previous experiences set the stage for how leaders approach equity and social justice.

To act as change leaders, it is important for leaders to engage in the type of learning coined by Chris Argyris in 1977 as "double-loop learning."[7] Double-loop learning seeks to bring to the surface the assumptions underlying one's actions rather than leave those assumptions unquestioned. It is a process that involves teaching people to think more deeply about their own assumptions and beliefs. This type of deep and continuous learning at the individual level ultimately moves to change at the organizational level.

WHAT IS AN EQUITY MIND-SET?

Scholars sometimes focus their discussions of an equity mind-set only on students. For example, Christine Johnson McPhail and Kimberly Beatty define *equity mind-set* as a mode of thinking that, when exhibited by practitioners, calls attention to patterns of inequity in student outcomes.[8] Erin Castro also positions equity in the context of higher education as the idea that students from historically marginalized and minoritized communities have access to what they need to be successful.[9]

We align our definition of *equity-mindedness* with the more expansive and multifaceted understanding of the term put forth by Eric Felix and colleagues in 2015. Namely, equity-mindedness is:

- being race conscious in a critical way, as opposed to color blind;
- being cognizant of structural and institutional racism as the root cause of inequities as opposed to deficiencies stemming from essentialist perspectives on race or ethnicity;
- recognizing that to achieve equity it may be necessary to treat individuals unequally as opposed to treating everyone equally; and
- being able to focus on practices as the source of failure rather than student deficits.[10]

Developing an equity mind-set as a leader involves recognizing that individuals start with different identities, different past experiences, and different awareness levels. Some have been acting as equity champions and supporting equity work on their campuses and in their communities for a long time. Others are just starting to develop their critical consciousness. Thus, developing an equity mind-set looks different for different people.

Data Spotlight: Voices from the Field

Alexis [all names provided in the Data Spotlights are pseudonyms] is a Black woman and the chief diversity officer at a midsized community college in the South who acknowledged that she has been engaged in equity work for almost forty years. She reflected, "I can't tell you how many times people tell me, 'I wish you could dump all the knowledge that you know into me.' I'll never be able to do that. What I know is based on my life and what I have learned. I tell people I'm not an expert[.] [W]hen people use the term *subject matter expert,* I denounce that and say I'm skilled in certain areas, and I have experiences in certain areas. I may have a number of years of experience, but I am not an expert. What we can do is create opportunities for people to continue to learn and grow and give them the opportunity to cofacilitate and do this work. Then, they can teach someone else, and it just continues to move forward." Thus, even when leaders have a heightened awareness of equity and lived experience as a marginalized leader, they never reach "expert" status. Leaders must continually reflect, learn, and deepen their understanding and knowledge.

Midlevel leaders surveyed for the 2021 National Survey of Community College Leadership for Social Justice described how equity-mindedness shows up on their campuses. Table 2.1 provides their perspectives in light of the definition put forth in this chapter.

Next, we explore some key considerations for leaders wishing to develop or enhance their equity mind-set:

- defining one's positionality
- understanding intersections of power and privilege
- recognizing and combating implicit bias
- developing critical consciousness
- growing one's humility
- abandoning a deficit mind-set
- being comfortable with productive discomfort

Engaging in continuous learning in each of these areas will help develop a transformative leadership identity that supports equity-mindedness.

Individuals can work on each of the elements individually and concurrently. The assumption is that ongoing individual learning must occur to continue to enhance one's equity mind-set. After exploring each of these considerations, we suggest ways in which community colleges, other organizations and associations, as well as graduate preparation programs can center equity-mindedness as a key competency for leaders.

TABLE 2.1 Evidence (or not) of equity-mindedness on campus

Factor of equity-mindedness	*Quotes from midlevel leaders*
Being race conscious as opposed to color blind	• We ground ourselves, and I ground myself[, in] looking first at primarily race. That's the beginning. • The color of your skin or your gender or your religion or your sexual orientation doesn't really matter[;] it's trying to do what's right and that's what I've always tried to do.
Awareness of structural and institutional racism as the root cause of inequities	• You still have to put the focus on the racial injustices, and how those have to be corrected . . . and that is one of the cornerstones of when we talk about structural racism[;] people's reactions to not understanding their knee-jerk response. • Let me throw these buzzwords out like *equity* and *social justice* and . . . *white fragility* and all these things. But without actually taking a mirror and looking at how to do real change, you continue to perpetuate these inequities.
Recognition that to achieve equity, it may be necessary to treat individuals unequally	• There's a lot of people who confuse equity and equality[;] you know, they think, well, "This person's being treated differently and that's not fair[,]" and they use the word *equitable* [and say,] "That's not equitable." And actually it is because some people need something extra or something different. • *Equity* would be defined as everyone having the same[,] not the same access[,] not equal access, but the access that they need. • I wanted to see fair opportunities be given to me, I wanted to see fair opportunities and that the playing field [was] equal, so I could have the opportunity to receive just as many job opportunities, athletic opportunities, academic opportunities, as my fellow person who may not share the same skin tone.
Ability to focus on practices as the source of failure rather than student deficits	• Students come from different ethnicities, different races. They have different orientations, and we try to see . . . those barriers that the students might face. • I find as the dean, I have a lot of things that will be sent to me, but that faculty will be using race as an issue for their students' failure when it really has nothing to do with that.

DEFINING ONE'S POSITIONALITY

Positionality, as a concept, is how one comes to understand one's identity and sense of self. As described by Mayra Puente and colleagues, "Positionality refers to an individual's intersectional identities and how they relate to systems of power, privilege, and oppression, which requires action to unlearn, deconstruct, reflect, and question beliefs, values, assumptions, worldviews, and epistemologies to actualize the sense of purpose that derives from the unfolding of self and through building/sustaining community towards collective liberation."[11]

Importantly, as one comes to understand one's positionality, the purposeful inner work of unlearning, deconstructing, reflecting, and questioning serves as the foundation for developing an equity mind-set. As Jennifer Perry Cheatham and colleagues explained, reflecting on identity is crucial because our identities can provide strength and insight, but they can also produce blind spots.[12] Taking the time to define one's positionality provides an opportunity to identify long-held assumptions and the role of previous life experiences and to begin questioning one's beliefs.

Positionality is sometimes considered relevant only to researchers and scholars and is not often discussed in the context of administrative leadership. By sharing their positionality both formally and informally with campus community members, leaders can enhance others' understanding of how they approach their role as a leader. Specifically, one's positionality can help to explain why certain decisions were made or lend insight into how a leader approaches a topic. As one leader stated, "It is important to do the self-work, especially because most higher ed administrators are white and more of our students are diverse, and [administrators] are not taking the time to intentionally speak of the privilege they have."

Once leaders have a conceptual understanding of positionality and recognize that it is pertinent to everyone, not just scholars and researchers, the next step is to do the intentional work of articulating their unique positionality. This work involves deep consideration of the questions, *Who am I?* and *Which facets of my social identity have informed who I am and how I make meaning of the world?* These questions must not only be answered with focused contemplation but also answered explicitly, outside one's consciousness, in one's writing and verbal communication. Leaders must speak their positionality out loud.

A positionality statement considers various dimensions of one's identity such as age, race, sexual orientation, class, geographic location, political ideology, religion, gender, military experience, partnership status, educational experiences, and nationality, as well as visible and invisible disabilities and other aspects of one's sense of self such as one's appearance. Positionality statements help us to become aware of our perspectives, our beliefs, and any underlying assumptions in our work, and they help us in understanding our place in the organizational hierarchy. When interviewed, leaders are often asked about their leadership beliefs and approaches, and writing a positionality statement can inform their thinking about leading. For leaders, a positionality statement should consider how various elements of identity, alongside life experiences, influence their approach to leadership and how they see the world. Assessing one's biases (and what shapes them) by creating a positionality statement can help leaders ensure that their leadership approach is well informed, intentional, and respectful of others.

While defining one's positionality begins as an individual endeavor, it can certainly benefit from interactions and discussion with others. When sharing one's positionality, whether in writing or verbally, engaging with a supportive group of colleagues can serve multiple purposes. Going through the exercise of stating one's positionality out loud may be a completely new experience for some leaders, thus providing an opportunity for others to gain an enhanced or new understanding of them. Having the ears of a supportive colleague can also ensure that you do not, consciously or unconsciously, downplay or censure yourself. For example, it might be tempting to answer the question, "Who am I?," with something like, "I'm just a middle-aged white woman with three kids." Having that critical but supportive friend who can point out the flaw of using the word *just* can have a significant effect on this exercise.

If articulating one's positionality is a new experience, it can be helpful to review others' statements. However, the statements of others should not necessarily be used as a template to follow but rather should expose the reader (or listener) to the many ways in which individuals come to a deeper understanding of their unique identity and the factors that have shaped their understanding of the world. In that vein, we present the following, not as a checklist of questions that must be answered but to highlight the unique ways that individuals can conceptualize their positionality and how their positionality influences their thinking about their leadership identity:

- What are my social identities, and how significant is each to my leadership?
- What significant life experiences have I had, and how have they shaped my leadership?
- How have my educational and disciplinary experiences shaped who I am professionally?
- How have my work experiences shaped my leadership?
- What are my values, and what do I hope to achieve as a leader?

Defining one's positionality is a foundational task of developing an equity mindset. To us, it is not an optional activity. One must become more self-aware by putting pen to paper and speaking aloud to then be able to enhance one's understanding of the intersecting systems of power and privilege pervasive in our colleges, communities, and society.

Why Does Positionality Matter in Research and Scholarship?

Some academic journals, such as the *Journal of Social and Personal Relationships* and *Personal Relationships*, encourage, though do not require, authors to include a positionality statement with their manuscript submissions. Authors are asked to share how their identities relate to their research topic and to the identities of their participants. In many instances, this requires the researcher to divulge personal life experiences that have shaped their research paradigm and their perspectives of others. For example, a researcher exploring queer intimate partner violence shared the following as part of such a submission:

> I am a 29-year-old, white, Christian, lesbian cisgender woman raised in a high socioeconomic status family in a rural town in the Southeast U.S. While I am now married to a wonderful woman who is the love of my life, I began my studies on Queer intimate partner violence just months after escaping an abusive lesbian relationship. As I recovered from my own complicated experience of Queer intimate partner violence, I realized just how privileged I had been to be able to leave my abuser when I did: unlike many of my clients and the clients my participants spoke of. I had the

> money, social supports, and freedom not only to leave my abuser, but to relocate over 1800 miles away.[13]

As another example, in an article on social media, Black online spaces, and the politics of *dis*respectability, Shardé Davis shared the following:

> Before I present the findings, and in the spirit of self-reflexivity, I acknowledge my standpoint as an educated Black American woman. I am not an avid participant in Black online spaces such as comments sections, but I have observed the interactions of other users, advocated for Black online spaces, and am intrigued by the use of language to mark and protect cultural identities. I acknowledge that my positionality influenced this project to some extent; my member resources proved to be important tools that helped me make meaning of the text.[14]

Such statements, whether divulging deeply personal information or simply providing a singular insight into one's identity, help to situate our understanding of a piece of research and may influence our interpretation of an author's conclusions.

UNDERSTANDING THE INTERSECTIONS OF POWER AND PRIVILEGE

Fully exploring one's positionality requires a critical examination of the intersections of power and privilege so that positionality is never reduced to a single facet of identity. Similarly, equity on campus must never be reduced to a single facet of identity because of the complexity of people's backgrounds and experiences. Limiting our understanding of equity to just race, ethnicity, or gender, for example, means ignoring the intersections of social identities and how marginalization and oppression are compounded for certain individuals.

When equity is equated only with *racial* equity, campus community members who identify in other ways—for example, as part of the LGBTQ community or as politically conservative—are often ignored and not given a voice. Similarly, we often exclude from our discussions of equity those with visible and invisible disabilities. Thus, leaders must apply an intersectional lens to their understanding of equity.

Intersectionality refers not simply to the intersections of identities; rather, it refers to the multiple nexuses of power in which identities are situated and the resulting consequences are shaped by institutional factors.[15] While power and privilege are often referenced in the same breath, it is particularly important for leaders to distinguish between the two concepts. *Power* refers to the ability to decide who has access to resources, and those in power, such as community college leaders, are in positions to direct and influence the behavior of others. *Privilege* refers to unearned access to resources that are readily available only to some individuals as a result of their advantaged membership to a particular social group.

Gareth Morgan argued that power in education is operationalized by creating, defining, encoding, transmitting, and evaluating claims to knowledge.[16] Privilege results in the use of dominant norms that in turn afford some more power than others. Figure 2.1 illustrates some of the dimensions of privilege and provides examples of privileged identities (those with more power) and oppressed identities (those with less power).

One surveyed leader reflected, "As an ally, I'm recognizing that I have all the privilege as a white educated Protestant man and in leadership at a college. So, being comfortable in that role as an ally and advocating for people who are uncomfortable advocating for themselves [means I have to understand my privilege]." This leader has thus recognized the power he has

FIGURE 2.1 Axis of privilege and oppression

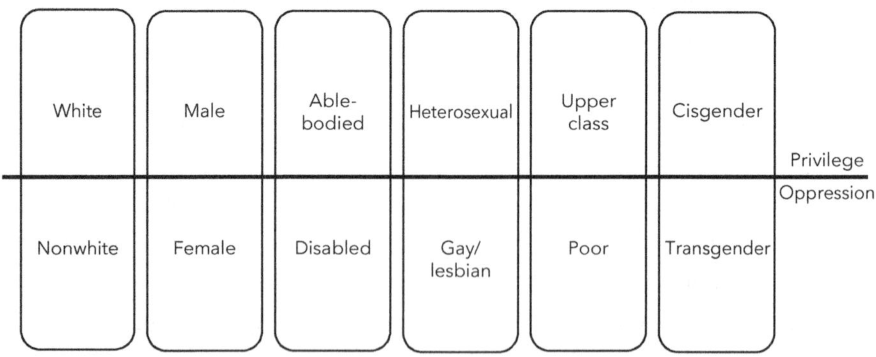

Source: Adapted from Kathryn Pauly Morgan, "Describing the Emperor's New Clothes: Three Myths of Educational (In-)Equity," in *The Gender Question in Education: Theory, Pedagogy and Politics*, ed. Ann Diller, Barbara Houston, Kathryn Pauly Morgan, and Maryann Ayim (Boulder, CO: Westview, 1996), 105–23.

in terms of gender, race, and position and has leveraged that power in his work as an ally.

Data Spotlight: Critical Reflection

Results from the 2021 National Survey of Community College Leadership for Social Justice reveal that a large majority of senior leaders had engaged in critical reflection on power and privilege; however, the level of reflection varied based on leadership position (figure 2.2). One out of four deans and one out of three director-level respondents indicated that they had never engaged in critical reflection on power and privilege. Comparatively fewer presidents (11.6 percent) and vice presidents or provosts (17.1 percent) indicated the same.

Given the importance of power and privilege in leadership, it is imperative for *all* leaders to engage in critical reflection of how their identities provide advantage (or not) relative to others. The fact that many top-level leaders surveyed did indicate engaging in such reflection is an encouraging sign; however, the lower levels of reflection for midlevel leaders indicate the role that position plays in the use of critical reflection, as well as differences in power based on position.

FIGURE 2.2 Survey prompt: During the past two years, have you engaged in critical reflection on power and privilege?

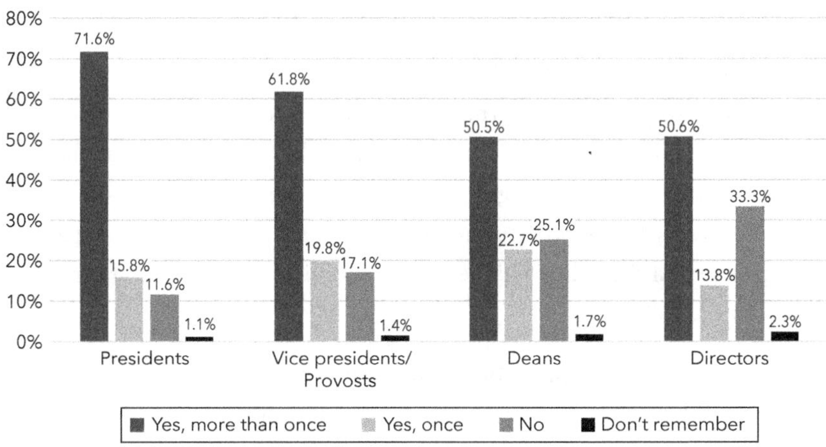

RECOGNIZING AND COMBATING IMPLICIT BIAS

Through their unique life experiences, every leader has implicit biases and engages in subconscious stereotyping. Stereotypical associations can be so subtle that people who hold them might not even be aware of them. Such biases affect the way we interact and socialize with others, and they affect how we practice leadership. Implicit biases are those stereotypical attitudes that we have accumulated over time about members outside our racial, ethnic, gender, economic, religious, and other circles of identity. Implicit bias involves attitudes and perspectives that are triggered automatically without mental awareness. Thus, implicit biases cannot easily be banished from our minds through simple interventions.

However, implicit biases are habits of mind that can be mediated when one is motivated to do so by becoming more aware and by putting in effort. Formal implicit bias training opportunities that include both experiential and educational components can help people become better equipped to identify their implicit biases and recognize the negative impact those biases can have on others. The facilitation of such training is paramount to combating implicit biases. Many colleges, therefore, contract with outside organizations and experts to create optimal learning environments to address implicit bias; however, limited evidence exists on the efficacy of these learning experiences.

Mandating Implicit Bias Training

In some states and in some fields, implicit bias training is required for licensure. For example, in 2022, the Michigan Department of Licensing and Regulatory Affairs (www.michigan.gov/lara) began requiring all health-care professionals in Michigan to complete three hours of implicit bias training every three-year licensing cycle. Focused on reducing disparities in access to and the delivery of health-care services, the mandatory training provides the following:

- information on implicit biases and cultural sensitivity, including the historical basis and present consequences of implicit bias
- strategies to remedy the negative impact of implicit bias

- an understanding of how implicit bias affects perception, judgment, and actions that may result in inequitable decision-making and a failure to effectively communicate
- a pre- and post-test implicit bias assessment

While debatable whether a three-hour mandatory training and a required assessment can change mind-sets, this requirement for licensure symbolizes a statewide commitment to reducing health disparities. Similar initiatives in educational settings have the potential to serve as an important symbol; however, limited evidence exists that higher education leaders have similar experiences to those of health-care professionals in Michigan.

One surveyed leader reflected on the changing role of implicit bias on his campus: "When you take your hiring practices that used to have implicit bias training and having to have so many people on a committee and ensuring that the committees were diverse, and now, unless it's at a certain level, you can pretty much hire whoever you want. We are not committed." The lack of effectiveness of required implicit bias training programs highlights how one-off or short training programs are potentially inefficient in making broad-based changes to increase representation. However, continuous learning at the individual level can provide a foundation for change. An understanding of one's own biases can lead to individual change and help people speak up in group settings when biased decisions are evident.

Implicit bias training for search committees is one way some individuals on campus become aware of their own biases. Such training can support people's learning over time, especially if no campus-wide or professional licensure requirement is in place. For example, because of the marked lack of diversity in STEM (i.e., science, technology, engineering, and mathematics) fields, implicit bias training for search committees hiring faculty has received attention.[17] Another way to introduce equity into hiring practices is to include equity advocates on search committees. Recognizing how structures build on implicit biases is also important and requires individuals to first recognize their own implicit biases in order to see the biases in policies, processes, and outcomes. Survey instruments like Harvard's Implicit Association Tests (www.implicit.harvard.edu/implicit/takeatest.html) are one tool for individuals to better understand their biases. Once identified, individuals can then take steps to address the ways in which their biases influence their leadership.

DEVELOPING CRITICAL CONSCIOUSNESS

Defining one's positionality, interrogating systems of power and privilege, and acknowledging implicit bias are all elements of enhancing one's critical consciousness. Critical consciousness and the intricate processes of engaging in critical self-reflection are first steps in developing an equity mind-set. To practice transformative leadership, leaders must first have a deep understanding of their own values, beliefs, and assumptions and how they are tied to systems that perpetuate injustice. This self-reflection must be in service of something greater than increased awareness itself—and that "something greater" is the possibility of making community colleges more equitable and just.

The idea of raising one's critical consciousness and engaging in critical reflection dates back decades, and many associate these concepts with the writings of Paulo Freire.[18] According to Freire, critical consciousness in education means being aware of social, political, and economic pressures and oppressive factors and finding the power to act to transform them. Freire proposed a cycle of critical consciousness that involves gaining knowledge about systems and structures that create and sustain inequity (via critical analysis), developing a sense of power or capability (critical agency), and ultimately committing to take action against oppressive conditions (critical action).

More recently, Sharon Radd and Bruce Kramer have described critical consciousness as an ongoing and growing awareness and knowledge of power, privilege, and oppression combined with a habit of openness and learning to disrupt injustice and create more just action, processes, structures, and circumstances.[19] As with other habits, then, developing critical consciousness is a constantly evolving and ongoing process. Fostering critical consciousness may be a goal to which we can all aspire but one that can never be fully achieved in an ever-changing society.

Embedded in the various definitions and understandings of critical consciousness is the key task of engaging in critical reflection. Alexis Jemal delineates critical reflection as encompassing the following three activities:

- thinking critically about accepted beliefs, thoughts, feelings, and assumptions

- detecting the hidden interests underlying personal and social assumptions and beliefs
- identifying how history affects the present details of everyday life and how ways of thinking and feeling serve to maintain and perpetuate the existing system of inequality[20]

Becoming aware of one's history and one's privilege and power is necessary to reflect critically and determine action steps to disrupt inequities.

Consider how one surveyed leader described the role of reflection: "To prepare people for leadership roles at community colleges, I think reflection is a huge part of being able to reflect on where you came from, you know[,] how you earned your education, what were the obstacles, and [reflecting] on the ability of a leader at a community college to use that education to either help others or to be a roadblock for others." Opportunities for critical reflection can be built into leadership development sessions or arise on an individual level as people seek to increase their understanding of equity.

Critical consciousness is theorized as consisting of two components: critical reflection and critical action. As with many constructs, researchers have tried to create reliable and valid measures of this complex phenomenon. In 2017, Matthew Diemer and colleagues validated the Critical Consciousness Scale, which includes items about perceptions of inequality and egalitarianism to measure critical reflection.[21] For example, the scale asks respondents to indicate their level of agreement with the following statements: "Certain racial or ethnic groups have fewer chances to get ahead" (a measure of perceived inequality) and "It is a good thing that certain groups are at the top and other groups are at the bottom" (a measure of egalitarianism). The measures of critical action include questions related to participation in social and political activities to change perceived inequalities. For example, the scale asks respondents to indicate how often they have participated in a discussion about a social or political issue and how often they have joined in protest marches, political demonstrations, or political meetings. It is important to recognize that critical action is not the same as civic engagement. Unlike civic engagement, or civic action, which can include direct service, *critical* action targets concrete and long-standing sociopolitical change against marginalizing forces and power structures. Instruments like the Critical Consciousness Scale can help leaders to better understand their current level of critical consciousness and identify areas of growth and opportunity.

While scholars and researchers agree that critical consciousness is conceptualized as critical reflection paired with critical action, another important consideration is one's motivation to engage in efforts to develop and enhance one's critical consciousness. Critical motivation reflects the interest and agency one has to redress societal inequities, and this type of motivation may mediate or moderate the relationship between reflection and action.[22]

Several opportunities exist to help leaders increase their critical consciousness. For example, Mayra Puente and colleagues recommend a group activity called "Item of Significance," which can be done in classrooms and in leadership development sessions.[23] In this activity, individuals are asked to bring a picture or item to present to the group that reflects something about their identity, heritage, or culture. A group discussion then provides an opportunity to reflect on relationships that support a sense of self, connection, and meaning. As leaders raise their own critical consciousness, they can identify elements that are important for their own sense of belonging on campus and in turn recognize how others can feel this same sense of belonging.

GROWING ONE'S HUMILITY

Humility is often thought of as an easily recognizable attribute, one of which we can say, "We know it when we see it." It is useful, however, to think deeper about the layered nature of humility and how a focused effort to become equity-minded is interconnected with humility. We propose two important layers of humility: leadership humility and cultural humility. Leadership humility encompasses the following:

- a willingness to view oneself accurately, in terms of both strengths and weaknesses
- a displayed appreciation of others' strengths and contributions
- engaging in continuous learning, being teachable, and being willing to learn from all people
- an understanding that the world is bigger than oneself[24]

Leadership humility is certainly not a new concept. In fact, Edgar Schein, a foremost expert on organizational culture, has published books entitled *Humble*

Inquiry and *Humble Leadership*.[25] But we assert that humility is not upheld as a necessary attribute that leaders must continuously develop because humility does not align with the "hero" and "great man" visions of past leaders. A leader who acknowledges their weaknesses and admits that they are not all-knowing might fall prey to being labeled a weak leader rather than a humble leader.

Measuring Humility

As with critical consciousness, researchers have developed scales to assess humility.[26] Leaders can self-assess their humility by critically reflecting on some of the following statements included in humility scales:

- I admit when I don't know how to do something.
- I acknowledge when others have more knowledge and skills than I do.
- I take notice of others' strengths.
- I am genuinely interested in learning more.
- I ask questions when I am uncertain about something.
- I am open to the advice of others.
- I sometimes act superior to others.
- Others sometimes perceive me as a know-it-all.
- I see myself as a small part of a larger whole.
- I believe that not everything is in my control.

After assessing oneself, it can be useful to try to answer these questions from the perspectives of those you work with. Further, you may want to actually solicit colleagues' perspectives to see how accurately you have assessed their perceptions of you.

Developing an equity mind-set is also interwoven with developing cultural humility. In the past, professional development opportunities for faculty and staff may have focused on developing cultural competence, defined as a set of skills that lead to effective and appropriate communication and interactions with people of other cultures. What may be more important in becoming equity-minded, however, is the practice of cultural humility. Cultural humility can indeed be seen as a component of cultural competence. Cultural competence is about gaining knowledge that results in an increased ability to interact effectively with people of various racial, ethnic, socioeconomic, religious, and social groups. Advancing one's cultural competence is an ongoing process that involves learning about the patterns of behavior, beliefs, language, values, and customs of particular groups of people.[27] However, developing cultural competence does not equate to developing cultural humility.

Cultural humility, in comparison to cultural competence, is an interpersonal stance that is other oriented rather than self-focused. It is characterized by respect for and a lack of superiority toward another person's cultural background and experience.[28] Similar to developing cultural competence, developing cultural humility is also an ongoing process. It involves a deep level of self-exploration and self-critique combined with a sincere willingness to learn from others. Cultural humility means entering into a relationship with another person with the intention of honoring their beliefs, customs, and values. It means acknowledging differences and accepting people for who they are.

The theory of cultural humility has been applied more often to health care and human services than to higher education because of its origins in Jean Watson's 2008 theory of human caring.[29] Based on Watson's decades of experience as a nurse, the theory stresses the importance of authenticity, trust, and intentionality in relationships between caregivers and those being cared for. For most people who have interacted with health-care professionals, a lack of adherence to the theory of human caring may be easy to envision. And a lack of care can have long-lasting consequences. For example, we might feel disrespected or feel that our experiences are being devalued or disregarded in negative interactions with health-care providers. Or we may feel that a provider is making inappropriate generalizations and not really listening to us. These types of interactions can have direct negative impacts on our health. If we apply these same types of experiences and feelings to other settings, such as interactions with leaders, the importance of care surfaces as one of the most important attributes of an equity-minded leader.

With the current state of incivility in society and the many examples of bullying in higher education, it seems appropriate to raise the question, *Why is care for others still considered primarily in relationships between patients and health-care providers rather than in other relationships, such as those between faculty leaders and administrators?*[30] Without care for others, leaders will likely never be viewed as having humility, as the two attributes go hand in hand.

Incivility in Higher Education

Humility has the potential to combat incivility and bullying in higher education. In 1978, James Appleton and colleagues identified behaviors that promote incivility and stand in stark contrast to humility:

- indulging in self-promotion
- showing intolerance or disrespect to others
- purposefully procrastinating or avoiding conflicts that result in harming relationships
- engaging in professional misconduct, such as breaking confidentiality, being a part of a rumor mill, or playing favorites
- having temper tantrums and displaying hostility during individual or group interactions
- avoiding taking a stand in support of someone else
- engaging in behaviors that perpetuate problems rather than solve problems[31]

While few leaders may be willing to publicly admit engaging in such blatant bullying behaviors, this list can be used to encourage a moment of self-reflection for leaders who wish to grow their humility and become more equity-minded.

Consider the Caring Campus initiative of the Institute for Evidence-Based Change, which involved close to thirty colleges.[32] The intention of the project was to provide coaching and resources to campuses to help build a supportive campus culture in which students felt a sense of connection and felt cared for. Critical to this program was a recognition of the roles staff and faculty have in building a caring environment. Researchers at the Community College Research Center analyzed data gathered from a subset of the participating colleges and found that a set of behavioral commitments were made by staff:

- developing cross-departmental awareness
- acquiring deep knowledge of college functions
- enhancing quality of staff interactions with students[33]

Staff turnover and burnout can impede the development of a sustained caring culture; so too can changes in campus priorities. Faculty participating in the Caring Campus program were selected by campus leaders to receive coaching. The behavioral commitments suggested by the Institute for Evidence-Based Change for faculty to adopt included elements from the literature on sense of belonging, as well as best practices in teaching and learning:

- Learn and regularly use students' names.
- Communicate clearly about the course.
- Create moments that matter.
- Provide frequent assignments and assessments.
- Practice situational fairness.[34]

Early results from participating campuses show increased student retention, improved faculty engagement, and changes in campus culture.[35] Leaders on the participating campuses used change theory practices to help support the initiative (e.g., communicating the vision, aligning with new and existing work, building relevant structures, and celebrating wins). Connecting the concepts of building a caring culture on campus to those of individual and cultural humility is important for individual leadership development. This individual action provides equity-driven leaders additional strategies to improve community college cultures.

ABANDONING A DEFICIT MIND-SET

Deficit thinking runs rampant in our educational settings. Although extensively studied and discussed in K–12 contexts, it is equally likely to occur in colleges and universities. Deficit thinking is not just being negative or "seeing the glass as half empty." Rather, deficit thinking occurs when blame is placed on individuals rather than the oppressive structures, policies, and practices that perpetuate injustice. Most often in educational settings, this type of thinking is applied to marginalized student populations and is evidenced when educators assume that students will not be successful because of their demographic characteristics or backgrounds. Richard Valencia has characterized deficit thinking as the justification for failing schools: "The deficit thinking paradigm, as a whole, posits that students who fail in school do so because of alleged internal deficiencies (such as cognitive and/or motivational limitations) or shortcomings socially . . . such as familial deficit or dysfunction. . . . The popular 'at-risk' construct, now entrenched in educational circles, views poor and working-class children and their families (typically of color) as predominantly responsible for school failure."[36]

Labeling a student "at risk" simply because of one demographic characteristic, which often occurs explicitly in higher education, exemplifies a deficit mind-set because it involves applying an entirely negative classification to an individual with no consideration of the systems that created the need for this particular label.

Leaders with an equity mind-set challenge these types of deficit discourses as they come up and refrain from using deficit language in their communications and interactions with campus community members. Before being able to challenge and disrupt these types of discourses and shift the blame from the individual to the system, however, leaders must banish some of the deficit thinking that has been infiltrating our educational spaces for decades, and this is not an easy or quick task.

Deficit thinking is akin to implicit bias in that we may be unaware that we are engaging in that line of thinking because it is so pervasive and ingrained in educational systems. A deficit mind-set is often not intentional, conscious, or deliberate. Rather, it is a result of existing systems, policies, and practices. Therefore, the first step in reducing deficit thinking is developing an internal awareness and recognition of deficit thinking when it is happening.

To shift their mind-set, leaders must be able to recognize when they, themselves, as people who hold positions of power, are engaging in deficit thinking. To this end, Valencia has identified six components, or what we might consider hallmarks, of deficit thinking, all of which are linked to oppressive power structures dominant in educational settings:

1. Blaming the victim: a practice in which people in power identify a social problem, assess differences between disadvantaged and advantaged groups, define differences as the cause of the problem, and intervene to "correct" those differences
2. Continuing the cycle of oppression: the vicious cycle in which victims and people in power remain separate by way of an unjust and imbalanced use of authority
3. Making false "scientific" claims: the supposed use of the scientific method to reinforce the assumptions and values of a dominant group and then use

of those as norms by which to compare marginalized groups without consideration for the norms of those groups

4. Making snap judgments and diagnoses: the social and behavioral science approach of describing a deficit in a group, explaining the deficit in terms of genetic traits, using that explanation to predict the perpetuation of the deficit, and prescribing a solution to remedy the deficit
5. Lacking awareness of context: ignoring the influence of the time period and the notion that how over time changes occur regarding cultural norms and ideology
6. Disregarding views that challenge the norms and ideas of those in power: not challenging the norms and ideas of a dominant group that perpetuate conditions of deficit thinking[37]

An understanding of the six components of deficit thinking can help leaders in two ways: through "internal speak," that is, the internal recognition of when deficit thinking is occurring, and through "public speak," that is, when deficit thinking is occurring in communication with campus constituents.

While deficit thinking is most often considered in terms of student outcomes, it is useful to consider the impact that deficit thinking has on perpetuating a culture of inequity whereby faculty and staff are continuously exposed to practices and policies that align with deficit thinking. To what extent are leaders perpetuating (whether through action or inaction) an organizational culture that in essence blames students for poor outcomes rather than interrogating the root causes of injustice?

Participating leaders in the 2021 National Survey for Community College Leadership for Social Justice were asked to what extent senior leaders on campus focused on the root causes of injustices because a focus on root causes, rather than blaming students for deficits, is critical in advancing equity on campus. Only 23 percent of respondents felt senior leaders were "very much" focused on identifying the root causes of injustices, whereas 40 percent thought leaders were "somewhat" focused on root causes, and 37 percent felt leaders were only "a little" or "not at all" focused on identifying root causes (figure 2.3).

Deficit thinking is a barrier that must be understood and overcome in order to achieve more equitable campuses. As one diversity, equity, and inclusion (DEI) leader noted, "There are people who are obstructionist, and their goal is to

FIGURE 2.3 Percentage of leaders describing senior leaders as focused on root causes of injustices

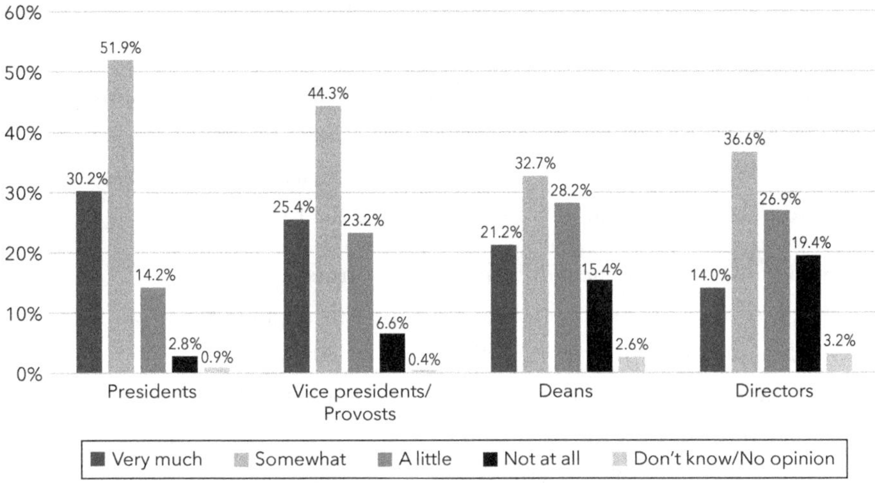

question every decision being made, and suggest a deficit model . . . we're slipping into that[;] it's not looking at what we're doing or [questioning] the system and who had benefits and who had privileges." Addressing a deficit mind-set is one of the first steps toward understanding how structures impede equity on campus.

BEING COMFORTABLE WITH PRODUCTIVE DISCOMFORT

While the process of becoming more equity-minded is critical for community college leaders, it can also result in what theorists such as Leon Festinger and Jack Mezirow refer to as cognitive dissonance.[38] Cognitive dissonance, likely a common occurrence for many leaders, is defined as the mental discomfort that results from holding two or more conflicting beliefs, values, or attitudes. The internal struggle and conflict of cognitive dissonance can no doubt cause discomfort.

Cognitive Dissonance

According to F. Scott Fitzgerald, "The test of a first-rate intelligence is the ability to hold two opposed ideas in mind at the same time and still retain the ability to function." This quote seems to encompass our modern-day understanding of cognitive dissonance and how it can affect our behavior.

Cognitive dissonance occurs when a belief, value, or attitude is challenged by new information that forces a person to hold two or more conflicting positions simultaneously. While it is important to be able to recognize this experience and the inner conflict that results, it is equally important to "diagnose" one's response to the dissonance. As new information is obtained that conflicts with a belief, value, or attitude that we hold, different responses are possible. We may do one of the following:

- Flat out reject the new information as untrue.
- Rationalize the original belief, value, or attitude in some way.
- Hide or mask our original belief, value, or attitude.
- Acknowledge only the information that confirms the original belief as true (known in research as confirmation bias).
- Shut down completely (and as F. Scott Fitzgerald referenced, we may lose our ability to function).[39]

Understanding both our own reactions to cognitive dissonance as well as those of others is a particularly important step for leaders in developing an equity mind-set. In DEI trainings and professional development opportunities, any of the responses described earlier may be readily apparent in the comments, behaviors, or reactions of attendees. Leaders can help others develop their equity-mindset by pointing out these common reactions to cognitive dissonance and individuals may find that understanding the list of common reactions is a helpful starting place for tackling difficult and complex topics in group settings.

A key task for leaders is to recognize the discomfort of cognitive dissonance and turn it into *productive* discomfort. Productive discomfort is the uncomfortable feeling experienced when discussing a polarizing issue with a person whose perspective differs from your own. What shifts the uncomfortable to the productive in discussions is the use of active listening to understand better the perspective of others with different views and to situate how past experiences (your own and that of others) and context (past and current) provide a backdrop for understanding the roots behind the issue at hand. Before being able to engage in dialogue about an issue related to the unequal distribution of power and privilege, however, requires individuals to "sit with" the discomfort they feel when confronted with the dynamics of power and privilege that may have personally benefited them in the past. At its base, productive discomfort involves a willingness in this self-examination to change one's thinking and understanding. In her 2023 book *Leading Within Systems of Inequity in Education*, Mary Rice-Boothe eloquently explains that discomfort must be seen as a gift.[40] The gift of learning and personal growth that occurs during and after periods of productive discomfort helps in individual development, and ultimately contributes to the evolution of dialogue in larger groups with differing perspectives.

One midlevel leader described how his campus used data analysis of their student body to jumpstart productive discomfort on campus. He noted that the data showed that despite what people thought was happening in serving marginalized student populations, the campus was not even serving its high-performing students: only 3.5 percent of the student body were completing thirty credits in their first year. Thirty credits is the number of credits anticipated for full-time students to complete in a one-year period. He stated, "That [finding] dropped everybody's jaws to the floor because they knew we had racial equity issues, but they didn't really see it. It created some cognitive dissonance for the college writ large." Helping campus members "see" the issue of inequity for students creates an environment of discomfort that can spur people to change. When individuals face this type of dissonance, they are motivated to change their own behavior, which ultimately spurs larger changes on campus. When the source of dissonance counters a person's beliefs, resistance can occur. Exposing individuals to the concept of cognitive dissonance theory can help reduce the amount of uncertainty or denial a person feels when addressing an issue like inequity.[41]

Comfort with Discomfort

The premise that becoming equity-minded should be a comfortable process is misguided. In fact, Kenneth Jones and Tema Okun suggest that the belief that those in power have a right to emotional and psychological comfort may be a characteristic of an organizational culture that supports white supremacy.[42] To ensure that an organization can create a culture comfortable with discomfort, the authors suggest the following:

- Understand that discomfort is at the root of all growth and learning.
- Welcome discomfort and learn to "sit with" it before responding or acting.
- Connect your personal experiences and feelings with the discomfort.
- Avoid taking things personally. Instead, welcome honest critical feedback.
- Seek understanding about whatever is causing the discomfort.[43]

When cognitive dissonance results from a disorienting dilemma, learning happens.[44] The process of learning may include an elaboration of an existing point of view, establishing new points of view, transforming an existing point of view, or transforming an ethnocentric habit of mind. While transforming an ethnocentric habit of mind occurs infrequently, at the root of the other types of transformative learning is cognitive dissonance, which leads to questioning assumptions and a change in perspective. Change in perspective is the ultimate outcome of productive discomfort.

An example of this type of productive discomfort was provided by one interview participant, a midlevel leader who described his campus's participation in the Truth, Racial Healing & Transformation Campus Centers initiative of the American Association of Colleges and Universities. His campus undertook a review of its policies and procedures to ensure the use of equitable language and the application of equity in standing committees and groups. Describing the outcome of the times of productive discomfort on campus, he said, "Everybody's getting a little more comfortable talking about those things, and I think because they hear other folks talking more comfortably, they don't feel reserved when they come up with a plan . . . and say, 'Hey, we could do this,' instead of 'That's crazy!' The consistency of the work and the discussions push people." When campus members can sit with discomfort and then move forward, rather than freeze into inaction, progress toward equity will occur.

LIVING A TRANSFORMATIVE LEADERSHIP IDENTITY THAT SUPPORTS EQUITY-MINDEDNESS

A critical examination of the self is needed before leaders can embrace a transformative leadership approach and engage in actions that result in equity-driven campuses. Specifically, it is through an understanding of one's positionality, by recognizing one's implicit biases and deficit thinking, as well as by acknowledging the existence of systems of power and privilege, that one's leadership identity begins to materialize and become recognizable as transformative. Important in this process is continually learning and examining one's perspectives.

Developing an equity mind-set begins with the foundation of an individual's schema. One's mental maps lay the groundwork for how one sees, understands, and makes sense of what they are learning. *Sense-making*, a term introduced by Karl Weick, refers to how we structure the unknown so that we can come up with a plausible understanding (a "map") to make sense of a complex and changing world. Sense-making is the activity that enables leaders to turn the ongoing complexity of the world into a situation that is comprehended explicitly in words and that serves as a springboard for action.[45] Given the role of experience in sense-making, it is important for leaders to challenge their own frames of reference because drawing exclusively on what one already knows limits one's ability to continue to learn and advance equity.

Sense-making is all about the sense-maker because this concept is grounded in identity construction and the answer to the question, *Who am I as a leader?* People create their own identities as leaders and then project those identity in various contexts. Sense-making is a key leadership capability, as it provides the means of making sense of one's own identity and recognizing the impact of how one's identity is experienced by others. One strategy to engage in meaningful sense-making and to become a sense-giver for others is exploring a wider systems perspective that seeks out varied perspectives so as not to make assumptions.[46]

For leaders to become sense-givers for others and help frame an understanding of equity on campus, it is first necessary for them to make sense for themselves. Thus, critical consciousness and an understanding of one's positionality are necessary components of learning to become an equity-driven leader. Learning with others and in a shared context setting helps in this process because sense-making is an ongoing process. Making sense about what is happening around them in their college's context helps increase shared understanding. Because individuals are inclined to believe what is plausible, the use of data is essential to dispel myths presented with plausible rationales (e.g., the erroneous idea that marginalized students bring deficits into higher education settings).

According to Jennifer Perry Cheatham et al., the sense-making process requires leaders to resist oversimplification, linear thinking, and their desire for clear causality.[47] Bringing an inquiry mind-set to their learning allows leaders opportunities to acquire a deeper understanding of equity and help others in making sense of equity efforts on campus. As one midlevel leader explained, "In my own personal journey, learning the language of equity and learning how to express those things that I know are happening to our students, that are happening to my colleagues and to our employees, and being able to translate that into meaningful work is how I learned to define equity for myself." This leader first had to make sense of the meaning of equity for herself, which was based on her positionality, her understanding of her own experiences and her interactions with others, and her understanding of how her institutional context influenced both her thinking and how equity occurred.

By combining the various elements of this chapter, we can create a model for developing a transformative leadership identity that supports equity (figure 2.4). Because every leader brings unique life experiences and approaches to their leadership, leaders will find that certain elements require more time and learning relative to others. The various components of the model assume that continuous learning occurs as individuals react to disorienting dilemmas.

The components of developing an equity mind-set outlined in this chapter are not intended to occur in a linear fashion; rather, as the model in figure 2.4 highlights, there are multiple entry points. The model also assumes dynamic relationships among the various factors, as represented by the dashed lines around each element in the figure. The presence of continuous learning around all components highlights that individual learning occurs on a continuum and that leaders can always learn more to develop their equity mind-set. For example, as one continues to develop critical consciousness, their positionality statement will change. Developing critical consciousness also allows individuals a means of "seeing" their implicit biases more clearly, which can help one identify when a deficit mind-set is present that should change. Instances of productive

FIGURE 2.4 Developing a transformative leadership identity that supports equity

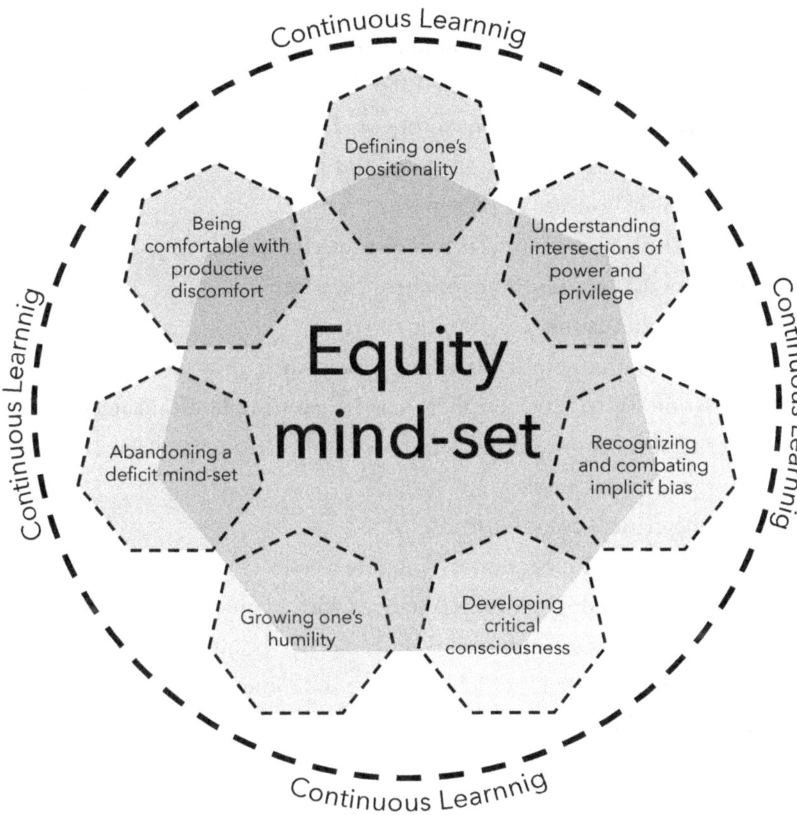

discomfort inform further development in the other factors, further contributing to the development of an informed equity mind-set. Because individuals will enter the model with varying degrees of advancement toward an equity mind-set, how the model operates for each person will differ.

CALL TO ACTION

This chapter described a series of considerations for leaders wishing to develop or enhance their equity mind-set. The following summarizes the elements involved and includes examples of action items leaders can take to work through each:

- Defining one's positionality:
  - Write a personal position statement that identifies the facets of your social identity.

  - Describe how your life experiences have influenced, reinforced, or challenged your positionality.
  - Identify your values, what you hope to achieve as a leader, and what you need to support your goals (the Life Values Inventory is a resource for this work: www.lifevaluesinventory.org/).
- Understanding intersections of power and privilege:
  - Reflect on the sources of power you possess.
  - Identify the dimensions of privilege that you have.
  - Use figure 2.1 as a resource for these exercises.
- Recognizing and combating implicit bias:
  - Take one or more implicit bias assessments (e.g., Harvard's Implicit Association Tests: www.implicit.harvard.edu/implicit/takeatest.html).
  - Use critical reflection to identify how implicit bias may have affected you during your work week.
- Developing critical consciousness:
  - Engage in critical reflection by keeping a reflective journal.
  - Participate in dialogues and exchanges with people whose perspectives differ from yours to understand multiple viewpoints.
  - Take action in areas in which you have individual agency.
- Growing one's humility:
  - Recognize your role as part of a bigger system.
  - Engage in building a caring culture on campus and recognizing the contributions others are making.
  - Solicit feedback from others to understand their perspectives of you.
- Abandoning a deficit mind-set:
  - Keep a list of the six components of deficit thinking handy to review whether you have fallen into any "traps" or taken any steps backward.
  - Work on developing a growth mind-set as a means of combating deficit thinking.
- Being comfortable with productive discomfort:
  - Identify times you experience cognitive dissonance, and note your reactions.
  - Note how instances of discomfort inform your future actions.

- Living a transformative leadership identity that supports equity-mindedness:
    - Generate a profile that articulates your leadership identity.
    - Identify areas of growth, and seek out further development opportunities.

Reflecting on issues of power and privilege and developing critical consciousness demonstrates an expansion of a leader's base of knowledge and understanding. However, it is only in taking action that critical consciousness becomes a practice of leadership. Before moving from critical consciousness to critical action, we posit that leaders also need a depth of knowledge and understanding of the various contexts and systems that affect justice. Campus context influences how leaders make sense of equity, both for themselves and others. In chapter 3, we take a closer look at the role of context in creating an equity-driven campus.

CHAPTER 3

Developing Contextual Competency

Context influences the development of equity-driven leaders and informs how leaders support equity and social justice on their campuses. Institutions of higher education, particularly community colleges, have historically been seen as a vehicle for social mobility and enhanced opportunity. According to Paul LeBlanc, higher education has been seen as a tool to offset societal inequality but in recent years has been seen as part of the problem.[1] And more so than at any other time in history, the value of higher education is being questioned. The devaluing of college degrees and the low funding of community colleges, alongside the lack of progress related to equitable outcomes, are contextual factors that significantly complicate the practice of leadership. On one hand, community colleges are seen as engines of the economy and social mobility.[2] On the other, the exodus of students of color, particularly Black men, during the COVID-19 pandemic and equity gaps across all metrics cast a long shadow of missed opportunities. In this chapter, we define contextual competency and discuss the various layers of context, especially in terms of diversity, equity, and inclusion (DEI) efforts. This layered understanding is necessary to develop an equity mind-set and embrace a transformative leadership approach.

CONTEXTUAL COMPETENCY

Lists of competencies are everywhere in higher education—from job descriptions and performance reviews to course descriptions and outlines of what attendees can "expect" to achieve during professional development opportunities. Competencies are often separated into areas related to developing new knowledge, skills, abilities, and behaviors. Competency-based frameworks serve as guides to assess how individuals are progressing and to mark achievements and milestones. As described in chapter 1, for example, the American Association of Community Colleges (AACC) leadership competencies act as a checklist of areas in which community college leaders at various levels should be competent or developing competency.[3]

While competencies are plentiful in higher education, contextual competency is often integrated into broader frameworks rather than being considered a stand-alone competency. For example, references to organizational culture have figured prominently in the various versions of the AACC competencies; however, these competencies are limited in focus to understanding traditions and previous accomplishments that paint a portrait of the college context. The latest AACC competencies report, the fourth edition, released in 2022, includes cultural awareness and community culture as competencies within the overarching competency of institutional and cultural awareness. True, the inclusion and recognition of the influence of the community on campus priorities provide an element of contextual competency, yet what remains ignored is how local context can also constrain the community college's vision for equity and social justice. Consider, for example, the ways states are seeking limitations on DEI initiatives. As Carolyn Shields has argued, transformative leaders seek to support democracy, emancipation, and equity to transform inequitable organizations.[4] Critical to supporting the public good generated by community colleges is recognizing the intersections of the college with civic life, the community, and educating citizens as active participants in democracy.

Other contextual elements are included in the AACC competency of governance and local, state, and federal policy, which examines how organizations work. New to this competency in the fourth edition of the competencies is reference to an equity agenda. This addition signals an assumption that all community colleges should have an equity agenda, with the tasks of developing and implementing the agenda falling under the purview of the CEO. Of note, the new listing of this competency states that the CEO seeks ways to improve services so that Black, Latinx, Indigenous, and other marginalized students have the resources they need to be successful. Thus, it is essential for leaders to understand contextual competency in order to have an awareness of the levers available for change and which to access to move their institutions toward equitable outcomes.

Background information and an understanding of the contexts of the institution, the community, the state, and the country all contribute to how leaders come to understand the contexts of their community colleges. We argue that contextual competency warrants more consideration and prominence, as does the importance of context for the practice of equity-driven leadership in community colleges. This chapter, therefore, explores how developing a deep understanding of the current context, both locally and nationally, and examining that context from an ecological and systems perspective are often overlooked but imperative skills for leaders. One midlevel leader reflected on his college president's strong contextual competency: "He's done a really nice job of framing the story of what we're doing in a way that everybody can get behind it within the college and outside of the college. I think that is a critical competency for everyone to develop over time, and it's something that seems to come more naturally to some than others, but I'm of the belief that we can all learn to have it [contextual competencies]." This chapter provides examples of how leaders can further develop their contextual competency.

By taking campus visits or doing extensive "homework" before accepting a campus leadership position, all leaders likely have a general understanding of the basic context of a community college. Yet despite this due diligence, leaders are sometimes surprised when they take on a new position and find they must quickly discern the "who, what, where, when, why, and how" of their college and the community in which it is situated.[5] Our purpose in this chapter is not to suggest that leaders do not understand their college's context or that their understanding of it is inaccurate. Rather, we seek to highlight how community college contexts have changed and the all-important ways that institutional and societal contexts interact to produce the culture that is experienced by the campus community. Organizational culture emerges from the values and beliefs of campus members. Edgar Schein's seminal work on culture identified three levels of organizational culture: artifacts (what is seen), values (what matters to institutional members), and assumed values (the unseen and unspoken assumptions guiding behavior).[6] Our understanding of organizational culture, however, cannot be situated in a vacuum and must be embedded in the larger local, state, and national contexts.

Interestingly, contextual competency is more often discussed in disciplines such as engineering, in which context is studied to ensure alignment with a potential design solution or process change. In explaining the importance of contextual competency in the problem-solving process for engineers, Cynthia Atman, Ken Yasuhara, and Deborah Kilgore defined contextual competency as the ability to recognize and consider the relevant interrelated aspects of a design problem's context, comprising the people, places, events, and socioeconomic systems that shape and are shaped by a particular engineering design process.[7] We posit that this definition is transferable to community college leadership.

Defining Contextual Competency

The essence of contextual competency is the recognition of the interrelated aspects of the community college by attending to people, places (or spaces on campus), events (both internal and external to the college), and the many systems embedded in and pressing upon the community college.

Understanding contextual competency begins with identifying the trends in national and state environments that are putting pressure on community colleges and their leaders. The influence of neoliberalism on this larger stage trickles down to affect elements of funding, perceptions of public good, and the value proposition of higher education. We suggest that a deep understanding of the macro-level context can inform a leader's understanding of outcomes and actions at the local institutional level because national and state contexts significantly affect an institution's readiness for change and ability to institute an equity agenda.

PRESSING EXTERNAL FACTORS OF INFLUENCE

Our understanding of justice in community college settings and how we create environments that support equity must be expanded to include other life circumstances of students and community members. While social justice has received considerable attention in college settings, other types of justice are equally important, including financial justice (i.e., earning a living wage), access to suitable and affordable housing, food security, and access to high-quality health care. Over time, the shift from considering higher education to be a public good to considering it an individual private good that benefits students and graduates directly with improved income potential and life chances has emphasized the privilege of underlying structures and policies afforded to some and not others.[8] By stepping back to take a macro view of their students, faculty, and staff, leaders can seek to better understand the lived experiences of those on campus and to understand the paths people have taken before stepping foot on campus. Here, a central question for leaders is, *What have I assumed?* At the heart of equity work is recognizing the uneven benefits that systems afford to some and not others. It is more likely that change can occur when equity-driven leaders have a solid understanding of systems and strong contextual competency. In this section, we review several components affecting the external landscape of community colleges.

Neoliberalism

The core operating principle of neoliberalism centers on the individual and their private good gains, absent any governmental interaction. Matt Hastings argued that neoliberalism frames the purpose of education in terms of investments made in the development of students' human capital: what students should learn and the value of education are relative to their individual prospects for future earnings.[9] This move to a consumerism perspective of education shows up in community college mission statements. In a review of 421 such statements, David Ayers concluded that the dominant discourse centered on economic activity and argued that local communities had no choice but to adapt.[10] Recent evidence of the influence of neoliberalism on community colleges in North Carolina occurred via a review of strategic plans. Like mission statements, strategic plans present what is important to a community college, its vision, and its goals. This study analyzed the strategic plans of fifty-five of the state's fifty-eight community colleges using a student success framework focused on completion, learning, labor market outcomes, and equity. Critically, the study found that the greatest focus of strategic planning goals was labor market objectives (36 percent), followed by attention to transfer/completion (31 percent) and learning (25 percent). Minimal attention was paid to equity (9 percent).[11] Consider one midlevel leader's comment regarding the focus of community colleges on market outcomes: "The research is pretty compelling in terms of both locally and nationally that most folks who engage with a community college are trying to advance their socio-economic situation in some way, shape, or form, and as a community college that is embedded in a local and regional economy, we are setting them up for success in their own mobility." Certainly, improving students' social mobility and financial well-being is important, and so, too, is supporting the larger public good, which affects the local community and beyond. Neoliberal ideals have seeped into community college mission statements and strategic plans at the expense of a focus on equity and outcomes of public good.

Thinking of education in terms of its contribution to improving human capital translates to thinking of education funding as a return on public investment. Yet, as Ayers explained, the inequality that has been growing since the mid-1900s—even during periods of high employment—can be seen to support the reasonable conclusion that economic development is not necessarily equivalent to wealth expansion for individuals. When market forces dictate curricular decisions and students are viewed only relative to their desirability by employers, the espoused mission of community colleges to be committed to democracy and justice becomes threatened.[12] Even when proclaiming the ideal of neoliberalism and private benefit gains, the outcome is not gains for all. Indeed, neoliberal ideals perpetuate systems of inequity. Knowing that this external context exerts an influence, often invisible, on community colleges, equity-driven leaders must contemplate how to resist this confining context to advance opportunities for students, staff, and faculty and to support public good benefits for the surrounding community.

Funding

The underfunding of community colleges has existed since their inception. Christopher Mullin illustrated the magnitude of funding inequities by sector when pointing out that community colleges received just 27 percent of total federal, state, and local revenues while serving 43 percent of undergraduate students in 2007.[13] This trend is also apparent in federal, state, and local combined funding for full-time-equivalent (FTE) students, with a 2017 study showing that public community colleges received $8,700 per FTE compared to the $17,500 public four-year colleges received. Because most federal funding goes directly to students in the form of financial aid, community colleges rely mostly on support from the state (33 percent), local sources (20 percent), and local tuition (17 percent).[14] Community college leaders have long been lauded for their resourcefulness under constrained circumstances, yet less money translates to fewer support services for students. Because community colleges enroll the most disadvantaged populations of students, they face the Sisyphean task of supporting the students most in need with the least funding for services. As one midlevel leader stated plainly, "You know our sector has been down for a couple of years pretty bad, so it is hard to find the money to do some stuff."

The recent use of college promise programs and performance-based funding have added a new wrinkle to community college financing. College promise programs in many states (thirty-three at the time of writing) offer scholarships to cover tuition and fees for eligible students. These scholarships are covered either by last-dollar, first-dollar, or middle-dollar financing. Last-dollar programs contribute funding after all federal and state financial aid has been used; first-dollar programs apply promise scholarships before other scholarships (e.g., Pell Grants, state grant aid); and middle-dollar programs act like last-dollar programs in guaranteeing some aid to all students after state financial aid has been applied but before federal financial aid has been applied. Performance-based funding for community colleges allocates some state funding (in twenty-five states) based on student outcomes (e.g., persistence, completion). Neither program, however, adds more dollars into the community college sector; thus, community colleges remain under-resourced.[15]

Issues of equity exist for both promise programs and performance-based funding policies. The requirements of promise programs (e.g., long-term residency, home ownership, service requirements) may favor affluent residents and exclude newcomers to a state. The conversion of schooling to an economic transaction undermines education as a universal entitlement of all minors in a democracy, irrespective of the wealth of their parents or their future economic value to a community. A consequence of performance-based funding policies for community colleges is an increase in short-term certificates, which have less of an effect on income potential compared to associate degrees over time. Further, these performance-based funding programs create incentives for colleges to limit enrollment to students more likely to succeed, which exacerbates the issue of equity. Because community colleges have a smaller resource base than their four-year counterparts, they are less able to offer meaningful support to students and therefore have less capacity to improve student outcomes.[16]

The value proposition of higher education as a public good

Traditionally, community colleges have received public support, even when questions were raised regarding the value of higher education relative to its cost.

American confidence in higher education overall fell from 57 percent in 2015 to 48 percent in 2018 and 36 percent in 2023.[17] Political affiliation correlates to degree of confidence, with 19 percent of Republicans indicating a great deal or quite a lot of confidence in higher education compared to 32 percent of Independents and 59 percent of Democrats.[18] The differences in degree of confidence based on political affiliation have grown over time, and the overall trend in confidence is down across parties. Yet a look at differences in sentiments across sectors shows that community colleges are seen as better than public four-year colleges and universities in contributing to a strong workforce, being worth the cost, and preparing people to be successful; community colleges are also seen as better than four-year colleges and universities in spending money wisely and being run efficiently.[19] Despite these favored public views of community colleges, enrollments have decreased over time—and plummeted during the pandemic, in particular for Black students.[20]

Davis Jenkins and colleagues argued that three strategies are needed to help community colleges improve student outcomes and close equity gaps. First, students must connect with and explore programs in personalized ways. Second, programs (both credit and noncredit) must be revamped with clear pathways and varied delivery modes to meet student needs. Third, dual enrollment (in which students are enrolled both in high school and college) must be reconceptualized to serve as an on-ramp to degree programs.[21] The value of community colleges in improving the economic return of graduates centers on economic justice, yet the community also benefits from having educated citizens. Because the value of these public benefits is not always visible, it is important for leaders to point out these trickle-down benefits to the community and to connect the dots between student outcomes and economic justice.

Figure 3.1 illustrates how local, state, and national contexts exert pressure on the cultivation of an equity mind-set. The work of developing an equity mind-set occurs on the individual level; however, it is influenced by society, the issues of the particular time period, history, and the interaction of individual identities with the community, state, national, and global contexts. Developing equity-driven leaders requires individuals to keep up with the larger issues influencing the operations of community colleges and the societal factors affecting students.

FIGURE 3.1 The influence of local, state, and national contexts on the development of an equity mind-set

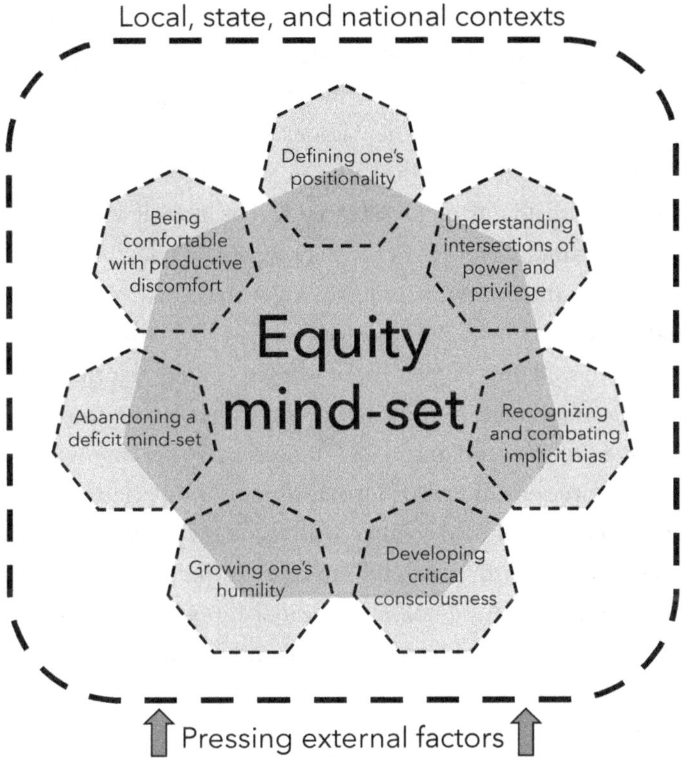

INSTITUTIONAL CONTEXT: THE PEOPLE, PLACES, AND EVENTS

Developing contextual competency requires leaders to have a systems view of the college and to understand the relationships among various activities. Paying attention to the people, places, and ongoing events on campus is aided by taking what Ronald Heifetz, in *Leadership Without Easy Answers*, would call "a view from the balcony."[22] In doing so, leaders can figuratively view the "dance floor" to see the interconnections among individuals, offices, and functional areas. Understanding more about the institution's context influences how leaders respond and how they can shape the understanding of campus members and help others to make sense of issues of equity. The internal context is influenced by the history of the college, including its founding story, traditions, previous decisions (in particular, those regarding funding and what is deemed mission critical), and how the institution reacts (and has reacted) to changes in the community. Consider how many community colleges work on retooling regional employees at times of plant closures or when new industries come to town, how many have opened their doors to immigrant populations and people fleeing wars. Simple practices like open-door policies and the degree of hierarchy in the organizational chart can also influence how things get done.

It takes substantial time for a new leader to gain a thorough understanding of the full context and stories of the campus, and, in some instances, contextual information is withheld during presidential hiring interviews. Incoming college presidents, for example, reported that they were not told the "whole" story of the college during the interview process. An American Council on Education presidential survey highlighted differences here, particularly for women of color. The survey found that only 53 percent of women of color felt that they had been given a realistic assessment of the current challenges facing the college relative to white women (68 percent) and men (70 percent).[23] Because women are often hired to lead institutions in precarious standing, it is especially critical for them to understand the institutional context in all its nuances. Michelle Ryan and colleagues have used the term "glass cliff" to refer to the tendency of women to be more likely than men to be appointed to leadership positions that are risky and precarious.[24] Thus, instead of facing a glass ceiling with little hope for advancement, women are often selected to lead institutions on the brink of failure and are thus susceptible to blame when things go badly.

To understand institutional context, it is important to know the level of people's readiness for change on campus. The starting point for infusing an equity orientation more fully on campus dictates how leaders begin. College members' readiness for change is influenced by the level of trust on campus, the commitment to change, and a belief in the capacity to make changes.[25] Importantly, many campus efforts result in performative equity rather than significant changes to structures and processes that actually improve equity on campus.[26] When leaders can identify campus actions that are performative versus those that result in deeper change, they acquire a fuller picture of the institutional context.

Readiness for change

In contemplating the types of equity work needed on campus, it is important to know and understand campus members' readiness for change. Readiness for change is both multilevel and multifaceted. A key element of being poised for change is a shared belief in the ability to implement the desired change, rather than simply talking about or envisioning it. Inherent in all change efforts is resistance, which can take many forms. Faculty, staff, and midlevel leaders may worry when change occurs on campus, wondering if they might end up worse off in their job or even let go. Getting early adopters on board is therefore critical, and celebrating small wins along the way helps.[27]

Central to assessing readiness for change is determining how consistent leaders are in their messaging, how information is shared, and experience with past change efforts. When campus members value the proposed change, it is more likely that they will support and help implement the change. Whether the institution has the time, resources, and information required to follow through on the proposed change all affect readiness for change. The institution's context and culture also contribute significantly to readiness to change. What change theorists often leave unaddressed in their models for change, however, is how trust influences the change process. Trust is influenced by several factors, including fear of reprisal if trust is violated; the history of interactions, which can either increase or decrease confidence that people will do what they say and assume the best of others; and the mutual understanding of intentions and shared desire for a particular outcome.[28] In chapter 5, we provide an expanded investigation of trust, given that it undergirds our blueprint for developing equity-driven leaders.

Eric Felix and Ángel González provided a conceptual way of looking at equity work based on the types and levels of resistance involved and the responsibilities inherent in various roles.[29] They argue that the more alignment there is between the efforts of senior leaders and campus members regarding equity, the more progress occurs. However, what is not included in this model is trust and how trust contributes to readiness for change. Trust is critically important when considering ways to mobilize action (in their model, Felix and González pose the question, "How can you listen to your team who are leading racial equity efforts and work towards building trust and transparency?"). Leaders must understand levels of institutional trust when working to support equity change on campus, and understanding the campus context helps determine the level of change in which the campus is ready to engage.

When Darren Osburn and Tammy Gocial administered the Higher Education Faculty Trust Inventory at three community colleges in the Midwest, they identified several factors influencing faculty trust in administrators.[30] The authors identified the following elements present in relationships of high trust between faculty and administrators:

- Administrators had high levels of regular interactions with faculty members.
- Administrators had previous faculty experiences, making faculty feel that leaders could relate to them.
- Administrators demonstrated openness, competence, and reliability.[31]

Osburn and Gocial found that a negative influence on trust emerged when faculty believed administrators were looking to move to another position.

As leaders seek to measure readiness for change on campus, they must assess what levels of trust currently exist. Importantly, if the campus has an environment of low trust, leaders must work to build more trust before campus members will be willing to engage in change. Simply getting out and about on campus provides leaders a means to learn directly from campus members, which in turn increases their accessibility to faculty, staff, and students. Knowing what is being discussed in the campus rumor mill can also help leaders dispel rumors and provide information that builds a shared narrative. When leaders show they are reliable and committed to the hard work of creating substantial change, trust increases.

Felix and González's model for advancing racial equity in community colleges (figure 3.2) illustrates how context influences approaches to equity on campus. Equity-driven leaders must first assess where their campus is located within the model to determine how collective action and movement to support equity can occur. Leaders should consider the level of trust individuals have in leadership on campus and how this level of trust contributes to the college's readiness for change. At the core of all change is getting individuals to change behavior and implementing new ways of thinking that will result in change.

Getting individuals to change their behavior is the basic building block of change efforts. Helping everyone on campus understand how implicit bias influences interactions, how deficit mind-sets limit people's expectations of others, and when polices reify privilege for some over others is critical to this process. Often, however, equity work is seen as the job of equity advocates rather than a larger collective effort. Expanding the buy-in to changes supporting equity and

FIGURE 3.2 A model for advancing racial equity in community colleges

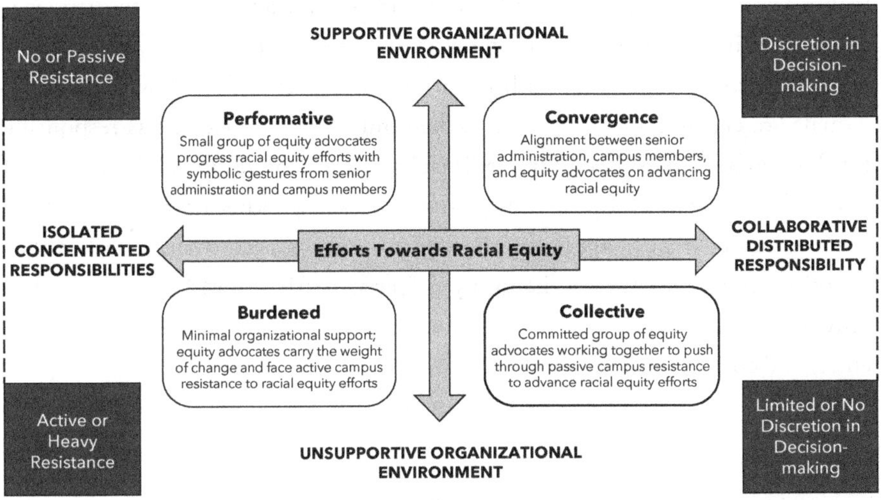

Source: Printed with permission from Eric R. Felix. Eric R. Felix and Ángel de Jesus González, *Mapping Organizational Support and Collective Action: Towards a Model for Advancing Racial Equity in Community Colleges* (Berkeley: University of California, Berkeley, Center for Studies in Higher Education, forthcoming).

increasing readiness for change on campus requires many concurrent efforts. First, people must be able to see value in the proposed change. In the case of equity-driven change efforts, leaders can help campus members see where equity gaps exist and understand why it is important to reduce those gaps. As reviewed in chapter 2, developing an equity mind-set requires abandoning a deficit mind-set that believes equity gaps result from shortcomings in students. Rather, campus members must be encouraged to see that they can change the way the college operates and eliminate equity gaps, and they must believe that that goal is important. Next, individuals must believe that there is institutional capability to accomplish the change. Here, leaders can help by highlighting which resources (including time, human resources, financial resources, and infrastructure) are available to support the implementation of the change. Reviewing past change initiatives and their outcomes can provide insight into how past successes and failures have influenced the college's culture and its readiness to change.

People get change fatigue when constantly bombarded by new initiatives, which are common when new leaders arrive on campus.[32] When the college engages in ongoing organizational learning instead, change is a natural part of the process, as policies and processes evolve when new information and feedback are considered.[33] When leaders start from an inquiry mind-set that assesses how things are going on campus, faculty and staff become accustomed to the idea of continuous improvement and are more ready for change.

As shown in figure 3.2, readiness for change is evident in how many individuals are engaged in the process. When only a few are viewed as responsible for the change, broad-based support is lacking (the change effort is "burdened"). Even when a small group of equity advocates are working on a change effort, without leadership engagement, the effort becomes performative rather than resulting in actual change (the effort is "performative" and "collective"). It is only when higher levels of alignment are present that a higher level of readiness emerges ("convergence" is present).

Data Spotlight: Voices from the Field

Omar is the associate dean of liberal arts at a small community college in the Southwest. He reflected on the challenges of doing equity work on campus resulting from funding issues and discrepancies between adjunct and full-time faculty: "We are like most community colleges who have [as few] full-time faculty as possible to try to save money by operating with as many adjuncts as possible, which causes equity issues right away. We have pay equity issues because we have a lot of adjuncts—we try to be careful but we still ask a lot more of adjuncts than I think is reasonable. But then adjuncts also don't do things, like they are not required to do a lot of the required things that full-time people are doing. So, if you're going to do something like have minimum qualifications that includes social justice, and pedagogy like training or experience, you're not necessarily going to expect that of your adjuncts. If you're going to have trainings that are mandatory for full-time faculty and staff, you're not going to have that for adjuncts. There's always going to be a discrepancy between how your department runs based on how many full-time faculty that you have." On this campus, issues of equity were apparent in the ratio of full-time faculty to part-time adjuncts with respect to workload, pay differences, and institutional expectations for equity work. Campus members felt burdened and less able to advance an equity agenda.

As Felix and González's model for advancing racial equity in community colleges and Omar's Data Spotlight highlight, it is important for leaders to understand the will of campus members to engage in equity change efforts and to understand whether change is seen as the role of only a few or as a shared commitment of everyone on campus. As Omar pointed out, equity issues regarding faculty status provide a context for how change efforts are seen based on role. When equity work falls only to full-time faculty members, the campus may be in the "burdened" category of Felix and González's model. Leaders must start by asking themselves questions such as the following:

- What is the role of adjunct faculty in supporting equity initiatives on campus?
- How is equity evident between full-time and adjunct faculty?
- What will it take for campus members to find value in supporting equity efforts on campus?
- What campus resources are available to commit to equity efforts?
- How do current levels of campus trust contribute to the college's readiness for change?

Performative equity

Performative equity occurs when leaders and colleges adopt positions that appear to value equity but do not have policies or practices in place to allow for systemic changes to the organizational structures that perpetuate racist practices.[34] Performative equity appears when change efforts are the responsibility of only a few individuals, when public responses of the college to racial violence and inequity do not result in changes to practices, and when equity is merely symbolic and not evident in representation among students, faculty, and leaders.

Faculty supporting equity efforts, even those who are "equity champions," face burnout from "racial battle fatigue," which results from the significant emotional labor they provide to support ethnic studies programming on campus.[35] When equity efforts are not supported on campus, individual advocates carry the burden and are unable to achieve broad-based change. One midlevel leader summed this up: "I mean, you have a chief diversity officer with no budget. So what is that supposed to do? Because if you don't put money behind something, it's not important." Budget allocations are where we see what an institution values putting its money and time toward. Recall that being ready for change includes having the resources needed to accomplish the proposed change.

When equity efforts are carried forward by only a few and not supported in the budget, the results are often performative.[36] In such cases, campuses "say" they are doing equity, but deep, real change does not occur. When equity champions face resistance on campus to working for change to support equity, they burn out or are silenced. One midlevel leader commented on resistance on his campus: "You know, sometimes it's the same person who's a champion in one space[; then] they can be a low-level resistor in other spaces." Yet there is power in numbers; when a collective group takes action, resistance can be overcome. Actions to support equity work on campus are recognized with national awards, and, in some instances, campuses have training programs for equity champions that help increase the number of those actively supporting equity efforts.[37]

Regardless of position and title, when equity champions are overburdened, efforts to achieve racial equity are limited and become reduced to performative equity. Jerel Ezell identified three action steps to help campuses move past performative equity:

- Actively recruiting, hiring, and retaining members of underrepresented groups for admission, faculty roles, and in administration. Representation on campus signals support for equitable opportunities.
- Creating anti-racism resources as part of mandated implicit bias training. Using evidence-based strategies to address bias helps build a culture of inclusion.
- Developing spaces on campus for community engagement, providing opportunities for community members to access academic courses, and including community members in campus committees. Strong connections between community colleges and their local communities provide a critical means to move from performance to real change.[38]

A campus's readiness for change informs the possibility and likelihood of leaders being able to help their colleges move beyond performative equity to taking the action required for the deep change needed on campus to address long-embedded practices that reify racialized organizations. Equity efforts in community colleges are often symbolically present in DEI units. In the following review of current DEI efforts, we highlight how many of these fall short of moving toward deep, long-term change and instead become merely performative.

CONTEXT FOR DIVERSITY, EQUITY, AND INCLUSION IN HIGHER EDUCATION

Centering equity and creating leadership roles that focus on equity have received renewed emphasis in higher education owing to the heightened public awareness of DEI issues since 2020 with George Floyd's murder becoming a tipping point for the nation in terms of racial equity. Yet legislative rollbacks on advances in DEI and attacks on DEI efforts starting in 2023 mean that community colleges in some states have had to recast their equity work. Work on the initial efforts of multicultural strategies to support minority student success in community colleges began in the 1990s and focused predominately on individual versus larger institutional efforts.[39] Robert Rhoads and James Valadez offered a voice of critique around this time as they put forth multiculturalism as a means to support the democratic mission of community colleges.[40] They pointed out that issues of power and privilege can limit roles for marginalized students and their future opportunities as workers and argued for the need to empower students, allowing them more self-direction. Early efforts in the 1990s by community college leaders often occurred in isolation on individual campuses. Consider how Zelema Harris, the president of Parkland College in Illinois, and Pauline Kayes, the director of Parkland's Office of Women's Programs and Services, reported in 1995 on their college-wide response to multicultural and international challenges. They stated that the local context had influenced the college's initiative to address changing demographics in the community, which included strategies to address and increase the attention paid to exclusive policies and procedures, the "hidden curriculum," implicit bias, and increasing campus awareness of issues of cultural diversity.[41] These strategies are remarkably similar to efforts underway in DEI centers at community colleges today.

Another campus-specific example is provided by Augustine Gallego, the chancellor of the San Diego Community College District, who wrote in 1996 that access to community colleges without educational equity and success for students of all backgrounds, races, and ethnic groups is not enough. A commitment to equity and success for a multicultural student body is still necessary today.[42] Chancellor Gallego argued that campus leaders must demonstrate a commitment to diversity and, like President Harris, noted the need to develop appropriate policies. Now, nearly thirty years later, issues of equity are top of mind and covering similar ground to provide the campus environments best suited to support the needs of the diverse student body enrolled in community colleges. Clearly, the deep change needed to move beyond performative equity did not occur with these early efforts to address issues of multiculturalism in the 1990s. Critical to advancing equity work is naming how color evasion ideologies and the hidden curriculum operate out of sight and discourage action.

The Hidden Curriculum

Hidden curriculum, or *invisible curriculum*, refers to the unstated norms, policies, and expectations of which students need to be aware to succeed in college but which are kept "hidden," or not made explicit to students. Thus, this concept may help to explain why retention and persistence rates have remained stagnant, even with significant investments in student supports. Organizational "insiders"—faculty, staff, and leaders—contribute to the hidden curriculum by making assumptions and failing (whether consciously or unconsciously) to be explicit in their expectations of students. For example, a faculty member that continually answers, "Read the syllabus," in response to student questions may not realize that much of the language in a syllabus is "academic speak" or jargon that students are unfamiliar with. Or when confronted with a student issue, a staff member may tell the student to visit the Dean of Students Office without explaining the role of the office or even how to go about making contact, a small detail but one that students may not understand. In creating equity-driven campuses, the "hidden" must become visible as we work to change the systems that perpetuate injustice. Dismantling the hidden curriculum through intentional educational opportunities for faculty and staff is one step in creating an equity-driven campus. A hidden curriculum exists for leaders, too, as they seek to advance in their positions. Ideal worker norms present particular expectations of how leaders are to look, act, and lead, but such norms are typically not made explicit.

Multiculturalism

One outcome of early efforts to address issues of multiculturalism was the founding of ethnic studies courses, which devoted space in curricula to learning about various cultures. However, a study conducted in 1992 found that less than one-third of community colleges offered ethnic studies courses.[43] Another study from the 1990s corroborated these early findings, reporting that 38 percent of the 350 community colleges surveyed offered courses in ethnic studies and that just 37 percent had courses in women's studies.[44] Efforts to combat the hidden curriculum by focusing attention on ethnic studies fell short in leading broad-based changes in terms of diversity in community colleges. Beyond the curriculum, community colleges, like their four-year counterparts, invested substantial institutional resources to create positions and offices to shepherd multicultural efforts on campus.

Movement from multicultural support on campus to DEI efforts represents a change in focus from support for different cultures and identities (e.g., the "melting pot" or "salad bowl" theory of blending various cultures) to inclusivity: how individuals from diverse backgrounds form a community in which all feel included and have a sense of belonging.[45] For many decades, institutions were focused on multicultural efforts and initiatives. Multiculturalism is an ideal that, when achieved, means that everyone—regardless of their differences—is recognized, accepted, and celebrated. Multicultural education has its roots in the Civil Rights Movement of the 1960s and 1970s and is most clearly reflected in curricular changes such as the inclusion of culture-specific courses in curricula and campus events celebrating a variety of cultures. Over time, multicultural centers grew from affinity groups to more comprehensive units on campus. It is not uncommon to find well-staffed multicultural centers providing many educational, social, and cultural activities that enhance the campus culture. These centers provide a safe space for students, especially in today's climate of backlash against DEI efforts.

As is certainly appropriate, the focus of efforts labeled "multicultural" is almost exclusively on students and their experiences. This focus, however, can result in a campus with a long list of activities celebrating difference but without a deeper commitment to equity.

An example of the change in focus from multiculturalism to diversity is provided by Manchester Community College. In 2006, Patrick Sullivan recounted how current diversity efforts had unfolded on the Manchester campus over time.[46] His case study outlined campus activities over a nineteen-year period beginning in about 1987, including the work of an active diversity committee that contributed action items to the college's strategic plan, a minority caucus and a women's caucus that provided leadership, and a Hispanic club and a gay and lesbian alliance that expanded inclusion. Key to this work was a focus on ongoing improvements that evolved over time and became institutionalized.

In late 2020, perhaps in response to the social unrest experienced during the previous few months, the AACC created a framework entitled *Diversity, Equity, and Inclusion: Framework for Action*, which included five essential elements.[47] Note here, too, how institutional context influences the DEI planning process. The five elements of the AACC framework are as follows:

- Defining what diversity, equity, and inclusion mean within your organization and communicating those understandings to all community members.
- Assessing culture, policies, and practices through the lens of equity and inclusion.
- Educating faculty, staff, and students about diversity, equity, and inclusion.
- Implementing policy reviews and scrutinizing operations to ensure alignment with diversity, equity, and inclusion principles.
- Ensuring that all voices are represented and welcomed.

Fast-forward to the current day, and we see that organizations beyond the AACC are working to support community colleges and providing strategies to advance equity in community colleges. Achieving the Dream released an equity toolkit to provide campus leaders with practical tools to improve equity on campus. The toolkit outlines eight equity principles and provides guiding questions to lead dialogue on campus, as well as tools and guides to working with data. It also gives real-world examples of where the tools have been working on campuses. The principles are as follows:

Equity Principle 1: Develop an equity mind-set.

Equity Principle 2: Interrogate institutional practices, structures, and policies; replace those that are inequitable.

Equity Principle 3: Integrate holistic supports throughout the student experience.

Equity Principle 4: Embrace cultural competence and culturally responsive pedagogy.

Equity Principle 5: Leverage existing and new data to support a culture of inquiry and evidence.

Equity Principle 6: Drive positive change through perseverance and power sharing.

Equity Principle 7: Engage with the local community to develop partnerships that lead to economic vitality.

Equity Principle 8: Acknowledge the pervasiveness of racism and discrimination in the United States of America.[48]

As in our model for developing a transformative leadership identity (see figure 2.4 in chapter 2), which has an equity mind-set at its center, Achieving the Dream includes developing an equity mind-set as its first equity principle. Our model looks more at the level of individual level development, whereas the AACC and Achieving the Dream frameworks focus on organizational levers for change to achieve equity on campus. We argue that to advance work in social justice, campuses must move past individual change toward organizational change. Community colleges must move from performative equity to transformative, deep change. A foundational first step in this process is developing equity-driven leaders equipped to advance change at the organizational level.

Diversity, equity, and inclusion

Diversity, equity, and inclusion have become ubiquitous in our organizations across all sectors. Alternative labels includes justice, equity, diversity, and inclusion (JEDI); diversity, equity, inclusion, and belonging (DEIB); diversity, inclusion, and belonging (DIB); and diversity and inclusion (D&I), among others. Many organizations have spent considerable time and solicited extensive feedback from constituents to create shared definitions of key terms related to equity. This shared understanding on college campuses then drives planning, initiatives, and public-facing representations of the institution, such as websites and institutional guidance documents.

Data Spotlight: Voices from the Field

Becca is a new interim diversity officer at a community college in the Northeast. Reflecting on her first year in the position, she stated, "I think for us, we just don't have the people. I'm an office of one. I'm not the only one who is alone leading an office as there are other places on campus that are single-person offices. A problem for me is that I haven't been able to do all the things I wanted to do this year. I just simply don't have the time. There are some practices that were engaging that just aren't sustainable, so I'm trying to help the college really move in a way to create more sustainable practices and more collaborative opportunities because I can't do it alone. Funding is also an issue. You have to put your money where your mouth is. People need to see the work of equity not just as the work of the Office of Diversity and Inclusion—it's not just up to me. This work is hard work and it's not . . . just hard . . . but it's emotionally and mentally draining." When the work of equity is relegated to a single office or a single person, real change cannot occur.

At the time of the 2021 National Survey of Community College Leadership for Social Justice, most leaders across all leadership positions (59 percent) indicated that their college did have a formal DEI plan (figure 3.3).

Most responses of yes to having a DEI plan came from presidents (66 percent), whereas the fewest came from directors (49 percent). This difference may be a result of awareness; perhaps more presidents initiated DEI plans than directors. If we assume this to be the case, then the lower response rate of directors indicates a gap in awareness of the existence of DEI plans. The differences in response may also indicate that DEI plans are not fully understood or embraced

FIGURE 3.3 Percentage of campuses with a DEI plan

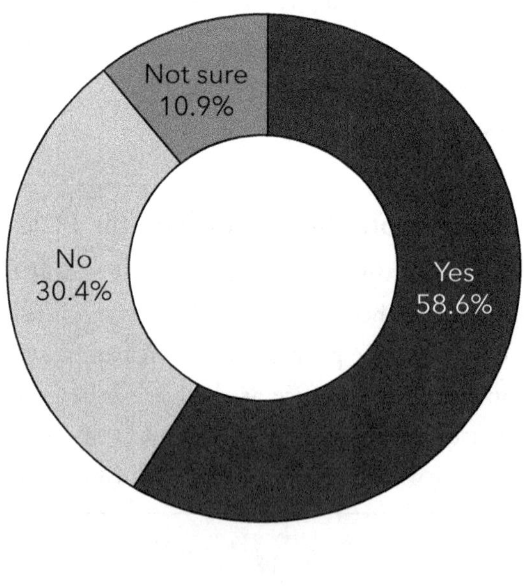

throughout the campus, a situation that can result in isolated efforts concentrated in just a few spots on campus, as noted in the archetypes illustrated in figure 3.2.

Components of a DEI Plan

The Education Advisory Board reviewed forty DEI plans from across the United States, Canada, Australia, and the United Kingdom and identified four key components of strong DEI plans:

1. Define a campus-specific DEI vision and vocabulary.
2. Create achievable goals by defining specific action items.
3. Facilitate follow-through by building in accountability measures.
4. Communicate transparently on current standing, and regularly update stakeholders on progress and roadblocks.[49]

While there are some differences in terminology, there is more commonality than difference across the public-facing definitions of DEI on college websites. Diversity, for example, is commonly defined as encompassing all aspects of human difference, including differences among social groups such as ethnicity, class, age, gender, sexuality, ability, religion, and nationality. The concept of campus diversity emerged in the 1970s and 1980s. During these decades, colleges focused almost exclusively on racial diversity and on the numbers and visual representation of people of color in higher education. Goals related to diversity are common across colleges and universities, and our collective understanding of diversity has grown to encompass many aspects of our social identity. However, when goals relate only to numbers and percentages of one group or another, institutions never confront the inherent systems of oppression that persist in all aspects of education. In such cases, leaders may simply hold up a figure and assume that their audience will equate representation with their college being an equitable and socially just institution. However, diverse representation, does not mean a campus is equitable, nor does it mean that the campus culture is inclusive.

The "E" of "DEI"—equity—is an important concept for institutions to clearly define and distinguish from similar terms like *equality*. *Equity* means acknowledging and addressing structural inequalities that advantage some and disadvantage others. *Equality* means treating people equally but ignores the inherent and long-standing policies and practices that have perpetuated injustice. Lily Zheng has usefully described equity as the measured experience of individual, interpersonal, and organizational success and well-being across all stakeholder populations and the *absence* of discrimination, mistreatment, and abuse for all.[50]

The "I" of "DEI"—inclusion—reflects the campus environment and whether community members feel respected, feel a sense of belonging, and feel engaged in a meaningful way on their campus. Perhaps because of the student-centered focus of colleges and universities, a "B" for "belonging," a concept related to inclusion, is often added to the "DEI" abbreviation. A sense of belonging is connected to the feeling of "mattering," and fostering this for students on campus is often sufficient to drive student outcomes. Terrell Strayhorn is the theorist most associated with the concept of a sense of belonging, and most of his work focuses on college students rather than the other campus community members. More recently, Strayhorn has begun addressing workplace belonging, which he defines as the emotional connection to a company that employees feel.[51] Workplace belonging is strongly correlated with equitable pay, meaningful work, and diverse suppliers, such as businesses owned by women and minoritized people. Further, a sense of belonging can take on heightened importance in certain contexts and intersects with one's social identities. Strayhorn's theory is a staple in our understanding of college student development and is now being applied in the higher education workplace for faculty and staff. Early research on workplace belonging in higher education contexts has found that workplace belonging is positively correlated with job satisfaction for part-time adjunct faculty at two-year community colleges, year-to-year retention for administrative support staff at historically Black colleges and universities, and a reduction in sick days at four-year research universities.[52]

What is evident in the data on DEI plans from the 2021 National Survey of Community College Leadership and in Becca's narrative (in the second Data Spotlight of this chapter) is that the current DEI work being done on community college campuses is largely performative. It is simply not enough to have a DEI office or a dedicated leader for diversity efforts. When DEI offices lack funding to do the work of centers, institutions are sending a message that equity work is not mission critical. Real change is not occurring because equity is not viewed as a shared value. The building blocks of a strong DEI plan rely on establishing a context-specific vocabulary and vision for DEI that can support real change, without these, equity work risks being reduced to performative equity. If measurable goals and action items are created and regular assessments put in place to ensure accountability, movement toward equity is more likely to occur. Leaders must constantly communicate updates, emphasize that equity is a core value for the college, and provide the resources to achieve the college's identified equity goals. Only then can real change occur.

THE CONTEXTUAL INFLUENCE OF IDEOLOGICAL WARFARE

While each component of DEI has the potential to become politically charged and create tension, the term that has caused the most debate in all layers of education is *social justice.* Indeed, when our survey on leadership for social justice in community colleges launched in 2021, we were surprised by the nature of some of the feedback we received. Consider the following responses to the prompt, "In what ways do you consider yourself to be a leader for social justice?":

- "The only thing I can say for certain is that few people can define for me what they mean by social justice. It's an amorphous concept that people use without any shared meaning among groups as to what we're actually talking about."
- "Haven't we gone a little overboard with this?"
- "I actually despise how the term is used today in our cancel culture. I am old school and we call it doing the right thing. I've always done the right thing for my 50+ years in the workforce. Treat people right and hold them accountable. So many of the recent "social justice" warriors forget about that accountability part. They believe it is justified to assault people, maim them, or burn down cities in the name of social justice. The movement has lost its focus and you are likely to see the pendulum swing the other way because of it."

These comments may be discouraging to some, but it is important to listen to all voices and to consider the backlash against social justice in the local, state, and national contexts. When leaders understand points of resistance, they can focus on what it means for individuals to come together from different starting points. As highlighted earlier in the diversity frameworks, it is critical to come to consensus on shared, context-dependent definitions of equity and social justice on campus.

Fierce ideological wars are being fought on college campuses among community members, as well as at the state and national levels. Despite their positions of power and privilege, senior leaders face significant constraints because of external stakeholders, local and state politics, and regional history. Consider the 2022 findings from a survey conducted by the *Chronicle of Higher Education,* in which Eric Kelderman reported the following:

> More than 80 percent of presidents chose national politics as one of eight topics that would cause them to self-censor their public remarks to avoid creating a controversy for themselves or their colleges (respondents could choose as many topics as necessary). Two-thirds of respondents chose state politics. Many also said they self-censor on topics that colleges have often identified as central to their mission and values, such as diversity, equity, and inclusion; gender and sexual identity; and racial justice.[53]

When DEI work looks like performative equity that is being done merely to improve a college's reputation and to show stakeholders that "something" is being done to improve representation and build equitable and inclusive systems, the work does not result in any real or deep change. When no real change has occurred in the past, it is tough to get individuals engaged in working on new initiatives to support equity. Likewise, when all change efforts are made at the individual level, change at the organizational level cannot occur. The type of checkbox mentality used in these types of efforts means that campus members lose trust in the process.

When asked what his campus's social justice efforts were, one midlevel leader commented, "Minimal, I think I would say. It seems like they address issues when they happen, and they do it on a surface level and then it's forgotten." Monitoring campus activity builds a certain context on campus, too. One midlevel dean of students recalled his office bringing in a speaker to review Native American history in the region: "They sent a delegate from the president's cabinet to attend, and not more than that, to ensure that we weren't overly emphasizing [a viewpoint]. So, it's very forefront for me to make sure we're not doing too much." These examples demonstrate that campus leaders often engage in minimal support for DEI efforts when their community context does not support a focus on equity. Campus members take note of how their leaders and the campus as a whole act or take a stand on DEI issues. The tension for some leaders is how to support deep change around equity in an environment that is openly hostile to DEI efforts. It is little wonder that many DEI strategies result in performative equity rather than systemic change.

Yet even when colleges make efforts to move equity forward, challenges occur. California Community Colleges, the state's community college system, has committed to making changes that move beyond merely checking the box on DEI. They released a diversity, equity, inclusion, and accessibility (DEIA) action statement that advocates for the promotion of equity through equity-minded policies and practices, including embedding DEIA competencies and criteria in employee evaluations and tenure review processes.[54] Several faculty members sued over this requirement, arguing that it makes them incorporate ideologies into their classes that they do not believe in.[55] At the time of writing, the lawsuit is pending, but its mere existence reveals that conflict over ideology is ripe in community colleges.

The existence and support of DEI has become so politically charged that some institutions, and their states, have banned DEI offices and any diversity programming or training. It appears to be more common to see negative, rather than positive, headlines about DEI efforts. For example, a 2023 *Forbes* article posed the following question: "Do campus diversity offices help or harm diversity?"[56] *Forbes* then published a follow-up article a few months later asking, "Is diversity, equity, and inclusion officially dead?"[57] While few scholarly articles in the field of higher education have been as blunt as *Forbes*, many opinion pieces have shared similar sentiments, such as a 2023 *Chronicle of Higher Education* piece titled "Higher Ed's DEI Lip Service: On My Disillusioning Experience as a Chief Diversity Officer" and a 2023 *Diversity Issues in Higher Education* article titled "DEI Efforts Are in Trouble. Here's How We Change That." Pieces like this suggest that there is potential for meaningful change—even against the current political backdrop.[58]

The backlash against DEI is certainly not limited to higher education and may in fact be more prevalent in business and industry. In 2016, a *Harvard Business Review* article by Frank Dobbin and Alexandra Kalev provided evidence that formal diversity programs in 829 midsize and large firms were not actually increasing diversity in terms of representation. Five years into required diversity training for managers, companies saw no improvement in the proportion of white women, Black men, or Hispanic people in management. Further, the percentage of Black women in management decreased by 9 percent on average across the firms over the same time period. The authors concluded that required diversity training simply does not work and may actually result in anger, resistance, and animosity toward such requirements. Instead, companies found success by focusing not on formal programs but targeted recruitment, mentoring programs, self-managed teams, and task forces that promoted social accountability.[59]

Efforts to advance DEI to date have often focused on what is public facing: how colleges *appear* to be making efforts to support change on campus. Certainly, establishing DEI positions, offices, and programming signals to various audiences the campus's interest in supporting these efforts. Yet, in DEI offices, it is often just one person leading the college's DEI efforts. Such efforts allow colleges to "check the DEI box," but without involving all campus members and providing the appropriate resources, the fundamental changes that are needed will not occur.

Anti-DEI Legislation

When DEI statements became a common topic in admissions and hiring about ten years ago, institutional leaders probably did not anticipate that these statements would become part of an intense ideological battle among colleges and universities and their respective state legislatures. As noted in the introduction to this book, the *Chronicle of Higher Education* started a DEI legislation tracker to document which states have introduced legislation, which have final legislative approval, which have new DEI laws, and which had bills that failed to pass or were vetoed. At the time of writing, nearly half the states (twenty-two) have collectively introduced forty bills, with only seven becoming law.[60] On one hand, the number of states introducing bills raises an alarm about the strength of the anti-DEI backlash and anti-DEI politics. On the other, the small number of states where bills have become law (five) indicates a high level of resistance to codifying into law specific elements of DEI offices, training, statements, and hiring practices yet still has a chilling effect in colleges across the country. By design, community colleges serve their surrounding communities, and students from low-income and minoritized backgrounds often comprise a significant proportion of the student body. The consequences of anti-DEI legislation are exacerbating the decline in enrollments witnessed since the COVID-19 pandemic that have already affected marginalized community college students. Consider the long-term effects of Proposition 209 in California, which banned race-based affirmative action in public universities in 1996. In 2022, Zachary Bleemer examined the effects of this legislation on the educational experiences and wages of underrepresented minority freshman applicants before and after the legislation (1994 and 2002) and found that the legislation had had a cascade effect. Following the legislation, underrepresented minority freshmen enrolled in lower-quality colleges, their degree attainment declined overall, and average wages in their twenties and thirties declined relative to their non-underrepresented minority peers. Moreover, many marginalized students who were qualified did not even apply to any University of California campus.[61] Early effects of current anti-DEI legislation are evident in the closure of DEI and LGBTQIA+ centers, faculty unease about what they teach in their classrooms, and changes to office names and position titles.

The weaponizing of DEI language by political actors is also evident since the increase in anti-DEI legislation. The midlevel leaders we interviewed noted that the use of critical language was based on local context. One midlevel leader located in the South said, "[You have to] know your context and knowing what verbiage and what phrases are going to resonate, and which ones have been potentially co-opted by politicians looking to find their own angle." This leader noted that they used the term *economic mobility* as a substitute for *equity*, as it was more acceptable in their state's ideological context.

INSTITUTIONAL CONTEXTS AND LEADER PERSPECTIVES ON DEI AND SOCIAL JUSTICE

Leaders, like all citizens, are bombarded by national media coverage of the cultural wars and other external contextual influences. Another layer is added to contextual competency when turning attention to their own institutional contexts. Administrative leaders on community college campuses have differing perspectives on DEI based on their positions, as well as on aspects of their identity. When asked to reflect on equity on campus overall, presidents and chancellors who participated in the 2021 National Survey of Community College Leadership for Social Justice were more likely to indicate that their campus was equitable compared to midlevel leaders. One-third of presidents and chancellors selected "very much" when asked whether the term *equitable* described their college overall. Top-level leaders in the survey were committed to supporting equity work on campus. The context of the institution, including its history, finances, and vision, contributed to how these leaders could enact strategies to make their campuses equitable.

Institutional Context: Survey Data Perspectives

The data presented next, while perhaps not surprising, suggest that there is substantial work to accomplish to create equity-driven colleges and thus ensure that a majority of leaders are able to describe their campus as equitable—and, more importantly, to experience their campuses as equitable. For example, the fact that only one out of five deans said that the term *equitable* "very much" described their campus is worthy of considerable contemplation given that deans, as midlevel leaders, are often in critical positions to directly influence policies and practices (figure 3.4). The fact that only a minority of surveyed leaders responded that the term *equitable* "very much" described their campus underscores the need to develop equity-driven community college leaders.

FIGURE 3.4 Percentage of leaders describing their campus as equitable

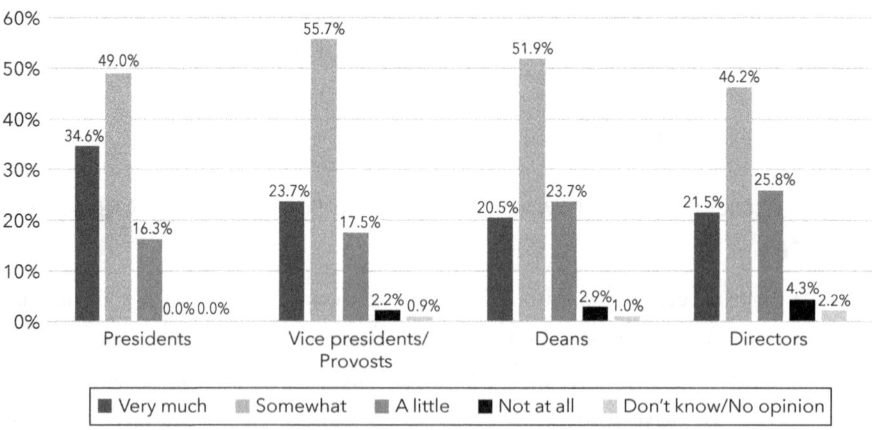

Similar patterns of difference between top- and midlevel leaders emerge in survey data about perceptions of inclusivity and other measures related to campus culture. A large percentage (44 percent) of presidents and chancellors indicated "very much" when asked whether the term *inclusive* described their college overall, compared with 27 percent of midlevel leaders at the director level (figure 3.5). These types of gaps in sense-making about equity on campus indicate that a culture of inclusion is not pervasive.

As yet another indication of a disconnect in perceptions of campus culture between college presidents and other campus members, 52 percent of presidents and chancellors selected "very much" when asked whether their college, overall, provides safe spaces for dialogue, compared with just 24 percent of midlevel leaders (figure 3.6). As we argued in chapter 2, it is important to have productive discomfort as individuals work toward becoming equity-driven leaders; if those in midlevel positions do not believe it is safe to have uncomfortable conversations on campus, progress in their development of an equity mind-set will slow considerably.

While survey data, such as that presented here, has limitations, the patterns in our data are telling. Midlevel leaders have different perspectives from senior-level leaders regarding DEI efforts on campus. To advance equity initiatives on campus, senior leaders must recognize that their perspectives and experiences of campus culture may often stand in opposition to those of a large segment of the campus community. This recognition is central to becoming

FIGURE 3.5 Percentage of leaders describing their campus as inclusive

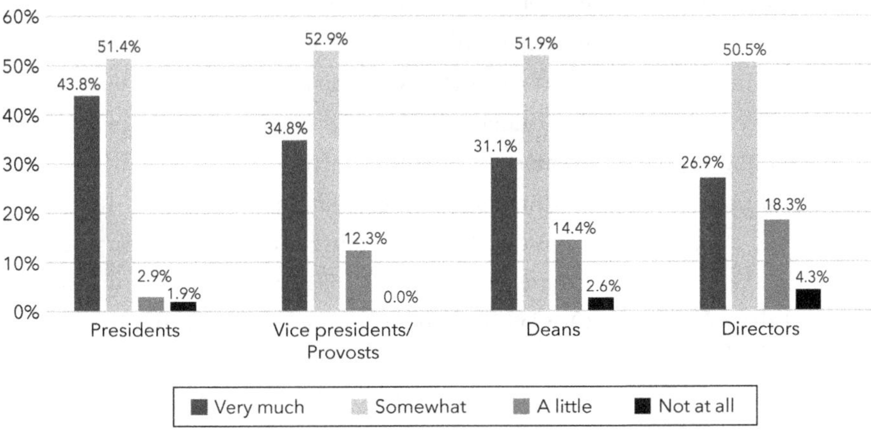

FIGURE 3.6 Percentage of leaders describing their campus as providing safe spaces for dialogue

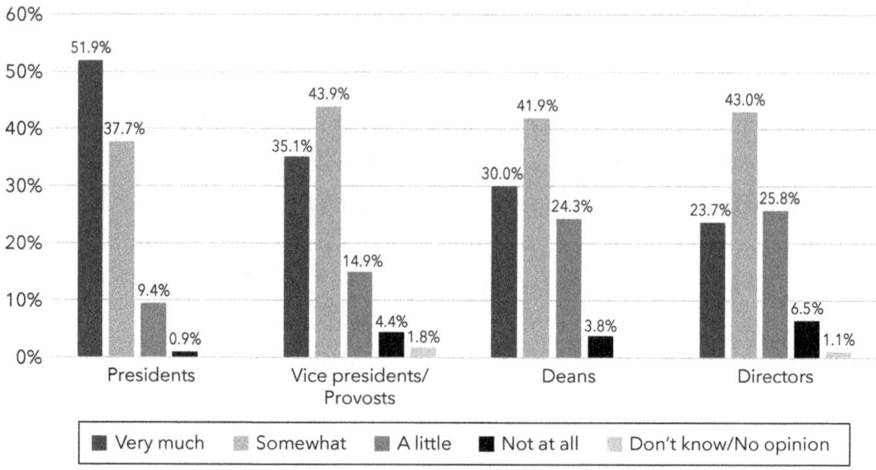

equity-minded. Because transformative leadership requires an environment in which organizational participants feel respected, included, and like they belong, it is important for top-level leaders to identify differences in perceptions of DEI on campus between top- and midlevel leaders and work to close these gaps. Chapter 5 presents strategies to develop a community of practice to help bridge existing gaps.

Who Is Responsible for DEI?

On many campuses, the position of chief diversity officer (CDO) is a recent addition to the administrative ranks, and the responsibilities of this role may be included in a variety of titles. Our survey respondents had titles including vice provost for student, equity, and community affairs; equity officer; and executive director of diversity, equity, and inclusion. The wide array of titles, joint appointments, and organizational arrangements makes it difficult to generalize about leaders serving in these mission-critical roles. Yet it is more important than at any other point in history to clearly understand the role that CDOs play in shaping and potentially shifting the culture of an organization.

Research, interviews, and reflections from senior administrators working in DEI serve as reminders of the unique challenges that CDOs encounter. One community college CDO described her experience as follows:

> My job seemed to have intense and unique levels of stress compared to others at the college. I, for example, had to negotiate the local politics of my organization while navigating the difficult terrain of educating and challenging fellow colleagues' deeply held beliefs about topics that most can avoid at work—religion, racism, sexism, oppression, power, privilege, and so on. . . . Comparatively, people do not tend to have strong emotions about academic advising, operations, or other functional areas. Employees in these roles have stress, but not the same kind of stress. . . . Though I always wanted to be in a position with so much potential for social impact, I often felt overwhelmed and isolated.[62]

These comments reflect the burdened archetype of Felix and González's model (see figure 3.2) in which equity advocates carry the weight of DEI efforts without broad support.

Just as the external contexts of the community, state, and nation influence the development of an equity mind-set, so, too, does the institutional context. As has been discussed, how DEI and social justice operate at the institutional level is influenced by many factors. The nesting of levels of context highlights that more than one element is at work as individuals try to expand their thinking about equity. The intersecting and sometimes competing factors and systems must be acknowledged, and individuals must understand how to build their contextual competency. Recall that developing contextual competency requires recognizing the interrelated aspects of the community college, which requires understanding how people, places, events, and systems are embedded in and press upon the college (figure 3.7).

Developing contextual competency

Aspiring and sitting leaders alike must fine-tune their ability to understand the context in which they work and where they are seeking to bring about more

FIGURE 3.7 Nesting an equity mind-set within institutional and external contexts

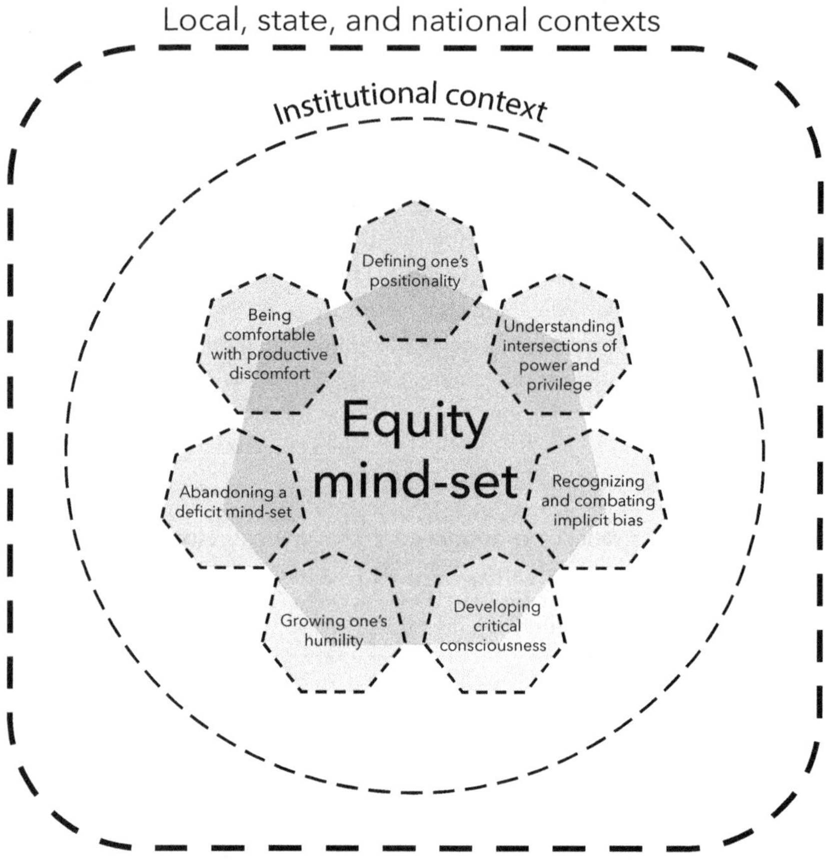

equitable outcomes. Adopting a range of the following strategies can help in expanding leaders' contextual competency:

- Read broadly:
  - On a daily basis, scan the *Chronicle of Higher Education* and *Inside Higher Ed* for breaking news and current events.
  - Subscribe to community college news outlets and research centers for updates on research and best practices (e.g., Community College Research Center, Office of Community College Research and Leadership, Belk Center for Community College Leadership and Research).
  - Access popular business presses to understand financial trends and explore best practices in business that are transferable to higher education.

  - Read about innovative strategies used in health care, the military, and nonprofit organizations that can be applied to community colleges.
  - Contemplate how your reading helps you question your assumptions.
- Leverage local community events:
  - Engage with community constituencies at local events to learn what is on people's minds.
  - Visit nonprofit organizations (e.g., food pantries, workforce development sites, organizations focused on criminal justice reform) to understand your community's needs.
  - Sit on local boards to learn more about your community's social and business needs.
  - Reflect on how these interactions expand your understanding of context and build connections between the college and the community.
- Use data to understand student needs:
  - Conduct focus groups with current students and high school students to gain insights into their needs and campus experiences.
  - Look for patterns in admission yield, persistence, and completion data that challenge campus narratives.
  - Identify equity gaps on campus, and build strategies to address them.
- Keep abreast of policy and governance changes and perspectives:
  - Track local, state, and national legislation affecting community colleges and their students.
  - Identify the ideologies and perspectives of governing bodies to understand how best to communicate campus requests.
  - Build relationships with a range of policy actors from state legislative offices, county-level legislative bodies, and local leadership councils.
  - Contemplate what types of beneficial connections might emerge by collaborating with other stakeholders.

CONTEXTS THAT SUPPORT EQUITY

Inequity infiltrates organizations. It does so by permeating the systems that have been created, have evolved, and have been upheld throughout an organization's life. Here, it is helpful to dissect what we mean by *system*, as the term is open to interpretation. For our discussion, *system* refers to the broad and interconnected policies, processes, and practices and the structure, culture, and strategy in a given environment that create and maintain certain outcomes.[63] How people interact with the context matters in terms of what is accomplished in addressing inequities. Understanding the campus context and its culture helps develop contextual competency and can help advance change, especially when the campus

TABLE 3.1 Examining where inequity exists on campus

Facet of institutional context	*Reflection questions*
Organizational structure, such as that represented in an organizational chart, including resource allocation, budgeting, and planning	1. How are decisions made regarding budgets and resources? 2. Who is involved in making strategic plans for the college? 3. Do women and marginalized employees receive the same types of opportunities? 4. How do organizational structures favor white men?
Written policies and procedures that govern all aspects of the college	1. How do campus policies support equity? 2. Do DEI efforts use SMART (i.e., specific, measurable, achievable, relevant, timely) goals? 3. What type of review has occurred to identify inequities in policies? 4. Do policies change only when campuses are "forced" to do so by law (e.g., family leave policies)?
Student admissions, access, and success	1. Who in the community is enrolling in the college? 2. Do student demographics mirror those of the surrounding community? 3. What do enrollment, persistence, and completion data look like when disaggregated by sex, race and ethnicity, or age? 4. What equity gaps exist?
Curriculum and pedagogy	1. Who is responsible for building the curriculum? 2. What anti-racist teaching strategies are used in classes? 3. Do faculty engage in inclusive pedagogies to reach all students?
Hiring, retention, and promotion of faculty and staff	1. What do campus data look like for hiring, retention, and promotion when disaggregated by sex or race and ethnicity? 2. How representative are faculty and staff relative to students? 3. Are hiring and promotion policies inclusive?
Institutional programming and events; employee education, training, and development	1. Who programs events on campus? Who decides what events are offered? 2. Do all faculty and staff engage in employee development programming? 3. How does participation in professional development relate to promotions and raises? 4. How is the impact of events and learning opportunities measured?

culture normalizes sexism or racism by devaluing women or marginalized leaders, faculty, staff, and students.

In higher education, inequity exists throughout the institutional context and institutional systems. We applied the anti-racism framework of the National Association of Diversity Officers in Higher Education[64] to a community college context to identify where inequities are found. Answering the questions provided in table 3.1 can inform and advance leaders' contextual competency.

Leaders must situate their own mind-set and competencies (shared in chapter 2) within the larger social ecosystem and context, which are currently entrenched in ideological wars and political quagmires. This chapter explored the need for leaders to develop contextual competency by recognizing the interrelated aspects of the community college. Leaders must attend to people (the wide array of stakeholders), places (or spaces on campus), events (both internal and external to the college), and the many systems embedded in and pressing upon the college. In chapter 4, we present action-oriented strategies and possibilities to drive equity on community college campuses.

CHAPTER 4

Giving Voice and Taking Action

Transformative leaders approach situations and relationships with critical reflection, critical analysis, and critical action to disrupt and dismantle inequitable and unjust practices.[1] As discussed in chapter 2, pursuing an equity mind-set requires individuals to do the necessary work of reflecting and examining their own implicit biases and increasing their critical consciousness. Further, and as detailed in chapter 3, a leader's development must be situated within a deep understanding and analysis of their college's unique context and campus culture while not losing sight of state and national contexts. In this chapter, we provide examples from the field that demonstrate strategies to promote equity. With these strategies in mind, we look at our survey data and interviews to see what is working—or not working—on the ground in community colleges across the nation, how context influences the application of the strategies, and what actions leaders might take. Equity-minded, transformative leaders must assess where to put their energy as advocates, where to take action, and how to give voice to equity to create an equity-driven campus. By knowing what levers exist to improve equity in community colleges, equity-driven leaders can determine the best use of campus resources and how to expand their practices for broader awareness and application at their colleges.

WHAT IS EQUITY-MINDED ADVOCACY?

Intent is not impact.[2] A leader's intentions and mind-set alone do little to advance an equity agenda. Leaders must be an integral part of creating a campus culture that provides unwavering support for advocacy. Advocacy goes beyond a change in mind-set in that it is a *public* display of support that can be observed. Thus, advocacy is a daily activity for many: we might honk our horn as we drive by union members on strike or post a positive reaction to proposed legislation that supports transgender students. Becoming an equity-minded advocate, however, is much more than just a honk of a horn or a social media post. It involves an iterative, continuous process that requires leaders to take on several attributes and behaviors that are then reflected back to the campus community in their decision-making and public actions.

As we will discuss in chapter 5, not *all* community leaders must assume the role of advocate. In fact, a variety of roles must be filled, based on individual strengths and spheres of influence, to create an equity-driven campus. However, without dedicated advocates taking intentional actions to advance an equity agenda, efforts are likely to be perceived as performative by various stakeholder groups, and there may be little to no advancement toward truly becoming an equity-driven campus.

Characteristics of Equity-Minded Advocates

Advocacy is discussed within the field of education but also within other disciplines such as health care, social work, and counseling. Some common themes that cut across the advocacy literature include the following characteristics that align with transformative leadership practices. Equity-minded advocates:

- continuously deepen their awareness of injustices occurring at the local level and in broader social contexts;
- proactively seek out knowledge of the unique needs of the various populations in the community;
- engage in self-reflection about their own role in perpetuating injustice;
- critically examine interventions, policies, and practices to address root causes of injustice and create systemic change;
- are fiercely committed and take on responsibility for ensuring equality, as evidenced by decisions and actions;
- lift up voices that have been silenced and challenge those who have knowingly or unknowingly silenced others; and
- empower others to question social injustices and become equity-minded change agents.[3]

While some of these characteristics, such as deepening one's awareness and self-reflection, are aligned with the process of developing an equity mind-set, the practice of transformative leadership cannot be achieved through an equity mind-set alone. Rather, an equity mind-set must be reflected in a leader's decisions, actions, and all forms of communication as leaders seek to create a community of advocates who will collectively drive the creation of an equity-driven campus.

Lists of the characteristics of equity-minded advocacy suggest that leaders must lift up voices that have been silenced and become equity-minded change agents through their decisions and actions.[4] However, these types of broad statements often do not answer the following critical questions: *What do equity-minded advocates actually do, and how do they create collective advocacy to drive a campus toward equity?* To answer these questions, we turn to our data and find examples of leaders instituting policy changes, providing space for courageous conversations, and altering titles, roles, and responsibilities to address inequitable structures. Leaders surveyed in the 2021 National Survey of Community College Leadership for Social Justice shared these experiences:

- "I advocated for and was successful in getting programming changes to reflect the chosen first name for our students and employees in our enterprise systems." This statement is an example of a policy change that creates a more inclusive environment for people of all gender identities.
- "We hired affinity leaders to assist us in looking through the lenses of different eyes, Pakistani, American Indian, elder, Hispanic/LatinX, LGBTQ+A, religious." This example describes the creation of campus affinity groups committed and often empowered (through the provision of campus resources) to create safe spaces on campus.
- "I am the leader of my campus's Diversity and Global Awareness Committee and I lead our college's civil discourse series, where we dive into potentially contentious social and political topics." This leader is describing the importance of creating opportunities for dialogue to ensure that voices that may have been silenced in the past are heard.

Before we discuss specific actions like these in more detail, it is important to note that becoming an equity-minded advocate is not restricted by a person's title or department. Anyone can be an advocate and strive to live out the tenets of advocacy. Senior leaders have a particular duty to display these attributes and support others in the role of advocate. However, despite their position of privilege and power, senior leaders may feel constrained in their advocacy. As explained in chapter 3, leaders may feel unable to take action because of pressure from external stakeholders, local and state politics, and regional history. Or a leader's actions may be delayed or perceived as lacking in urgency because of contextual factors, which can convey a lack of care on the part of the leader. Top-level leaders often self-censor on diversity, equity, and inclusion (DEI) topics based on state and national politics.[5] Events related to anti-DEI legislation in 2023, as described in chapter 3, prove the extent to which colleges have been drastically affected by state-level politics and legislation, with the removal, in some instances, of critical race theory from the curriculum and negative attention drawn to DEI programming.

A question from the 2021 National Survey of Community College Leadership for Social Justice asked whether respondents viewed senior leaders as advocates for social justice. The data suggest that, from the perspective of campus community members, leaders' intentions might not be translating into action. Just over one-third of all respondents indicated "very much" in response to the question of whether senior leaders were advocates for social justice. Another one-third indicated "somewhat," while the remaining one-third indicated "a little" or "not at all." Analysis by position, however, reveals a trend that we found throughout the survey data: senior leaders have significantly different perspectives from those of midlevel leaders. Close to half (49 percent) of surveyed presidents and chancellors believe strongly that senior leaders are advocates for social justice. In comparison, just 33 percent of deans and 19 percent of directors felt similarly (figure 4.1).

Perception is reality. If a large segment of the campus community does not perceive that senior leaders are advocates for social justice, as the data summary in figure 4.1 suggests, senior leaders must take visible action to create a sense of collective advocacy. In the next section, we provide examples of actions that equity-driven leaders can take to demonstrate to campus community members that their campus is equity-driven.

FIGURE 4.1 Survey prompt: To what extent does the following describe senior leaders at your college: advocates for social justice?

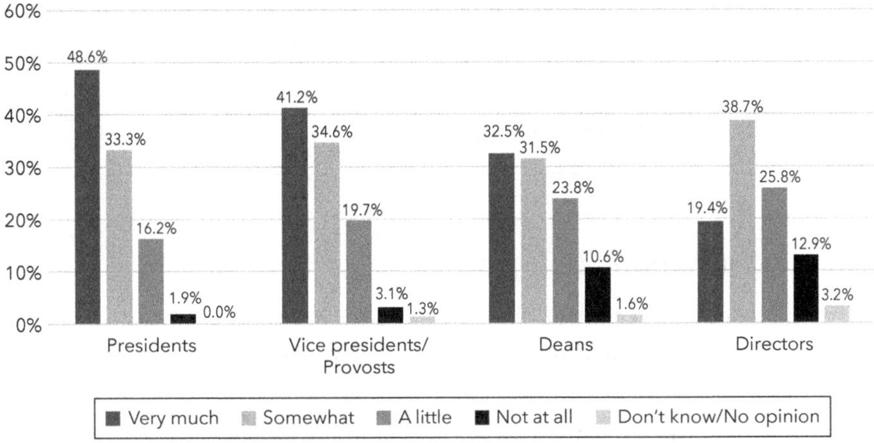

Data Spotlight: Advocacy for Others

The 2021 National Survey of Community College Leadership for Social Justice asked leaders to indicate whether they had advocated for someone who had been treated unjustly. Across all titles, the majority said yes (16.1 percent said no, and 5.6 percent said that they did not remember or that the survey question was not applicable). Similar percentages

FIGURE 4.2 Survey prompt: During the past two years, have you advocated for someone who was treated unjustly?

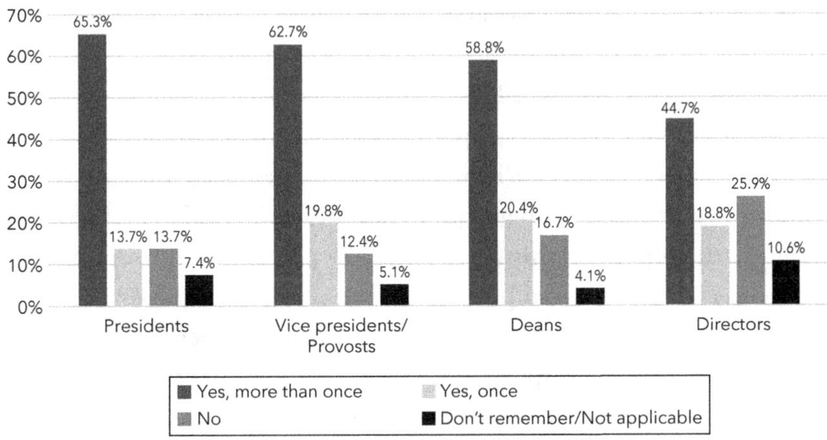

of presidents, vice presidents, and deans said yes, while one out of four director-level respondents said no (figure 4.2). It is important to note that some leaders may not have been aware of or recognized unjust treatment and therefore did not see a need to play the role of advocate; in such cases, leaders may have selected "not applicable."

ADVOCACY IN ACTION

Advocacy *is* action. The result of doing advocacy work is visible change, including changes to policies and practices. And the accumulation of those changes is the creation of a campus culture that exemplifies collective advocacy. However, transformative leaders can be stifled by the many policies and practices that perpetuate the status quo. In the 2021 National Survey of Community College Leadership for Social Justice, participants were asked whether they had engaged in any policy changes between 2019 and 2021 that specifically addressed an unjust policy. A similar pattern emerged in their responses as in other areas of the survey data. Presidents were the most likely to have been involved in examining or changing unjust policies, with 80 percent responding, "Yes, more than once," or "Yes, once." In comparison, 69 percent of vice presidents, 45 percent of deans, 42 percent of directors responded, "Yes, more than once," or "Yes, once" (figure 4.3). This finding suggests that policy changes occur centrally but perhaps not at the local level of units or departments, which indicates a missed opportunity to examine policies and create change.

Moving from policy to implementation often means adjusting one's own practices. Given the need for leaders to increase their critical consciousness, how they adjust their professional practice serves as an indicator of their growth as an equity-driven leader. When participants were asked whether they had examined and changed an unjust professional practice, differences were again evident based on position. Most presidents (78 percent) reported having made changes to their professional practice because of something they perceived as unjust. In comparison, 71 percent of vice presidents, 54 percent of deans, and 50 percent of directors responded that they had examined and changed an unjust professional practice. Clear differences were apparent between top- and midlevel leaders (figure 4.4).

FIGURE 4.3 Survey prompt: During the past two years, have you examined and changed a written policy that was unjust?

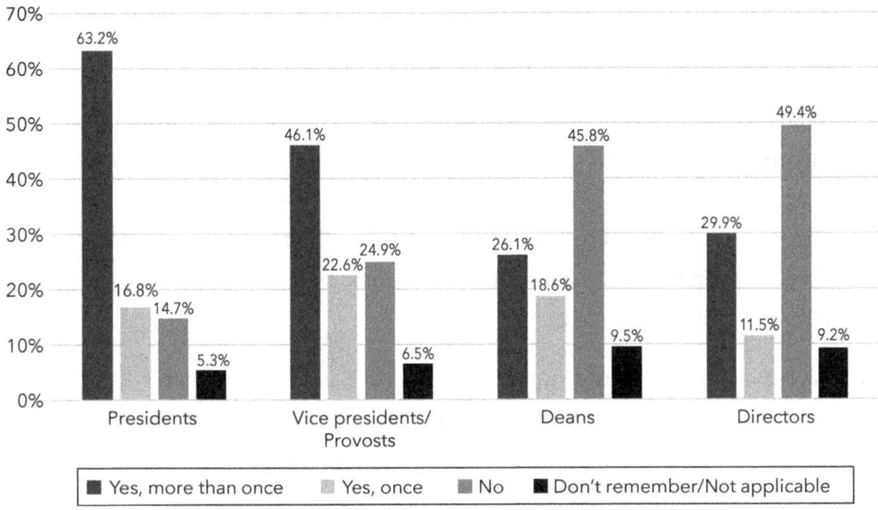

In this chapter, we have drawn on evidence-based practices and popular strategies to provide potential actions for leaders. Where possible, we also provide examples from survey responses that provide additional insight. The

FIGURE 4.4 Survey prompt: During the past two years, have you examined and changed a professional practice that was unjust?

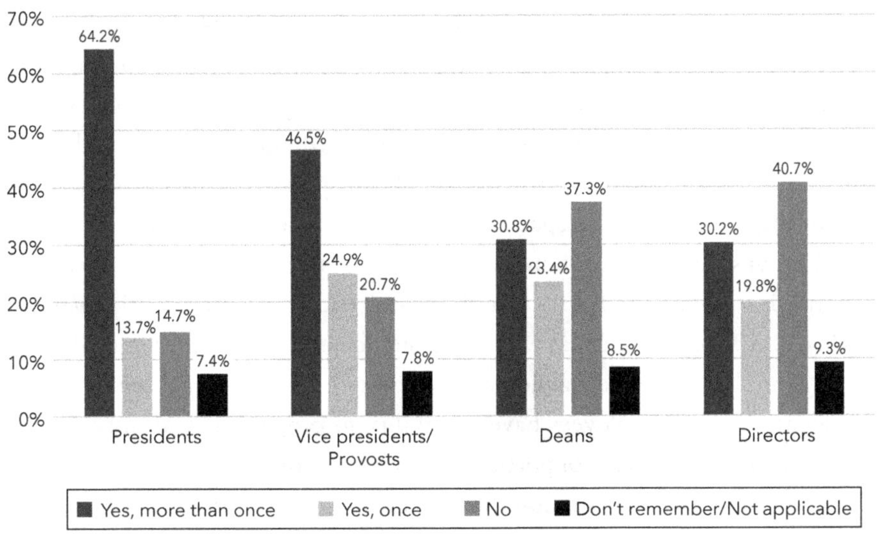

following actions have implications for both policy and practice and have the potential to support equity on campus:

- Creating and supporting campus affinity groups.
- Reconceptualizing mentorship as a form of allyship.
- Recognizing and encouraging advocacy work in the community.
- Encouraging curricular change to support equity-driven classrooms and teaching practices.
- Offering professional development opportunities that support equity.
- Creating opportunities for rational discourse by combating microaggressions and silencing bullies.

While this list is certainly not exhaustive, our intent is to share examples of tangible steps leaders can take to move beyond intent to action. In chapter 5, we take these individual actions to the next level by describing how communities of practice can be used as a mechanism for change.

Creating and supporting campus affinity groups

Affinity groups are gatherings of people who share common characteristics, identities, and life experiences. These gatherings allow people to share experiences, build community, engage in dialogue, identify shared issues, and share resources.[6] In a systematic review of the literature on affinity groups within higher education, Emiko Muraki and colleagues found that the stated purpose of affinity groups fell into one of three categories: creating a sense of connection and belonging among individuals, providing empowerment through shared resources and strategies, and a enacting social change (a more visible external purpose).[7] When affinity groups are well resourced and have clear goals, they can also increase campus community members' sense of belonging.[8]

Affinity groups provide spaces that can center the unique needs of various social groups. Everett Community College in Washington State, for example, has affinity groups for Asian American and Pacific Islander, African/Black, Latinx, and queer students, as well as a group focused on decentering whiteness. Each group has a defined mission and purpose that have been approved by the president. And all employees have the ability to propose new affinity groups. While the groups provide opportunities for professional development, mentoring, and engagement, a common theme is creating a safe space.

In our interviews, one midlevel leader noted the value of belonging to an affinity group in relation to his leadership development: "I have become very engaged with a local group here. There's a group of African American males that come together and focus on leadership development." A midlevel leader at a rural community college commented on being aware of the need to support student affinity groups: "A lot of rural Latino males are generally struggling more, and so we are figuring out how we can engage with them and provide better support." Recognizing the need to build support structures via affinity groups is an important part of a larger equity plan. Implementing affinity groups within the college signals that the institution is a champion of social justice through its provision of resources and support.[9]

Equality Maricopa: An Affinity Group Taking Public Action

Established in 2006, Equality Maricopa is a dynamic group of Maricopa Community Colleges employees in Arizona who identify as LGBTQIA+ and allies. As of 2023, the group has been fundraising to launch the first-of-its-kind LGBTQIA+ license plate, as Arizona law requires nonprofit organizations to raise $32,000 to cover production costs. Once the funds are raised, the plate will be submitted to the state for approval. Once passed by the Arizona legislature, $17 from the $25 state license plate fee will benefit Maricopa Community Colleges' LGBTQIA+ students through the PRISM scholarship, which recognizes the importance of increasing educational accessibility and supporting LGBTQIA+ students.

Reconceptualizing mentorship as a form of allyship

Leaders often take on the role of mentor or sponsor throughout their careers. At times, these relationships are informal, occurring organically, and in other instances, community colleges have formal, structured leadership mentoring programs. Traditional mentoring relationships involve a seasoned mentor working with a junior colleague, with outcomes affecting career development and psychosocial functions.[10] Carol Mullen and Cindy Klimaitis identified nine types of mentoring ranging from informal to formal, including peer, group, multilevel, collaborative, and diverse and cultural mentoring.[11] Previous research on the benefits of mentoring in community colleges highlights that participants want more focus on career development, that female leaders with a strong bond between mentor and mentee believe mentors play a role in their career satisfaction, and that sponsorship and other critical approaches to mentoring help address historical mentoring challenges for women and people of color.[12] What we know is that effective mentorship involves planning, training for mentors, and resources and that women and people of color often lack access to programming that could help them advance. Indeed, the recent American College President Survey by the American Council on Education identified mentoring as necessary to address the lack of progression of women and people of color into the presidency.[13] But is mentoring really what is needed to close the gap in community college leadership that views women and people of color lagging behind their white male counterparts?

To put it bluntly, there is limited evidence that formal mentoring programs advance the representation of women and people of color into senior leadership roles. What would signify a commitment to advancing equity would be shifting the role of mentor to the role of ally and changing mentoring programs into allyship programs. Jamie Washington and Nancy Evans explained that allies are dominant-group members who work to end oppression, both personally and professionally, by supporting and advocating for oppressed populations.[14] Allyship is often exhibited through supportive individual relationships such as those in sponsorship and mentoring. Dominant-group allies amplify the voices and perspectives of nondominant group members, for example, in spaces such as cabinet meetings, professional sessions, and when asked for recommendations of individuals for new opportunities. As one midlevel leader noted, "Being able to turn to different leaders on campus, and say, you know, 'This is what I'm struggling with,' particularly as a woman of color . . . to have allies, people I can turn to for support, has been really helpful." Equity-driven leaders must engage in actions on campus to prevent midlevel leaders from feeling isolated or overlooked for promotion and other advancement opportunities.

Recent higher education research has begun to explore the intersection of the traditional role of mentor or sponsor with allyship work. For example, researchers have found that white male faculty and administrators constructed and made meaning of the complexities embedded in allyship work at the individual, rather than institutional, level.[15] While allyship at the individual level is critical for individual development, this type of support fails to make changes to college structures or processes that may serve as barriers to equity. Without larger system changes, improvements in equity will not occur beyond the few individuals who benefit from having a mentor, sponsor, or ally.

Recognizing and encouraging advocacy work in the community

Community colleges and their communities are intricately linked. Separating advocacy work on campus from efforts off campus creates an artificial boundary that may create a divide for leaders in terms of their work and nonwork personas. For example, leaders may feel strongly about a social justice issue and participate in a rally in their community (figure 4.5), or they may boycott a product, service, or company (figure 4.6), but they may feel unable to share that experience with students or colleagues. In some instances, these limitations may result from formal policies that specify what college representatives are able to share on social media or college-managed LISTSERVs. While such policies exist for a reason, they can limit the perceived value of engaging in advocacy in the community

FIGURE 4.5 Survey prompt: During the past two years, have you attended a rally in support of a social justice issue?

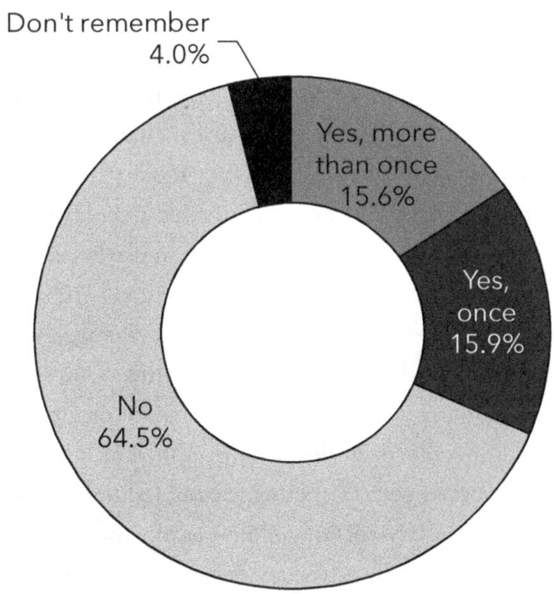

FIGURE 4.6 Survey prompt: During the past two years, have you boycotted a product, service, or company because of a social justice issue?

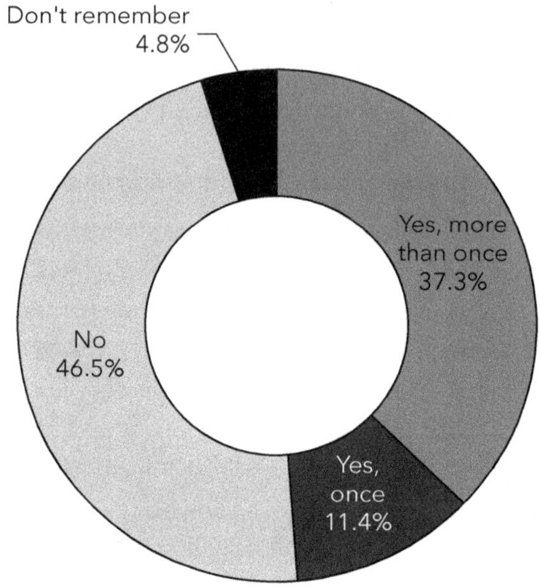

when on-campus advocacy is not encouraged or recognized as an important part of creating an equity-driven campus.

For some, the term *activism* may conjure up visions of violent demonstrations or angry mobs. However, this characterization is not accurate, nor is it helpful when considering how community colleges can advance an equity agenda. Activists work to spur broader social and political change by organizing others.[16] A shared definition of activism is elusive, but most agree that an activist displays certain behaviors. An activist organizes constituents, articulates concerns, and negotiates with powerholders to develop strategies to shift power.[17] From a conceptual standpoint, then, activism is in many ways indistinguishable from advocacy work in that both seek to make systemic change, and both affect the practice of leadership. A midlevel leader from our interviews reflected on how his previous experience in direct service working for a nonprofit and doing community organizing set the stage for his leadership approach: "One of the nonprofits I worked at before, I worked with formerly incarcerated individuals and at another nonprofit, I worked with survivors of gender-based violence. I think working on the ground level and doing the advocacy helped bridge to my leadership role."

When leaders can reconcile and make sense of their equity work in both the college and the community, they experience a critical element of transformative leadership: recognizing the interconnectedness and interdependence of individuals and systems.[18]

Encouraging leaders to engage in their local, regional, and state communities and bring those experiences to their leadership practice acknowledges the value of viewing equity and social justice through a socioecological lens that breaks down the artificial divide between a campus and its community. Izhak Berkovich described a socioecological approach to social justice in which leaders *must* act as social activists in the community, specifically within policy arenas, to promote social justice efforts.[19] This approach is undergirded by the belief that if students are constrained because of community contexts (e.g., poverty, violence), anti-oppressive work within the confines of a singular organization—such as a college—will not make much difference.[20] Therefore, rather than subtly or overtly discouraging activities that fall into the realm of community activism, community colleges should celebrate and recognize the importance of such activities.

While we are quick to recognize student achievements and their impact in the community through awards and scholarships, we are less likely to publicly acknowledge the work of faculty, staff, and administrative leaders. One obvious strategy, then, is to create awards and opportunities for public recognition that reward activism among all campus community members. For example, Alfred State College of Technology, a two-year institution in New York, offers civic engagement awards that recognize students, faculty, and staff who have demonstrated a commitment to engaging in the community, whether locally, nationally, or globally, through community service and activism.[21] While a seemingly small gesture, acknowledging activism as worthy of an award signals that the campus supports and publicly recognizes actions that advance equity—not just on campus but also beyond.

Encouraging curricular change to support equity-driven classrooms and teaching practices

A manifestation of the core mission of the community college and what it values is reflected in the curriculum and in what happens in the classroom. Equity-driven leaders can empower faculty and staff to become equity-minded advocates who guide the curriculum and interact with students both inside and outside the classroom. Several recent publications have focused on equity-driven teaching. For example, the 2023 book *The Norton Guide to Equity-Minded Teaching* provides tangible examples of teaching practices that strive to realize equal outcomes for all students.[22] Leaders must have a deep understanding of how equity is—or is not—infused into the curriculum, and they must take action and support those on the front lines of curricular change.

Equity-minded teaching has also been conceptualized as culturally relevant, or affirming, teaching. For example, in response to the fact that students of color do not see themselves or their experiences reflected in course readings, assignments, and assessments, J. Luke Wood and Frank Harris have used the term *mirroring* to describe a strategy that faculty can employ to review course content and materials to ensure cultural relevance and the inclusion of materials in which all students can see themselves.[23] Culturally relevant pedagogy is built on three foundational elements: student success requires students to engage in their academic development, students' cultural identity can be expressed and is viewed as an asset, and students must increase their own critical consciousness as a means of critiquing societal norms.[24] Gloria Ladson-Billings, the seminal scholar associated with culturally relevant pedagogy, encouraged educators to think more about culturally *sustaining* pedagogy.[25] Culturally sustaining pedagogy focuses on the need to foster and sustain cultural elements that students bring to classrooms as valid, critical contributions to education and as a response to societal change. Having faculty interrogate their own identities serves as a starting point in engaging in culturally responsive teaching.

Erin Doran conducted an exploratory study that examined how community college faculty teaching English applied the strategies of culturally relevant, sustaining, or responsive pedagogy in their classrooms. Doran found that faculty prioritized content and delivery, did not make connections to systemic inequality or student success, and did not reflect on their identity as a teacher. Of note, a third of the respondents opted out of defining *culturally relevant pedagogy* or said they were unfamiliar with the term.[26] Even though this study was exploratory and included a limited number of teaching areas, it is one of the few looking at the role of culturally relevant pedagogy in a community college context. Some disciplines, like nursing and social work, include issues of cultural difference in their curricula. A midlevel dean of nursing noted, "Integrated throughout our curriculum, the first thing students do is a cultural project where they present a poster presentation about the specifics of the culture and then how their health belief systems affect how they interact with people from that culture." Whereas some disciplines build issues of diversity and equity into the curriculum, others must start doing so.

Leaders often fail to mention the role of classroom pedagogy as a lever for improving equity in community colleges. The 2016 National Survey of Community College Leaders asked respondents for their definition of *leadership*, and scant few mentioned students or supporting faculty teaching. The fact that all students engage with faculty more often than any other type of campus member points to the critical need to support faculty development in inclusive teaching practices. Strategies to infuse equity into the curriculum include the following:

- Validation theory: Laura Rendón introduced validation theory in 1994 as a way to support low-income, first-generation immigrant students. Here, validation is the intentional and proactive affirmation of the ability of students by campus members, including faculty and staff. At the core of interactions with these institutional agents is the validation of students as creators of knowledge and valued members of the college learning community. Validation also occurs when these agents foster students' personal development and adjustment to the college setting.[27] Faculty development programs can provide opportunities to learn how to validate students and their experiences. For example, faculty members acknowledging the fact that many students juggle their education with many responsibilities outside college can make students feel seen and validated.
- Stereotype threat strategies: Claude Steele and Joshua Aronson coined the term *stereotype threat* to mean the risk of confirming a negative stereotype about a person's racial, ethnic, gender, or cultural identity. When a personal characteristic or something one says or does appears conforms to a negative stereotype, it makes the stereotype more plausible as a characterization of the person in the eyes of others and perhaps even in their own eyes. Effective interventions to combat stereotype threat include belief-based strategies that change one's beliefs about the negative stereotype (e.g., role models, enhancing feelings of social belonging) and identity-based strategies that build up positive feelings of self (e.g., activating a positive

alternative identity).[28] An example of this strategy in practice is the Scientist Spotlights Initiative (https://scientistspotlights.org/), which provides faculty with resources to associate curriculum content with examples of counter-stereotypical scientists.[29] Assigning student-created scientist spotlights can encourage students of diverse backgrounds to see themselves in the scientists they highlight and spark organic conversations about issues of diversity.[30] Instructor-created scientist spotlights can do the same and encourage students to reflect on what they have in common with successful scientists.[31]

- Universal Design for Learning (UDL): David Rose and Anne Meyer established the Center for Applied Specialized Technology in 1984, and in the 1990s with their colleagues, they introduced the UDL framework to enhance teaching and learning.[32] The UDL guidelines are organized into three overarching areas: providing multiple means of engagement, representation, and action and expression. Flexible approaches to learning move beyond one-size-fits all teaching strategies. By providing access to learning in varied ways and building on their learning, students ultimately internalize ways to self-regulate their learning and comprehension and expand their executive functions.[33]
- Labor-based grading: The rhetoric and composition professor Asao Inoue drew on anti-racist teaching practices to offer his students labor-based grading contracts. Labor-based grading emerges from the co-construction by students and the instructor of how much time or labor is spent on learning compared with the quality of the final work; it is an alternative to the traditional approach to grading, which has historically privileged white learners. Here, the focus is on the process, rather than the outcome, of learning.[34]

Equity-driven leaders can provide opportunities for faculty development programming, and individual faculty can engage in their own professional development activities to develop inclusive teaching strategies. Leveraging faculty members as catalyst for change is a strategy to scale institutional and regional change. Kristin O'Connell and colleagues reported on a five-year program involving eighty community college faculty engaged in structured professional development, and they have created a faculty change agent model that can be replicated.[35] Their model builds on the iterative process of providing professional development activities on teaching strategies, allowing faculty the opportunity to practice new techniques and make incremental changes and then share what they have learned with others before iterating another round of changes. The authors found that the use of evidence-based teaching practices in professional development sessions resulted in changes in classroom practices and in improved student outcomes at the program level.

Offering professional development opportunities that support equity

When an issue or problem arises and must be addressed, it is common for higher education professionals to go into reactionary mode, saying something like, "I know a great speaker that we can bring to campus," "Let's put out a quick survey to ask people what they think," or "Let's create a taskforce." In many instances, there is nothing inherently wrong with wanting to take immediate action and appear to be responsive and transparent in the process. However, there is little to no evidence that many current endeavors undertaken by colleges, often with genuinely good intentions, actually advance equity in a meaningful and sustainable way. Next, we describe some traditional forms of equity work on campus and the responses from midlevel leaders we interviewed regarding the utility of each.

Training programs. While many training programs are offered on community college campuses across the country (examples are "safe zone" and ally training),[36] not much is known about their lasting effects. Lily Zheng has argued,

> Poorly executed training can reduce complex issues spanning centuries of conflict into reductive lists of "good" and "bad" behaviors; foster resentment among participants who are blamed for causing harm they don't understand; lack safeguards to prevent conversations from becoming emotionally distressing, verbally abusive, or highly triggering for one or more parties; force individuals to self-disclose personal identities they aren't ready to share; or push them to take on educator roles and create an inflated sense of efficacy in participants to create organizational change.[37]

The intention of DEI training is certainly not to be ineffective, but without a level of critical consciousness, training experiences will be experienced differently by different people. On this topic, one midlevel leader said, "So we as leaders are required to take diversity training. I think it's six hours long. And then there are different trainings on LGBT [issues] and becoming an ally. You know, those types of things, so we have them available. But I don't know how effective they are because I think when you mandate things . . . that's like just checking off that box on the list of things, and therefore how meaningful is it to an individual versus if they seek it out of their own volition like they're curious now, and they want to learn more?" Central to improving DEI trainings is assessing individuals' motivation for participating because when training is seen simply as an exercise to "check a box," real change does not occur. Equity training programs should not be implemented in a one-and-done format; rather, they should be designed for continuous learning.

An example of an intentional training program that aims to support continuous learning was provided by a midlevel leader serving in the role of vice president of diversity who described their campus's approach to providing learning opportunities for campus stakeholders. The campus held a five-part series that first included training on implicit bias and then "courageous conversations" to help people become comfortable with the uncomfortable. The next sessions focused on reflective practices and how to advance equity in student success and examining what was happening in classrooms and with support services. The final part involved applying an equity lens to policy, which the leader described as follows: "We finally applied an equity lens to our policy development with multiple sessions, as well as bringing in external training. It helped people move from the training to action by providing small [group] huddle meetings guides." What is clear in the approach taken by this community college to provide real support for equity on campus is the amount of background development and attention to raising critical consciousness that occurred before the focus turned to reviewing policy. This example describes an intentional approach to bringing about real structural change via reform and emphasizes the foundational work that must be done before such change can occur.

One strategy to address the ongoing learning needs of faculty is to establish faculty learning communities that promote collaboration and ongoing reflection.[38] Also, as discussed earlier, the positive outcomes observed by O'Connell and colleagues from the use of their faculty change agent model occurred in part because of the iterative nature of the structured professional development activities used. This approach gave participants a chance to try out new teaching strategies, assess what worked and what did not, make incremental changes, share learnings, and then engage in subsequent rounds of learning and practicing.[39] Another important part of the program highlighted in the model was the provision of opportunities for participating faculty to lead faculty development sessions on their own campuses, thereby amplifying the reach of the structured professional development and allowing participants the opportunity to advance their own continuous learning.[40] Central to the positive examples highlighted in this section were the intentional planning of the training sessions and allowing time for reflection and practice.

Diversity Efforts in Business and Industry

A 2016 *Harvard Business Review* article by Frank Dobbin and Alexandra Kalev examined five years of data from more than eight hundred midsize and large US firms to ascertain the relationship between various diversity programming efforts and the proportion of women and people of color in management and leadership roles.[41] While not suggesting any causal relationships, the authors found evidence that companies were able to increase the representation of women and people of color in management and leadership positions when the following elements were part of the organizational fabric:

- voluntary, rather than mandatory, trainings on issues of diversity
- self-managed, nonhierarchical teams
- cross-training that exposed people to different groups of people
- mentoring programs
- diversity task forces that promoted accountability among members
- having one or more people in the role of diversity manager

The authors surmised that companies were successful in diversifying when they were able to forgo control tactics and create opportunities for more meaningful engagement for people throughout the organization.[42]

Guest speakers, keynotes, and lectures. It is common to highlight a DEI speaker either as part of a speaker series or to demonstrate publicly that the campus is making an effort to address DEI issues. Yet these speeches are often performative and seen as being done just for show. Attending a lecture may count as participation in professional development or fulfill a campus requirement to engage in DEI efforts, but it is only when speakers are part of a larger campus effort that involves group discussion, investigating practices, and fulfilling an action plan that real change can begin to occur.

One midlevel leader in our study reflected on the role of keynote lectures and forums as a means of supporting equity in community colleges:

> I think we have had one or two forums that address social justice, and these were large forums where all faculty, all college staff were invited with guest speakers and so forth. But that seems to happen periodically and only when certain instances might take place, whether it be in society or on campus, there seems to be this call to a forum. I've noticed that there are some leaders here that feel professional development is above them or meaning they're above professional development and I'm well known on campus for saying that professional development is for everybody.

As evinced by the perspective of this leader, when individuals think they do not need to hear a lecture or when a forum is offered only in response to a triggering event, there is less buy-in to the intended message. Without a holistic design for equity development on campus, keynotes and lectures run the same risk as DEI trainings: being seen as a way to show support for the cause but not actually changing anything or questioning individual behaviors or the responsibilities of the college. A focus on getting individuals to "change" through short trainings rarely advances real change on community college campuses. Certainly, a cumulative influence on changing the campus culture is possible when a number of individual actions are stitched together over time, but the more intentional development of an equity community of practice (as described in chapter 5) can more purposefully advance equity on campus.

Task forces and other ad hoc groups (volunteer or appointed). A common leadership tactic is to form a task force or ad hoc committee to investigate an issue and report back to the larger campus. A great deal of time and effort goes into these efforts, with many who have volunteered (or been "volun-told") believing deeply in the work they are doing. Yet these groups seldom have the power or authority to actually change policies and practices. Rather, the outcome is often a list of recommendations for those who *do* hold the power to make changes.

Think of the adage that task forces are where good ideas go to die, and you can see the traditional shortcomings of these types of actions.

However, change can occur via task forces when equity-driven midlevel leaders engage in the process. Take, for example, a dean of nursing in our study who commented on the work she was doing on a task force to improve equity in the area of nursing admissions:

> We have admission testing and we look at the individual scores. I guess the catalyst that made me look at that was that the students that are admitted to the program are not representative of the students that are applying to the program as far as cultural and ethnic diversity. And even, I think, gender diversity. We had to consider the way that we look at scoring to decide if it is the best practice to look at these individual components versus the whole score—so looking at scores versus the weight of other things that may be considered more that make people well-rounded individuals, as well. Do they have health-care experience? What life experiences do they bring to the table? Do they speak other languages? There are other things that they bring to the table that are skills that we're not capturing in our admission process, and I feel like that skews it to where it's like we're only looking at whether they can take a test well.

The dean in this example held a position of power that could result in changes to enhance equity, and she, herself, was an equity-driven leader. Telling in her comments was the inequity she discovered in the admissions data, which showed a lack of representation that could be traced back to the single criterion of test scores determining admission. The dean's efforts of contemplating the bias inherent in admission tests and identifying a more holistic way to assess ability showcase an actionable strategy to improve equity.

Data Spotlight: The Role of the Dean

Deans responded differently from presidents and other senior leaders in the 2021 National Survey of Community College Leadership for Social Justice. Compared with presidents and other senior leaders, they were less likely to indicate that they had taken actions such as examining and changing unjust policies and practices. Given the important role that deans play in college decision-making, it may be that deans are "stuck between a rock and a hard place" when it comes to change efforts. They must navigate the sometimes tenuous situation of pleasing faculty through their decisions and actions while also being highly attuned to the administrative, financial, and curricular challenges facing the college overall. Our interviews with deans spotlighted both the challenges and the successes of deans in their efforts to create equity-driven campuses.

Example 1*: I'm a dean, right, so I kind of sit in between upper leadership and our faculty, making sure that there's equity and advocacy. I've tried to help change our hiring practices to make sure that they're more equitable, trying to get rid of implicit bias, those kinds of things. And I try to live that way in my life outside of work, as well—as a member of the community, as a coach, and [as] a father. We don't do leadership development well. We have not formally integrated the work of regular professional development and training. I started a dean's leadership academy and then we did a survey of the competencies, so things like budgeting and, you know, accreditation and things that are foreign to people were [rated as areas where people wanted more training]. You don't get training in [these areas] as a faculty member, for sure. But then DEI was a thing that was a desire for training, but it tends to come kind of after the logistical stuff. So, I do think that the AACC approach—which is to put the lens of DEI and social justice in front of all of those things, so it's recruiting faculty with a DEI lens, doing your budgeting with the DEI lens, doing your enrollment and recruiting with that lens—I think that's the best approach.*

For this dean, recognizing that attention to equity was an "add-on" in leadership development programming presented an idea to change their leadership academy by borrowing a strategy from the American Association of Community Colleges: applying an equity lens to all aspects of leadership. As an equity-driven leader, this dean influenced change on their campus that will have a ripple effect via the equity-focused leadership development program now in place.

Example 2*: I was the power user of data at my first college, so I was already using data and addressing equity with data. And our college at the time joined Achieving the Dream. And so, we see a whole cohort of people going to Achieving the Dream for that specific training. And we had a data team at our college, and the data team was led by me. So, for me, the training has always been,* *from my own perspective, grassroots. Let's make sure that we're addressing equity and identifying where our disproportionate impact groups are so we can talk about what are the interventions to resolve [them]. I had the opportunity to return to academic affairs three years ago and now I'm working with our dean of institutional effectiveness here. We're able to bring data and facilitate conversations in a way that you could say cross-pollinate[s] where this data may live.*

The use of data to tell a story about where equity gaps exist on campus provides a tool to debunk long-standing myths about students, student progression, and completion. Having a data agenda for campus initiatives, such as guided pathways, helps shape campus conversations and identify an actionable agenda for change.

Example 3: *I'm the dean of engineering and advanced technologies, so a lot of advanced manufacturing skill trades, and we know there's a dearth of diverse talent when it comes to these types of fields, but at the same time they are very lucrative fields, they're challenging career years. It's important for me as a Black man who is in education to try to reach out as much as I can to others who have been left out of the social and educational mainstream to allow them to take advantage of the opportunities that are there to support their families and their communities. In the process of doing that, I look for opportunities to get engaged in those initiatives that involve social justice and equity. So that's not just something that I'm doing as an individual, but I'm contributing to the culture change at, you know, at the institution level, so that we're making a much broader impact than any one person can do alone.*

This dean described how midlevel leaders can become border-crossers who bring together different groups and how his identity as a leader of color provides a visible representation of possibility for others. As a leader, this dean was conscious of how his individual efforts contribute to organizational change that benefits students and the community.

Example 4: *I'm in frequent contact with deans and other directors, and [I am] learning how to recognize that desire to do the work for social justice and work on leadership development and then turn around and help others identify or communicate that. I'm coming from a driver of being in the dean role for the past year to where I've had more specific faculty interactions. That's where I've had the most opportunity to really step back and try to implement some of the things I mentioned. Really focusing on how we go about bringing teams together, and it's simple things such as the RSI [Regular and Substantive Interaction] standards that we had last year with regular team interaction and all. Or on our accreditation work, when we're bringing people together. So how am I creating this team? How am I asking questions when we're trying to approach a subject now? I think it's had a very large impact with how we're processing information.*

Translating knowledge gained from individual leadership development into support for faculty is a central role for midlevel leaders. What this dean points out is the power of teams to advance learning (in this case, use of the RSI standards) and then to implement it in practice. Reflective practice by this midlevel leader created an opportunity for changes in practice on campus.

The lack of action on the part of midlevel leaders, particularly academic deans, in investigating policies and changing personal practices that are unjust requires further investigation. On one hand, if midlevel academic leaders are in the pipeline for senior positions, we must ask where and when they will develop leadership acumen in policy work and engage in a reflective practice that questions their own beliefs and actions. On the other hand, the bureaucratic structures of community colleges may limit the range of power and influence of deans regarding policy work. But the limitations of positional responsibilities should in no way stunt the growth of individuals as they focus on their own learning and their development of critical consciousness. (See chapter 2 for a range of approaches leaders may take to expand their critical consciousness.)

Creating opportunities for rational discourse by combating microaggressions and silencing bullies

Equity-minded leaders create opportunities for rational discourse that build trust. This type of discourse allows for extended and repeated conversations that evolve over time into a culture of careful listening and cautious openness to new perspectives. An important caveat is that rational discourse is not about consensus but rather deeper and richer understandings of our own biases, our colleagues' perspectives on particular issues, and how each person uniquely constructs those issues.[43] When leaders provide meaningful and appropriate opportunities for rational discourse, they create bridges that bring together diverse communities. These bridges then enable individuals and groups to overcome barriers that have prevented them from sharing, trusting, and engaging in dialogue.

The possibility of rational discourse assumes that a certain level of trust exists on campus that can create a space where people are comfortable engaging in uncomfortable discourse. The presidents in our study were more likely than other leaders to describe their colleges as providing safe spaces for dialogue, and they were more likely to describe senior leaders as regularly engaging in honest, authentic dialogue. More specifically, half the presidents said that they provided those safe spaces for dialogue and that they engaged in authentic dialogue with campus personnel. Yet vice presidents (35 percent) and other midlevel leaders (30 percent of deans, 22 percent of directors) did not agree that senior leaders were providing safe spaces for dialogue. Without safe spaces for difficult and courageous conversations, it is hard to imagine that organizational change will occur.

Additionally, our findings show that women and people of color differed in their perceptions of campus. Leaders of color were less likely than white leaders to describe their colleges as providing safe spaces for dialogue (figure 4.7), and female leaders were less likely than male leaders to describe senior leaders as regularly engaging in honest, authentic dialogue (figure 4.8).

FIGURE 4.7 Survey prompt: To what extent does your college provide safe spaces for dialogue?

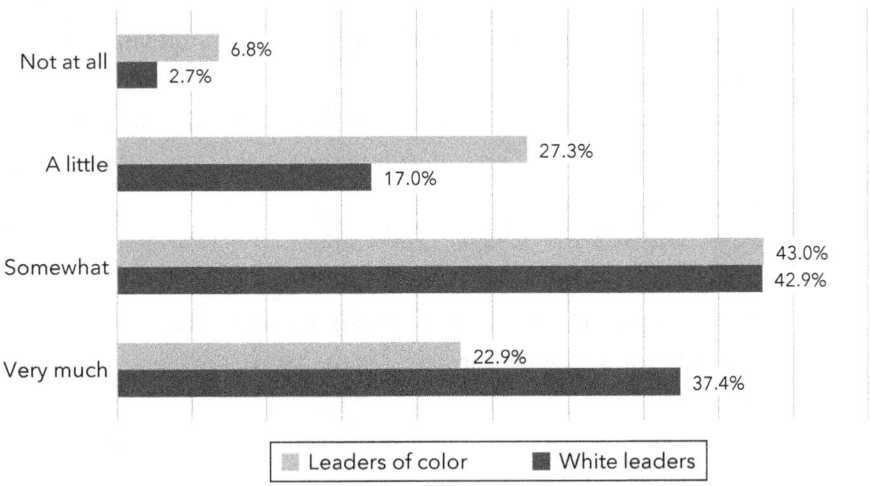

FIGURE 4.8 Survey prompt: To what extent do senior leaders regularly engage in honest, authentic dialogue?

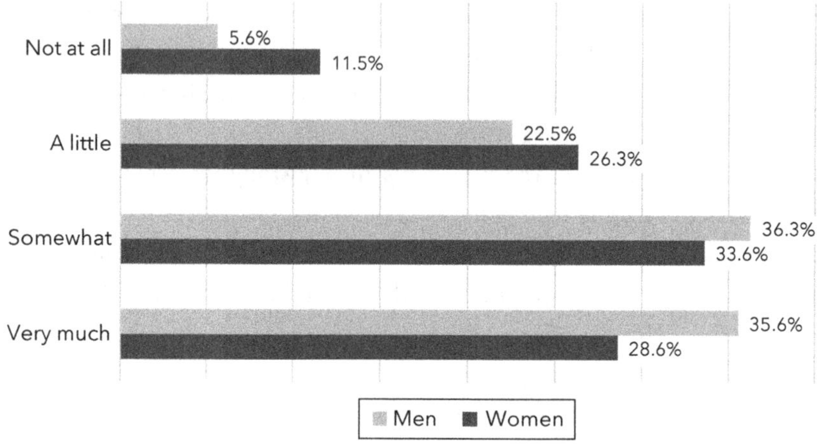

Examining adult learning theories can lend insight into how to create the ideal conditions and safe spaces needed for rational discourse. Jack Mezirow, well known for his transformative adult learning theory, provided a list of essential elements that can help leaders set the stage for meaningful and potentially transformative discourse.[44] Expanding on Mezirow's ideas, we believe that the conditions required for rational discourse include the following:

- having accurate and complete information to guide the discussion; ideally, information is shared well in advance of the planned discussion to allow individuals time to review, absorb, and supplement the information, as appropriate
- ensuring people do not feel coerced into the discussion; allowing individuals to decide how much they want to contribute verbally, rather than putting them on the spot
- having the ability to weigh evidence and evaluate arguments; not rushing to judgment or a conclusion
- allowing time for critical reflection; recognizing that people process information in different ways and that some require more processing and reflecting time
- being open to alternative perspectives; not shutting down if one experiences cognitive dissonance

- providing opportunities for all to participate in the discourse; ensuring everyone has an opportunity to speak; providing follow-up discussions for those who need or want additional time for reflection

Mezirow also provided guidance on how a group with divergent beliefs, values, and attitudes might reach consensus. He suggested that individuals should be willing to "accept an informed, objective, and rational consensus as a legitimate test of validity."[45] However, this concept of consensus warrants more thought in the context of creating equity-driven campuses—we must be willing to engage in discourse about the foundational premises guiding our educational institutions, since they have historically perpetuated injustice and oppression. Therefore, in the 2020s, promulgating the idea of "rational consensus" seems potentially misguided given power differentials embedded in certain positions and policies. Thus, we argue that the act of problematizing consensus, in and of itself, can help further rational discourse. For example, it may be useful to debrief after a "consensus" decision has been made, questioning who drove the viewpoint that ultimately became the "consensus" decision and who the holdouts or dissenting voices were in the decision-making process. Observing patterns in reaching consensus may allow one to determine whether the voices of those with privilege and power continually dominate discourses or whether broad representation was achieved in the final decision. Reflecting on the role of power and privilege in decision-making can help turn a critical eye toward everyday processes that contribute to barriers to change.

Data Spotlight: Leading Discussions

Leaders have a responsibility to create opportunities for rational and meaningful dialogue among campus community members. They also have a responsibility to ensure that there are safe spaces for such dialogues to take place on campus. When asked whether leaders had led a discussion with a group of people on a social justice issue in the previous two years, 38 percent of survey respondents, across all positions and roles, said no (figure 4.9). One interpretation of this finding is that rather than leading discussions, leaders may delegate the facilitation of discussions to those with more expertise or experience, such as leaders of DEI offices. For example, one DEI director commented, "We started in 2017 a series of workshops that I developed for the college . . . we are taking people back to the [equity] basics." While this director had institutional support, the tasks involved in developing the workshop series were squarely on her shoulders. The work of implementation is often regulated to DEI offices rather than being seen as a responsibility of all leaders.

FIGURE 4.9 Survey prompt: During the past two years, have you led a discussion with a group of people on an issue related to social justice?

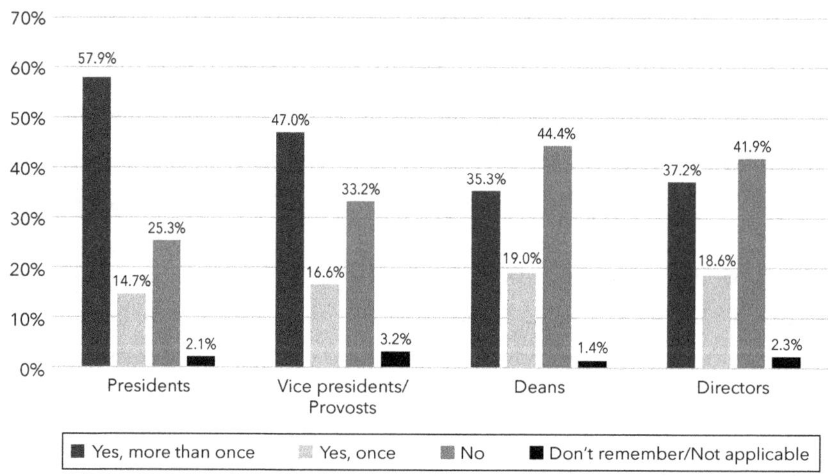

Confronting others. In the context of social unrest, it is often said that "silence equals consent," meaning that a lack of response to a comment or behavior implies tacit approval of that comment or behavior. It is worth reiterating that our national survey data revealed that a large percentage of leaders indicated that they had *not* confronted individuals whose language or behavior was offensive or discriminatory. When asked whether leaders had confronted an individual whose language or behavior was offensive or discriminatory in the previous two years, 32 percent of respondents, across all positions and roles, said no (by position, this was about 19 percent of presidents; 30 percent of provosts, vice presidents, and deans; and 48 percent of directors), and 5 percent said that they did not remember whether they had confronted others (figure 4.10).

FIGURE 4.10 Survey prompt: During the past two years, have you confronted an individual about offensive, discriminatory language or behaviors?

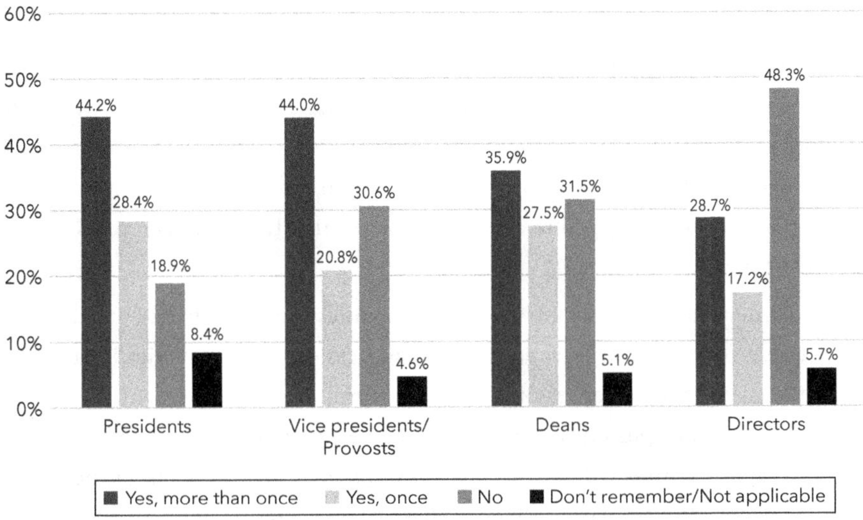

The data points in figure 4.10, when examined in light of other measures and perceptions of advocacy in action, indicate several areas of consideration for advancing an equity agenda—specifically with regard to confronting others and providing opportunities for rational discourse. As with the other survey questions, a pattern emerged based on position. Midlevel leaders responded differently from senior leaders. Those in director positions have less power than presidents and are less in the spotlight. Those in midlevel leadership positions, however, interact more frequently with faculty, staff, and students, potentially making their actions even more critical. One midlevel director discussed how she uses her voice for advocacy: "I've had to train myself to speak up . . . it's so unnatural, it's very hard. I am speaking up for others—I'm speaking in an advocacy role in terms of justice." The work of speaking up is difficult, and it comes with risks. This quote also illustrates that leaders must intentionally practice and, in essence, train themselves to advocate for others.

Combating verbal microaggressions. Rational discourse cannot exist in a culture in which microaggressions are regular occurrences. Leaders must take clear and public action to raise awareness of and combat microaggressions. Discriminatory language and behavior can be subtle and often materialize as microaggressions. Over time, microaggressions have come to replace more overt and explicit displays of discrimination. They are defined as brief (hence "micro") instances and include regularly experienced verbal, behavioral, or environmental indignities that communicate hostile, derogatory, or negative slights toward individuals or groups of individuals.[46] Many leaders may not recognize or even be aware of the microaggressions that some people experience in the workplace and thus may not confront the offenders. In addition, some leaders may feel ill equipped to address those committing microaggressions one on one or publicly.

To some, microaggressions may seem harmless or just a buzzword, but the cumulative burden of a lifetime of microaggressions can have significant and lasting negative consequences on campus community members, which are then reflected in the campus culture and how people experience the campus. A common metaphor connected to microaggressions is "death by a thousand cuts," which reflects the cumulative effect of these types of aggressions. In addition to the toll that regularly experiencing microaggressions might have on one's physical health, the cost to one's mental health can be great. Anger and depression are two commonly cited outcomes but so, too, are loss of confidence, lowered work productivity, and decreased problem-solving capabilities.[47]

Types of Microaggressions

According to Derald Wing Sue and Lisa Spanierman, authors of *Microaggressions in Everyday Life*, microaggressions are expressed in three forms, all of which can have significant negative effects on people and campus culture:[48]

- Microassaults are conscious and deliberate in nature. In 2023, a member of the United States Congress referred to Black people and African Americans using the term "colored people" during a debate on the House floor. While the representative later stated that he "misspoke," this use of derogatory and offensive language is an example of a microassault.
- Microinsults are verbal, nonverbal, or environmental actions that are insensitive, rude, or demean a person's identity and are more subtle than

microassaults. When, for example, only men are called upon in meetings to report out, the subtle message conveyed is that men's input is more important that the input of those with other gender identities.

- Microinvalidations are used to dismiss the psychological thoughts, feelings, or experiences of individuals or groups of people. The concept of gaslighting, described by the *Washington Post* as a trendy buzzword in 2022, involves the manipulation by one person over another by using actions that make the victim question their own reality and perceptions; both gaslighting and the associated behaviors can be viewed as microinvalidations in that individuals are made to question their own deductive reasoning. Another example of a microinvalidation is the suggestion that racism is a thing of the past.

Having the language to define the various forms of microaggressions apparent in community colleges can help individuals on the receiving end of these actions better understand what they are experiencing and help advocates identify these actions when they occur and address them in the moment.

Recent research on workplace microaggressions has sought to distinguish between types of microaggressions and determine the impact on individuals when advocates and allies intervene. When individuals experience a microaggression, having someone to talk to can trigger a redemptive sense-making process that can build resilience and counter the negative effects of microaggressions. The role of advocates and allies in countering the negative impact of microaggressions further distinguishes the role they play from that of others who may be supportive of those who are transgressed but prefer not to intervene. An advocate or ally will publicly address a microaggression, usually without prompting by the person experiencing it, whereas a supporter may offer sympathy in private. One midlevel leader described her experience with microaggressions during virtual calls: "There are detracting voices who, you know, I laugh because you can always time it. Especially it's going to come on the chat. He's never going to come off on the camera[;] it's always just going to drop in the little comments on chat. So there is that. Then there's when it comes in several different words that are microaggression form and that also comes in the form of 'aggression' aggression."

As evident in this case, this leader had to address the issue on an individual level because no one else on the virtual calls spoke out against the microaggressions occurring in the chat. Because of her experiences, however, this leader is poised to advocate for others experiencing microaggressions.

Gender Microaggressions

Experiencing a gender microaggression is similar to experiencing sex-based harassment because both denigrate an individual based on their gender. However, differences exist in that harassment is often intentional, with perpetrators being motivated to protect their social status or dominance in the workplace, whereas microaggressions are often unintentional. Because gender microaggressions may be unintentional and lack an identifiable motive, the researchers Jennifer Kim and Alyson Meister explained that it can be difficult to have a meaningful dialogue during an experience of a gender microaggression (e.g., during a DEI training session). Those committing microaggressions may become defensive or defiant, saying things like, "That is not what I meant," or "You are overreacting!" When gender microaggressions are experienced by women, it can have a destabilizing effect by preventing them from forming positive professional identities and may result in women leaving their roles and organizations. Leaders must seek out ways to intervene, raise awareness of what constitutes a microaggression, and address the negative effects of gender microaggressions.[49]

Disability Microaggressions

People with disabilities face microaggressions on a regular basis, whether in the classroom or the workplace. While many leaders may be aware of outdated and ableist language harmful to people with disabilities, many may be less familiar with some of the unintended microaggressions that people with disabilities experience in our colleges and universities. Examples include the presumption of incompetence, speaking to people with disabilities in a condescending way, and "harmless" disability jokes. For example, when passing by a person using a wheelchair or scooter, a seemingly harmless remark from a nondisabled person might be, "You got a license for that thing?" While possibly said because the nondisabled person feels awkward and thinks that saying something is better than saying nothing, these remarks, like all microaggressions, add up over time and can have a significant negative effect on a person's well-being. Admitting mistakes, accepting critical feedback, and thanking those who point out microaggressions when they occur are key tasks of combating microaggressions in our organizations.

Silencing bullies. Just as opportunities will be squashed for rational discourse if there is an undercurrent of verbal microaggressions, it is also true that rational discourse cannot happen if bullying exists on a campus. Leaders who wish to be advocates and advance an equity agenda must silence—or remove—bullies. While microaggressions can be subtle, bullying is not. Bullying is characterized by direct intentional verbal assaults such as yelling and public displays of aggression targeted toward a person or group of people.[50] Bullying is repeated behavior that aims to hurt, undermine, or silence others. An example is repeatedly spreading rumors or lies about a colleague to damage their reputation or credibility. Leah Hollis reports that workplace bullying affects 58 to 62 percent of higher education faculty and administrators—and a higher percentage of underrepresented minority campus community members.[51]

Accusations of Bullying

In 2023, the president of a Connecticut college resigned among accusations of bullying by the dean of institutional equity and inclusion. Although the president had overseen the creation of the Institutional Equity and Inclusion department, the dean accused the president of bullying and creating a toxic administrative culture of fear and intimidation.[52] The 2024 suicide of a Black female vice president who was allegedly bullied by her president demonstrates the insidious nature of bullying, especially by those in power.[53] While these examples illustrate public bullying, most bullying behaviors remain out of the public eye between individuals in private conversations and actions, and all forms of bullying cause lasting harm.

While it is not our intent to provide step-by-step instructions for how leaders should confront and silence bullies, a strategy that many institutions are implementing is the creation of an antibullying policy. Suffolk County Community College in New York, for example, has an antibullying policy that defines bullying, explains procedures for reporting bullying, and lists available educational resources on bullying. In 2022, a working group from Highland Community College (HCC) in Illinois created an antibullying policy described on its website as "a policy to support a culture of trust, accountability, and respect, and demonstrate HCC's cultural beliefs, core values, and mission."[54] The college's website further explains that the discussion of the group and the resulting policy stemmed from concerns about racism, political divisiveness, and hate crimes; the increased emphasis on anti-harassment and bullying on campuses; and the work at the college to improve culture and create a welcoming and inclusive environment.

GIVING VOICE

Lifting up voices that have been silenced is a key attribute of an equity-minded advocate. The idea of giving voice or *verbally* "speaking truth to power," however, no longer encapsulates our reality, given the wide array of communication vehicles that exist in our society. Social media and various technology innovations have infiltrated our lives in a way that makes advocacy efforts visible in real time. In the past, campus community members might have learned of a particular initiative during a weekly staff meeting or via a campus newspaper article. Now, there is no such "wait time."

The immediacy of information is both a blessing and a curse for leaders. On the plus side, information is accessible and allows for voices to be magnified. On the minus side, we are bombarded with misinformation that can spread rapidly and the sharing of information without context. The number of public relations crises on college campuses has grown exponentially. Consider the public platforms of voices of no confidence, rogue board of trustee actions, and how campuses have reacted to the cessation of and threats to DEI efforts. Rather than serving as a springboard for meaningful action, the rapid spread of information often turns into a public relations nightmare that distracts from building an equity-driven campus.

When Magdalena Martinez and Deanna Cooper examined the public discourse used by administrators and policy makers, they found that the presence of accountability rhetoric overshadowed social justice and equity goals.[55] With regard to the importance of language, they advised leaders to take nothing for granted (e.g., ask who is at the table and whose views are included); engage in deconstruction (e.g., investigate the various meanings people hold of social justice and equity); determine who benefits from a particular way of thinking about the organization (e.g., understand the values and privilege of upper management); give voice to traditionally silenced groups (e.g., elevate voices of historically underrepresented groups); embrace paradox (e.g., engage in Janusian thinking); and integrate moral reasoning into professional development (e.g., open up safe spaces for dialogue on differences).[56] Understanding how leaders make sense of social justice can provide a foundation for how they advocate for social justice on campus through their communications.

As noted earlier, positionality and identity affected how leaders in the 2021 National Survey of Community College Leadership for Social Justice perceived the opportunity to engage in safe and authentic dialogue on campus. Our findings corroborate existing research showing that anti-Blackness, gender bias, and other institutional barriers result in differences in people's experiences of work based on identity. Given this backdrop, it is critical for campus leaders to attend to how critical conversations on social justice occur and to provide forums and development opportunities to help build a culture of equity on campus. This work requires heightening the awareness of the entire institution about people's different experiences and recognizing that not all campus community members feel that the campus offers safe spaces.

In part, the language of leadership is central to how other campus stakeholders understand their college context and buy in to change efforts on campus. Thus, how leaders use the language of equity and social justice matters. Framing involves how leaders present information to others and where they direct campus members' attention. Thinking of the perspective of the glass being half full or half empty provides a simple example of the use of framing and leaders' influence on how others "see" the glass. In framing a vision for others, leaders highlight how the current status quo falls short and portray what a better future looks like, a process that involves "frame breaking."[57] Frame breaking occurs on multiple levels. First, as they develop their critical consciousness, leaders may break an old frame (i.e., change their perspective) of how they see issues of equity and social justice. Second, when leaders provide a view of equity gaps on campus, they help break through assumptions about the experiences of students, faculty, and staff and break up existing mythologies explaining particular campus outcomes.

Finally, individual campus members engage in their own frame breaking when they, too, engage in raising their own critical consciousness. Given models of social ecology and the various influences on the college, creating a new understanding for others relies on leveraging the values of the campus culture because institutional and community history can play an important role in this process.

Leaders must be savvy in understanding the context in which they lead. Regional differences highlight complicated histories of the country that involve race, economics, and belief systems. Take, for example, one vice president in the South who offered, "Now, we don't refer to it as *social justice*. I think that's a key, knowing your context and knowing what verbiage and what phrases are going to resonate and which ones have been potentially co-opted by politicians that they will find on their own. We use *mobility—economic mobility*."

The use of language that is acceptable to campus members and to surrounding community members, in this case the choice to use the term *economic mobility*, ties in directly with prevalent neoliberal influences on higher education. In this example, the term *social justice* had been weaponized in the region by political influencers.[58] Now, consider the perspective of an academic dean from the West Coast who provided an example of how he advocates for social justice on campus:

> As I'm trying to advocate it [social justice], I try to make sure that we've got good information out there. In a project we recently did we were really focusing on Black student success and to kick that off, we frankly first put out a lot of information to dispel some of the rumors that were on campus about where our Black students were coming from. . . . We showed our top 10 feeder schools for our Black students were in fact in our service region. . . . Another standing myth was that Black students are all student-athletes, and we showed only 10 percent are student-athletes. . . . We have this sort of perpetual myth that all Black students are poor students, and yes[,] a lot of them do use financial aid, but it's not that different from our general student body.

This midlevel leader worked on frame breaking the notions of what it means to educate Black students and provided the space for campus members to engage in generative dialogue around race and student success.

In framing, leaders have the power to lift the voices of campus and community populations that traditionally have been silenced. The actions they take, how they advocate for others, how they model being an ally for others on campus, and how they challenge the status quo all contribute to how campus members will react to seeing equity become a core guiding value on campus. Given the difference in mid- and top-level leaders' views of equity efforts on campus, an important first step is for top-level leaders to take action to understand why divergent views and perspectives are held by those leading in the middle.

Giving voice to equity on campus occurs via the many actions identified in this chapter. When leaders build a culture with advocacy at the center, all decision-making is guided by equity. Thus, policy reviews and standard operating practices start with questioning whether processes are equitable. This questioning can occur only when safe spaces for dialogue exist. Who is included in decision-making and whose perspectives dominate matter. Change occurs when leaders are equity-minded advocates.

CALL TO ACTION

This chapter began with the definition of what it means to be an advocate, and we clarified that advocacy goes beyond a change in mind-set. It is a public display of support that can be observed in a leader's actions. Advocates empower and support others to take action that will drive equity. The actions explored in this chapter that have implications for policies and practices include the following:

- Creating and supporting campus affinity groups:
  - Provide safe spaces on campus for affinity groups to meet.
  - Engage in strategies to improve a sense of belonging for all members of the campus community.
  - Actively support affinity groups through resources, staff, top-level leader and participation to show campus commitment to these groups.
- Reconceptualizing mentorship as a form of allyship:
  - Expand opportunities for mentoring to allow for more participation.
  - Provide training for mentors, sponsors, and allies in career development strategies.
  - Examine who on campus engages with mentors, who has allies, and who is left out.
- Recognizing and encouraging advocacy work in the community:
  - Build in processes that provide space for campus members to learn more about advocacy work in the community.
  - Celebrate the activities of campus members working as advocates in the community.
  - Identify where community advocacy helps support campus priorities.

- Encouraging curricular change to support equity-driven classrooms and teaching practices:
    - Provide faculty development for culturally responsive pedagogy and inclusive teaching strategies.
    - Require data analysis on classroom outcomes disaggregated by demographics to identify equity gaps.
    - Address barriers to persistence for marginalized students (e.g., the application process, financial holds on accounts, unclear degree pathways).
- Offering professional development opportunities that support equity:
    - Revamp professional development offerings to infuse equity in all programming.
    - Provide opportunities for continuous learning and practice for newly acquired strategies.
    - Encourage faculty leaders to help conduct professional development sessions.
- Creating opportunities for rational discourse by combating microaggressions and silencing bullies:
    - Engage in trust-building activities to provide a foundation for rational discourse on campus.
    - Ensure that accurate and complete information that expands transparency is widely available to all campus members.
    - Provide training on conflict resolution, microaggressions, and bystander strategies to combat bullying and the tacit acceptance of microaggressions based on race, gender, ethnicity, and ability.
- Ensuring that all campus voices are heard:
    - Provide safe spaces for dialogue.
    - Engage in frame breaking to highlight problems with the current status quo and keep equity at the center of all decisions and actions on campus.
    - Identify who is at the table in decision-making and how to include the voices of those not currently present.

In the final chapter, we offer a blueprint for how equity-driven community college leaders can move to larger organizational change that will outlast individual leaders, propel teams of leaders, and retain hard-won changes that are fully integrated into the organizational culture.

CHAPTER 5

Building an Equity-Driven Community College

Even with labels like "open access" and "democracy's colleges," community colleges continue to be sites of deep and pervasive inequality. The pervasiveness of the gap between what is espoused and the reality on campus is evident when we examine trends in student outcomes, interrogate policies and practices that perpetuate the status quo, and ask leaders for their perspectives, as we did in the 2021 National Survey of Community College Leadership for Social Justice. While many campus community members may point to advancements and achievements in their diversity, equity, and inclusion (DEI) initiatives, quantitative and qualitative evidence supporting the notion that campuses have become substantively more equitable is lacking.[1] Good intentions and changes in individual mind-sets are not enough to change organizations. Further, it is naive to believe that actions such as a couple hours of diversity training, forming an affinity group, or challenging a microaggression during a meeting could shift an organization's culture substantially. Certainly, it is important for leaders to employ a range of actions such as these to support equity, but individual actions alone cannot address issues of embedded structural inequity. Thus, in this chapter, we unite some of the ideas presented earlier in the book to create a blueprint for developing equity-driven leaders.

A blueprint for developing equity-driven leaders encompasses the key components of transformative leadership while also attending to context and the many pressing factors unique to leading in the twenty-first century. As equity-driven transformative leadership is cultivated, opportunities are created for communities of practice that can do the collective work of shifting campus culture and building organizational trust in equity-driven initiatives. To this end, after describing the blueprint, we discuss how a group of equity-driven leaders can create conditions for collective action. However, the success of collective efforts depends on leaders from across the college using their unique talents, strengths, and skill sets to create the conditions for change. Hence, in the last section of this chapter, we pay particular attention to leadership roles that transcend the traditional view of a single leader or individual change agent to create an equity-driven campus.

A BLUEPRINT FOR DEVELOPING EQUITY-DRIVEN COMMUNITY COLLEGE LEADERS

The blueprint for developing equity-driven leaders in community colleges starts with individual change, considers the influence of context, and promotes actions that characterize equity-minded transformative leaders (figure 5.1). The foundation of the blueprint is individual change that leads to collective change. Chapter 2 explored the components necessary to develop and expand individual equity-mindedness by adopting a transformative leadership approach. Chapter 3 argued that developing contextual competency is a critical task of leadership. Context provides the backdrop for the practice of leadership, and an intricate understanding of context is necessary to propel equity-driven initiatives. Chapter 4 described how an equity-driven leader moves from intentions to action. For the blueprint to be meaningful in building an equity-driven campus, organizational trust is paramount.

Transformative leadership identity

The development of equity-driven leaders begins with looking inward to assess the influence of positionality on one's worldview. This work requires a deep level of self-reflection about privilege, both implicit and explicit biases, and stereotypes and how one's mind-set may be perpetuating inequity. In addition to self-reflection, leaders must also strive to engage in continuous learning to enhance their critical consciousness. Learning more about how positionality contributes to implicit bias and about raising one's own critical consciousness and that of others requires leaders to regularly ask questions and interrogate current practices. Because this type of self-examination can result in cognitive dissonance,

FIGURE 5.1 Blueprint for developing equity-driven leaders

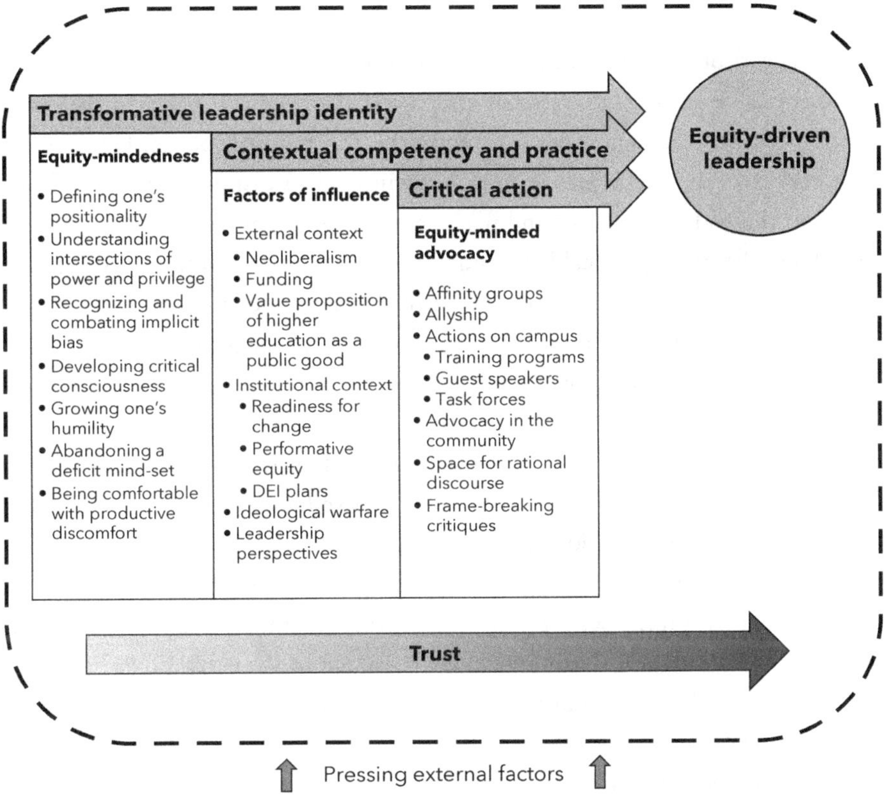

a key attribute of transformative leaders is learning to be comfortable with the uncomfortable.

Developing a transformative leadership identity is more than just changing one's mind-set, however. It is the move from critical reflection to critical action that is at the core of transformative leadership. Transformative leaders focus on equity and justice, understanding the interconnectedness of people and systems that contribute to structural barriers that perpetuate inequity. Transformative leaders take intentional action to change unjust structures. In practice, transformative leaders challenge current frameworks that embed inequities into policies and practice. Recognizing the inequitable distribution of power drives the transformative leader toward change. And it is through leaders' development of a transformative leadership identity that other campus community members build trust in the change process and share in the responsibility of creating an equity-driven campus.

Contextual competency and practice

We have defined *contextual competence* as the ability to recognize the interrelated aspects of the community college by attending to people, places (or spaces on campus), events (both internal and external to the college), and the many systems embedded in and pressing upon the community college. Understanding context requires leaders to look both inward to campus culture and outward to the wider influences and many pressing external factors on the college. The long history of permeable boundaries between the community college and the community serves as an advantage in developing contextual competency. Understanding community needs is embedded in college operations. Furthering contextual competency requires identifying pressure points in the community that could derail equity efforts. These pressures include the move toward neoliberalism, a view that places value on the individual rather the larger public good; changes in public education funding, which have increased the burden on students to fund their education and limited the availability of college services; and the need to promote the value proposition of education to the public.

Situated within the college context are efforts that fall under the DEI abbreviation. The political and ideological environment of the early 2020s has weaponized DEI work and created a difficult context for equity-driven leaders to work in. Findings from the 2021 National Survey of Community College Leadership for Social Justice highlighted the perspectives of campus leaders, with about one in four respondents stating that they could not describe their college as equitable despite the fact that most community colleges have a DEI plan and engage in various DEI initiatives. Of critical importance is that fewer people of color and women in the data set felt that their campuses provided safe spaces for dialogue, suggesting that the conditions for creating a culture that supports DEI may be lacking in many places.

Critical action

Moving from critical reflection and the development of contextual competency to critical action is the linchpin to changing inequitable systems. Becoming an advocate means publicly supporting others and encouraging campus community members to also take on the role of equity-minded advocate. In the 2021 National Survey of Community College Leadership for Social Justice, senior leaders were more likely than midlevel leaders to indicate having confronted an individual about offensive, discriminatory language or behaviors. This difference in response based on leadership position was also seen when participants were asked whether they had examined or changed a written policy or practice that was unjust, with more senior leaders than midlevel leaders answering yes. It is worth reiterating that approximately one-third of survey respondents indicated that they had *not* examined or changed unjust policies or practices in recent years. Without changes to policies and practices, we contend that efforts to create an equity-driven campus will not succeed. Investigating admission policies, policies governing financial holds on student accounts, drop-add policies, transfer policies, and staff and faculty promotion policies can help leaders identify systemic equity issues such as racism.[2]

Beyond explicit changes to policy and practice, critical action can be taken in many areas. Recognizing and combating microaggressions, for example, is one form of advocacy. And because most of the interactions students have on campus are in classrooms, building inclusive classrooms and teaching practices, through professional development opportunities, is an essential aspect of creating a culture that supports equity. Creating space for rational discourse has been achieved when campus members feel safe, bullies are silenced, and microaggressions stop. Giving voice to marginalized and historically silenced campus members begins to build a culture in which equity practices thrive. Taking actions such as confronting someone who has perpetrated a microaggression or publicly acknowledging that some voices have been silenced is hard work. But it is work that must be done. And it is important to note that the actions taken by leaders may depend on their career stage, positional authority, and level of awareness, as well as whether a sense of trust exists in the organizational culture. When leaders engage in frame-breaking activities, new practices emerge to support equity in community colleges.

Trust

Trust is the foundation of an equity-driven campus. Traditional leadership theories refer to honesty and trust as the essential building blocks of leadership.[3] Honesty aligns with candor and involves leaders providing clarity and transparency. In other words, saying what they mean and meaning what they say is crucial for leaders. Being honest allows leaders to use humble inquiry to engage with others. This form of inquiry involves asking questions of others based on genuine interest in what they have to contribute (referred to as "listening/hearing mode") and is in opposition to the form leaders often employ, which involves telling others their ideas; (referred to as "transmitting mode").[4] Trust in individuals is built through honesty, transparency, and a willingness to engage in humbly inquiry. And it is through individual trust that campus community members build collective trust in the organization. Barriers to trust-building occur when individuals have different interpretations of the messages conveyed by leaders and when leaders' actions do not align with their words.

Equity-driven leaders must build or regain trust, especially with those in the campus community who have been marginalized or disenfranchised, as well as with those who have lost confidence in performative DEI efforts.[5] One midlevel leader in our study reflected, "Your focus as an equity leader is you need to have the time to cultivate relationships. The trust, the understanding . . . you really have to activate your committee members to move messages beyond just the leadership." When trust is broken, campus members become wary and start to question leaders' intentions. One midlevel leader offered an example of how the degradation of trust nationally has influenced levels of trust on campus: "Coming off a [Trump] presidency where trust had eroded completely, and now trust is having to be rebuilt . . . you're seeing leaders that led through the pandemic in honorable ways with integrity and now their motives are being questioned and it's [because of] nothing they are doing. It is reflective of the national vibe." Collective trust levels are affected by both the internal and external experiences of campus members.

As shown in figure 5.1, external factors influence what occurs on campus. The decline in public opinion regarding the value of higher education also influences general trust levels about the value of colleges, which can infiltrate campus environments in one way or another. Thus, in thinking about trust, it is imperative to consider how trust moves beyond the individual to the institutional level. When advancing equity, it is about *collective* action creating long-lasting *collective* trust. This type of trust creates a positive feedback loop of organizational functioning and change.

Trust is important in all spheres of life but when attempting to advance DEI initiatives, it is a requirement. Simply put, without trust, equity efforts will fail. In her 2023 book *DEI Deconstructed: Your No-Nonsense Guide to Doing the Work and Doing It Right*, Lily Zheng explained how DEI efforts can look very different based on the level of trust in the organization. In high-trust environments, leaders can take risks, and stakeholders are patient when it comes to change because they are willing to give the benefit of the doubt to one another and to organizational leaders. When challenges do arise in high-trust organizations, community members believe that their interests are always considered by decision-makers. In this type of environment, if harm is done that could reduce trust, action is swift to rectify the situation and "do right" by those who have been harmed.[6]

In medium-trust environments, a critical incident in the past may have eroded trust that organizational members have not yet fully regained. A lack of trust can linger for years or even decades after an event or after a particular leader has left the college. According to Zheng, because community members may not have high trust in senior leaders, for an organization to grow into a high-trust environment, it is critical to engage grassroot leaders and create accountability groups, such as councils, committees, or task forces with wide representation from across the college, that can legitimize change. It is through the efforts of colleagues and peers, rather than senior leaders, that others in the organization may develop more trust in organizational efforts.[7]

Organizations in which members have a low level of trust face many challenges, including those related to DEI efforts. In low-trust environments, there have likely been repeated breaches of trust through many critical incidents. In this environment, stakeholders become cynical, bitter, outwardly hostile, and antagonistic. In low-trust environments, any DEI effort that requires stakeholders to trust one another is "dead in the water" almost as soon as it is proposed.[8] In environments with low trust, the primary goal should be to gain and build trust to advance to a medium level of trust. Similarly, the goal of an organization with medium trust should be to advance to a high level of trust. When an organization has achieved and is able to maintain a high level of trust, change efforts can succeed even if there are starts and stops or mishaps along the way.

The use of grassroots groups can help build collective trust, but it is the efforts of a larger, more systematized community of practice and collective action that help institutionalize mechanisms for organizational trust to exist at high levels in the long term. A community of practice includes people with shared goals of advancing equity. To understand how a community of practice can be leveraged to move from individual change to institutionalized change, it is important first to understand the change process in general.

THE CHANGE PROCESS

Copious books, articles, and public writing exist about change and change leadership. Many change theories rely on leader-centric models of leadership, which can come up short in creating lasting change. We are certainly not the first to suggest that without individual change, organizational change will fail. But perhaps this is the tension that exists in the organizational change literature: not enough attention is given to the different roles of individuals, and change seems to depend on the efforts of a single leader. In the remaining sections of this chapter, therefore, we consider the following question: *How can community college leaders who practice transformative, equity-driven leadership cultivate an environment in which others, and the organization overall, are equity driven?* Our answer is threefold. First, leaders must understand the process of change, understand where they will face resistance, and put in steps to increase levels of trust to foster sustainable change efforts. Second, an equity-driven community of practice has the potential to advance meaningful change by tapping into collective action. Third, tapping into the various roles that individuals play in the process of change provides opportunities to use a fuller range of leadership approaches to support equity-driven solutions.

Becoming an equity-driven leader of an organization must take into account what we already know about successful change initiatives, as well as the challenges and roadblocks embedded in complex organizations like community colleges. Of particular note in the literature is that organizational change initiatives are rarely successful. In fact, John Kotter, well known for his linear eight-step organizational change model, reported that 70 percent of change efforts fail. He argued that if his model is employed, more success can occur.[9] The first step in his model is for leaders to convey a sense of urgency regarding the need for change. Step 2 is building a guiding coalition to engage in the work of change, with diversity of position, thought, and experience helping to move past a group-think mentality. The coalition builds a strategic vision for the change (step 3); leaders then must work toward removing barriers (e.g., bureaucratic processes, cumbersome rules) that stand in the way of change (step 4). Step 5 is to involve the larger campus community with particular actions, and step 6 is for leaders to broadly convey the motivation to move in new directions. Celebrating short-term wins (step 7) helps maintain momentum and sustain the acceleration of change ideas. The final step (step 8) is to institute change and ground it in institutional practices.[10]

Critiques of linear step-by-step models of change include the lack of questioning of the existing infrastructure of the college and its policies and practices, which were developed in a way that privileged historically dominant groups over marginalized groups. Membership in coalitions driving change is often exclusionary, too, meaning that these groups often fall short of achieving equity goals. While an assumption in the initial step of creating urgency may involve situating the issue in the larger societal landscape, the role of context and the pressure of external factors are not called out in many traditional models of change.

Moving from individual change in one's critical consciousness, which results in the development of an equity mind-set, to change at the organizational level, in which equity is woven into the fabric of the institution, is a missing link in many organizational change models. Becoming an equity-driven campus *requires* individuals within that community to change. Critical reflection can change one's mind-set, and this individual-level change can manifest in critical action or taking on a new role that changes the organizational landscape. A first step in organizational change can be hiring a person whose role is to lead equity-driven initiatives on campus. The number of mid-level leaders in the 2021 National Survey of Community College Leadership for Social Justice leading DEI offices attests to the energy community colleges have devoted to DEI efforts since the beginning of this century. This change (in the number of leaders heading DEI offices) can be gleaned by reviewing changes in titles or to names of departments. Yet even though these types of initial changes have been well underway over the last few decades, there is limited evidence that changes in titles or naming conventions have resulted in more equitable institutions—because these individuals or centers are often viewed as solely responsible for advancing equity on campus. The potential for change is lost when DEI staff and centers are not funded, when it is assumed that the work of equity can be done by individual advocates or small groups, when equity is not a collective goal, and when DEI efforts result merely in performative equity.

Examples of Change: Creating Centers for Social Justice and Other Initiatives

The founding of different types of centers to support equity on community college campuses has increased over time and provides a visible example of organizational change (though some of these entities are increasingly under attack owing to state legislative actions). One prominent example comes from the Housatonic campus of the Connecticut State Community College system. The college built on its mission to promote equity by establishing its Center for Equity and Social Justice. The college's DEI statement provides a clear commitment to efforts to improve equity on campus:

> The Connecticut State Community College commits to bold and disruptive change by actively: identifying, naming, and dismantling structural racism, systemic poverty, and other barriers; establishing equitable and anti-racist policies and practices; and empowering students, faculty, staff, and administrators to advance racial, social and economic justice. Our core collective responsibility is to continuously assess practices and polices and transform the world we live in by eliminating inequities.[11]

Likewise, the Race, Equity, and Social Justice Center at Los Angeles City College was established in 2020 to improve racial equity and social injustices. A commitment to challenging systemic barriers that support oppression is at the core of its mission. The founding of centers on community college campuses to support equity and social justice is encouraging, yet many of these newly formed centers are now facing challenges and initial momentum has waned. To continue moving forward, equity-driven leaders must institutionalize an equity perspective within the culture of the college.

COMMUNITIES OF PRACTICE AS A MECHANISM OF CHANGE

The blueprint we propose for developing equity-driven leaders (see figure 5.1) provides some considerations for larger institutional change. To make meaningful and lasting change, communities or groups of equity-minded individuals must unite to create a culture that supports equity. Building an equity-driven community of practice helps engrain equity into the campus culture in ways that last beyond the efforts of individual leaders and helps sustain change. The ability to have a lasting effect is particularly important given the short tenure of college presidents and other senior leaders. Change cannot depend on any single individual. A leader of color emphasized this point, stating, "I look for opportunities to get engaged in initiatives that involve social justice and equity. So that it's not just something that I'm doing as an individual, but I'm contributing to the culture change at the institutional level, so that we're making a much broader impact than any one person can do alone." Key here is having all individuals at the college recognize the importance of collective action in achieving change at the institutional level.

When a high level of organizational trust exists, colleges are able to create groups of people to help drive collective change. Building communities of practice (CoPs) can advance changes in culture that result in more pervasive support of equity efforts. A CoP differs from a task force and ad hoc committee in the underlying assumption of wider group involvement and its operating elements. A CoP is made up of individuals who share similar goals, in this case of creating an equity-driven campus. CoP members learn how to do the work effectively through regular and varied interactions. The components of a CoP include domain, community, and practice. *Domain* refers to members' commitment to a set of practices or a shared competence (e.g., equity). Community emerges through shared activities and dialogue that help members expand their understanding through shared learning and information. Practice provides opportunities for members to refine tools and resources that are ultimately shared and made available for others to use.[12] Building community is essential to achieving change goals.

Supporting learning in communities of practice

Adrianna Kezar, Sean Gehrke, and Samantha Bernstein-Sierra identified seven general principles as important foundational steps of supporting learning that leads to change. As equity-driven leaders look to engage other campus community members, developing environments for learning requires building spaces for their development. The principles of CoP learning identified by Kezar and colleagues are as follows:

- organic design for the community that allows for evolution
- open lines of communication that permit opportunities for dialogue among members
- different levels and forms of participation that allow for more inclusion
- the formation of both public and private community spaces that permit an individualized approach

- emphasis on the possibilities and value of participation in the community to help sustainability
- the building of space for learner-directed opportunities that also couple with the power of group processing
- a predicable cycle of engagement opportunities to sustain the community[13]

Moving beyond individual to collective learning in a CoP is supported in high-trust campus cultures. One midlevel leader described how her campus amplified collective learning: "Deans and other directors are learning to train ourselves to recognize talent on campus, and those who have the desire to do the work of social justice require leadership development, and we need to turn around and help others identify or communicate that." When high trust does not exist, it must be developed to create a culture that advances equity.

However, the work of building a CoP and shared understanding on campus leaves space for dissenting views and respectful dialogue, as one of the strengths of this type of group is that it is a "community." The limitations of a CoP emerge when the community involves only a narrow group of individuals, rather than being open to the entire campus. In this case, a CoP can reinforce the notion of the existence of insiders and outsiders, the "haves" and the "have-nots." It takes time and intentionality to create a CoP—two things that are often limited in higher education because of the demands on leaders and the college, as well as the academic calendar. One of the first steps, then, is to allow timelines for CoP activities to be flexible rather than strict, as is common in academic committee or task force work. A CoP is not the same as a formal college-recognized committee; thus, it takes on different characteristics. Further, some initial questions must be asked and answered to guide the work of a CoP.

Previous chapters addressed how people can develop an equity mind-set and what actions might emerge from doing so to support equity on campus. Bringing equity-minded individuals together and focusing group efforts on building a CoP that centers equity requires interrogating systems of inequity and working through a set of foundational questions together, such as the following:

- What are the communal values, ideals, and beliefs related to equity on campus?
- Even though campus community members may have different values, ideals, and beliefs, do members share responsibility equally to create an equity-driven campus?

- What about the college context connects people? What alienates people?
- What current practice or policies support equity on campus? What current practices or policies perpetuate inequity?
- Whose voices are prominent in discussions of equity on campus? Whose voices are excluded?
- Who holds the power, resources, and motivation to create an equity-driven campus?

Shared Responsibility for Justice

Creating equity-driven community colleges is a shared, collective responsibility that acknowledges and addresses structural injustices. In the 2011 book *Responsibility for Justice*, Iris Young explained that "individuals bear responsibility for structural injustice because they contribute by their actions to the processes that produce unjust outcomes. . . . All who dwell within these structures must take responsibility for remedying injustices they cause."[14] Young defined *structural injustice* as a "moral wrong" existing within the limits of accepted social rules and norms: "Social processes put large groups of persons under systematic threat of domination or deprivation of the means to develop and exercise their capacities, at the same time that these processes enable others to dominate or to have a wide range of opportunities for developing and exercising capacities available to them."[15]

To advance the idea of shared responsibility, Young presented a social connection model of responsibility that can be helpful for formulating equity agendas and making organizational decisions about how to rectify structural injustices. According to Young, several features of the social connection model must be present to advance social justice. All those who engage in perpetuating structural injustices share responsibility for those injustices. Therefore, the idea that creating an equity-driven campus is the responsibility of only certain individuals is a flawed conclusion. Moving beyond individual change to collective, shared responsibility can therefore be supported by a CoP. Further, addressing structural injustice is not backward looking, assigning blame or fault, but rather forward looking, as individuals join with others to organize collective action to reform structures.

The ingredients needed to build an equity-driven community of practice

High-functioning groups and teams have been the subject of extensive study and contemplation. Why do some groups of people seemingly flourish when combining efforts while others fail? In part, an equity-driven CoP can emerge when the campus is a high-trust environment and its culture is conducive to change. Building a culture that advances change requires a number of ingredients.[16] First, a sense of safety that allows people to feel supported and gives them a sense of belonging to the larger collective is needed. Second, critical consciousness at the group level must be established. Third, a sense of shared responsibility for change must emerge within the campus community. Instead of thinking that someone else will take care of all required changes, with top-level leaders considered the default change leaders, everyone on campus must understand that they have a role to play in making change happen. Finally, because an equity-driven CoP, like the college itself, operates in an ecosystem, a social change ecosystem framework is needed. This type of framework provides tools to align roles in the change process and build networks committed to solidarity, justice, and equity. The following elaborates on each ingredient:

- *A sense of safety within the group*
  When people feel safe and have their basic needs met, they are able to engage more fully with others on shared problems and change efforts. A community of any type must be equipped to deal with conflict. With conflict an ever-present facet of our lives, we must return to some of the basic premises of human interactions in which the focus is not on the individual but on the issue at hand. Thus, instead of personalizing a conflict (e.g., "I don't like you or the change you suggest"), the conversation should focus on the root cause of the issue (e.g., "I don't like changing this practice because it means I have to disrupt how I have done my work in the past"). As noted previously, not everyone feels their community college campus is inclusive or that it provides a safe space for dialogue. As one midlevel leader noted, "I like to use the term *brave space* rather than a *safe space*. Let's have a conversation and don't be afraid to ask the questions that you want to ask. . . . I think that it helps empower us to feel like we can have those conversations outside of that space where we have the information and the knowledge to be able to." Thus, a critical first step for equity-driven leaders

is to build a culture that provides spaces for courageous conversations to occur.

- *Collective critical consciousness*
Once a culture of safety exists, CoP members can work on developing the group's collective critical consciousness, which must start with members developing their individual critical consciousness. Introspection helps identify one's positionality and understanding of their power and privilege. Here, one identifies any of their personal resistance to change as represented in implicit biases and a deficit mind-set. It is through growing one's humility and becoming comfortable with productive discomfort that individuals become comfortable sharing their vulnerabilities with one another. As one midlevel leader said, "I think that constant learning for ourselves has been very helpful in the equity work that we're doing at the college." When transformative leaders foster a feeling of safety, more campus members can engage in transforming individual critical consciousness into collective critical consciousness. When CoP members share a collective consciousness, they can identify the range of experiences of campus members and the influence of larger societal pressures that perpetuate inequity in campus operations and in the experiences of campus community members.
- *Shared responsibility for change*
Many change theories involve a step that centers on having a shared vision or moral purpose that helps guide everyone on campus toward a goal. When campus members have a shared sense of purpose, it is possible for them to develop a collective equity mind-set and to understand the need to share responsibility for achieving institutional goals. Essentially, people feel like they have "skin in the game" and are willing to move to action. As one vice president offered, "We have a social justice responsibility to them [students] to provide not just access but a means of success for their completion." This responsibility must be shared for greater results to occur. Shared responsibility involves voluntary collective decision-making. Determining the motivation for this level of involvement requires a consideration of how decisions are made and what positive or negative outcomes might emerge. In doing this work, campus members will evaluate how much personal effort is involved, whether there is a sense of social inclusion, and whether they believe fairness grounds the decision-making process.[17] The

pull toward shared responsibility anticipates the positive energy of pooling everyone's ideas, which results in better outcomes compared to working alone or at odds, and that credit will be shared across all involved.

- *An understanding that the community of practice exists within a social change ecosystem*
  Communities of practice exist within an ecosystem. The skill of contextual competence involves recognizing the interrelated aspects of the community college by attending to people, places (or spaces on campus), events (both internal and external to the college), and the many systems embedded in and pressing upon the college. An ecosystems perspective can help make sense of how people, relationships, community, and societal structures interact and influence one other, creating dynamics responsible for a variety of behaviors, including those that perpetuate bias, discrimination, and injustice. How people on an individual level (i.e., microsystem) interact with their immediate environment (i.e., mesosystem) is influenced by external factors (i.e., exosystem) and societal culture (i.e., macrosystem) over time (i.e., chronosystem).[18] One of the DEI directors we surveyed noted that his campus had engaged in environmental scanning as a means of understanding the social change ecosystem: "One of the aspects to it [the environmental scan] is looking at the demographic population, and more specifically, racial equity across the region and externally, so even just kind of having these key focuses that are relevant to us." To support a social change ecosystem, campus members must be open to change and experimentation, have a futuristic perspective beyond short-term outcomes, and understand the interdependence of functional areas of work on and off campus, and they must not have a zero-sum perspective of winners and losers among the group.[19] When the larger benefits to the community and to student success drive action, change to support equity can occur.

A CoP comprising equity-driven leaders has the potential to create the conditions and culture to support an equity-driven campus. Because change is complex, it takes leaders from across the campus to accomplish goals and establish a culture of shared responsibility. It also requires a recognition that our stereotypical image of who a leader is and what a leader does is limiting and may hinder change efforts.

LEADERSHIP ROLES IN AN EQUITY-DRIVEN COMMUNITY COLLEGE

Community college leaders are present in every office across campus and hold a range of roles, some positional and some informal. However, decades of scholarship and rhetoric on leadership have created a mythical and unattainable image of what makes for a "good" leader. This image is often referred to as the quintessential "hero" leader. As outlined in chapter 1, nearly half the respondents in the 2016 National Survey of Community College Leaders defined *leadership* in leader-centric ways. Particularly in light of the contextual challenges and pressures facing community colleges today, the notion that one person could possess all the required competencies to successfully lead a college must be debunked. We have purposely referred to all the administrators who responded to our two surveys as leaders, regardless of whether their titles were coordinator, director, assistant dean, or vice chancellor.

The perspective we hope to leave you with is that *every* campus member has a leadership role to play and can actively participate in a community of practice and in change efforts. While some will have very visible "out-in-front" roles and others will work behind the scenes, all roles are important. And many of the possible roles do not and should not align with the mythical and unattainable images of successful leaders often presented in the scholarly literature. Continuing to elevate leaders based on title only may be perpetuating the lack of progress toward advancing equity. We maintain that traditional leadership practices are not substantially advancing an equity agenda in our community colleges. Following the blueprint for developing equity-driven leaders (see figure 5.1) and cultivating the characteristics of transformative leadership are key, but so, too, is recognizing the unique roles that leaders can play that capitalize on individual strengths. Those individual strengths then coalesce to create collective strength, which translates to collective action, which drives an equity agenda. Communities of practice provide a valuable tool for this work.

Our discussion of the roles that leaders play is guided by the following works: *Social Change Now* (2022) by Deepa Iyer, *DEI Deconstructed* (2023) by Lily Zheng, and *Redesigning Collegiate Leadership* (1993) by Estela Mara Bensimon and Anna Neumann.[20] Applying a range of leadership roles to the work of creating an equity-driven campus provides a new perspective for thinking about who can lead and may provide pathways for greater involvement for individuals who fill roles outside the leadership norm. While it is widely understood that traditional leadership roles must be filled, other critically important roles may be left unoccupied, thus potentially explaining why change efforts fail and why we are not seeing greater advancements in creating equity-driven campuses.

Traditional leadership roles

Traditional leadership roles involve taking charge of situations by setting goals, developing strategy, and deploying people to implement plans. Ample writing exists to help these types of leaders achieve change. Before discussing nontraditional leadership roles, the following provides a brief summary of traditional roles and what leaders in these roles intend to accomplish:

- Visionaries: Visionary leaders proclaim bold goals and define future possibilities. Getting others to buy in to the campus vision is a key outcome for visionary leaders. The prototype of "great" leaders often centers on a single person at the helm providing direction and vision for others and looking to transform institutions.
- Strategists: Strategists are focused on effectiveness on a macro level. They preoccupy themselves with the "why" and "how" and work with others to make effective decisions.[21] Often working to assess plans, strategists synthesize information in a way that highlights linkages to find effective solutions.
- Doers or organizers: This type of leader executes plans, especially for new processes and ways of doing work that allow for the implementation of new ideas and the vision of the institution. The work of doers or organizers is often relegated to midlevel leaders and is not always recognized as leadership.
- Change agents: Change agents disrupt the status quo and try new approaches, often through trial and error and taking risks. Change agents are seen as the forward thinkers on campus who show the path forward to achieving institutional goals.

The work of traditional leadership roles is often carried out in silos, with hierarchical positions determining the functions of authority and scope of work tied to positional roles. As evident in the data from the 2021 National Survey of Community College Leadership for Social Justice, midlevel and top-level leaders differed in their perspectives, actions, and experiences. These differences highlight a gap in establishing shared understanding in community college cultures, which can hinder progress toward advancing equity. There may be several reasons for this gap. For example, leadership may be seen as primarily the responsibility of those in the most senior positions, rather than as dispersed throughout the college, and ownership for advancing equity may not be viewed as a shared responsibility.

Tempered Radicals

Tempered radicals are a unique type of change agent. They are individuals who identify with and are committed to their organizations. But they are also "committed to a cause, community, or ideology that is fundamentally different from, and possibly at odds with, the dominant culture of their organization."[22] They use several strategies to create change that run the gamut from quiet and cautious to explicit and strident. Some quietly act in ways that express their personal values, subtly calling into question taken-for-granted beliefs and work practices. Debra Meyerson called this use of different strategies "disruptive self-expression" because of its potential to shake up the status quo:

> Many tempered radicals make a difference through little acts of self-expression—their dress, language, or leadership style. A tempered radical who was a department manager told me that, even though it was not the norm in his office, he insisted on taking off work for the Jewish holidays. This seems like a minor issue, but it signaled to his employees that it was legitimate to observe religious and cultural traditions. His actions made it easier for others to take off for non-Christian observances. Over time, as his colleagues were promoted, they mimicked his behavior. Eventually, the company adopted a personnel policy that facilitated such observances, validating behavior once considered deviant.[23]

Organizational learning can form a base for tempered radicalism as institutions evolve and adjust to external pressures such as new technologies, market demands, and employer demands for newly skilled workers. Many change efforts are incremental and implemented slowly, but tempered radicals push and prod the system through a variety of subtle processes, rechanneling information and opportunities, questioning assumptions, changing boundaries of inclusion, and scoring small wins.[24]

Expanded leadership roles

Less traditional leadership roles that individuals can play in creating an equity-driven campus include those that fall into the categories of relationship builders and connectors. Moving beyond traditional leadership roles that rely on "take-charge" and leader-centric norms requires thinking more expansively about the leadership roles of those in roles throughout the campus.

Relationship builders. Relationship builders nurture people's interactions with one another in the institution and support the foundational elements necessary for building a CoP focused on equity (i.e., a sense of safety, collective critical consciousness, shared responsibility, and recognizing the elements of a social change ecosystem). Relationship builders may serve in the following roles:

- Nurturers: Nurturers cultivate an environment in which all campus members feel included and have their needs met. This work requires a consideration of the personal and emotional needs of individuals. Creating and sustaining a community of care signals that people can feel safe to express their authentic selves at work. Part of the role of a nurturer is helping heal traumas caused by oppressive systems and working to prevent future trauma.
- Responders: Because relationship builders have their finger on the pulse of the institution and its people, they are able to quickly respond to the needs of others and of the institution. Responders help remove obstacles in the way of getting people to work together. They can tap into their networks to provide needed resources and expertise. Responders know who has the skills and knowledge to address various situations.
- Reformers: Unlike change agents, who seek to disrupt the status quo, reformers use a process of steady, incremental change. They rely on feedback loops and organizational learning processes to make change. Reformers are focused on processes rather than outcomes and seek to use the existing tools of the system to better it.
- Early adopters: Early adopters play the critical behind-the-scenes role of moving ideas of reform into the mainstream of acceptance. They support change optimistically and provide a sense of legitimacy to the process. They are similar to grassroots leaders in that they identify changes needed given

their positions throughout the institution, and they are first to take action to move toward change.

Connectors. Connectors have roles often seen as the "glue" that connects people within and outside the college. Notably, the work of these roles requires that some of the work of relationship builders has been done or is ongoing, as such efforts are needed to set the stage for making connections. The types of strategic partnerships that emerge through the work of connectors help advance change. Connectors may serve in the following roles:

- Storytellers and sense-makers: These types of leaders help campus members make sense of ongoing changes and help build the narrative of new realities and new ways of "doing business." Building a culture of equity means change, which can cause fear as old ways are jettisoned and new ways take hold. The storyteller helps campus members interpret new processes and visualize intended outcomes. The work of this role is done in both one-on-one interactions and in groups.
- Educators: Change requires campus members to learn. In the case of transformative leadership, it is critical to engage in learning. Educators help campus members develop an accurate working understanding of a range of topics. Educators help others deepen their critical consciousness, acquire a shared meaning and language, and meet people where they are in their current understanding.
- Boundary spanners: Bringing people, units, and work areas together is the central work of boundary spanners. They cross borders, both internally and externally, to make connections. Being the conduit to different networks helps spread and support equity work and taps into the social capital of boundary spanners. Given the demands of pressing external factors, connectors help in bridging those outside the college with those inside, which builds understanding and provides information needed to take action.

Table 5.1 summarizes the various leadership roles that can each play a critical part in advancing equity. Individuals can play multiple roles concurrently and at different times. Leaders can also shift between roles as needed, based on context. This more expansive understanding of leadership roles ensures that each individual on campus can use their unique talents, strengths, and skills to advance equity. Importantly, change efforts can fail when even one of role is left unoccupied.

TABLE 5.1 Leadership roles to advance equity

Role	*Attributes*	*Actions*
Visionary	Establishes goals based on anticipated future needs	• Environmental scans • Scenario planning
Strategist	Understands the moving parts and systems of the institution	• Designs plans for change • Identifies partners
Doer/Organizer	Knows how to implement plans and work with others	• Conducts audits, uses data • Builds coalitions
Change agent	Willing to test new ideas and take risks	• Critiques current practices • Applies innovative ideas
Nurturer	Pays attention to the needs of campus members	• Active listening • Meeting the emotional needs of others
Responder	Reacts to changes in the landscape	• Responds to the needs of others • Aligns resources to needs
Reformer	Breaks from dated practices to improve culture	• Synthesizes options • Implements changes
Early adopter	Engages in change early and brings legitimacy to actions	• Supports new ways of operating • First to try new ways of working
Storyteller/Sense-maker	Uses stories to explain change and make sense for others	• Creates a shared narrative • Fosters a shared reality
Educator	Supports learning about equity	• Supports learning opportunities • Exposes people to new ideas
Boundary spanner	Brings people together across networks	• Convenes individuals and groups • Bridges perspectives

Source: Adapted from Deepa Iyer, *Social Change Now: A Guide for Reflection and Connection* (Washington, DC: Thick, 2022); Lily Zheng, *DEI Deconstructed: Your No-Nonsense Guide to Doing the Work and Doing It Right* (Oakland, CA: Berrett-Koehler, 2023); Estela Mara Bensimon and Anna Neumann, *Redesigning Collegiate Leadership: Teams and Teamwork in Higher Education* (Baltimore, MD: Johns Hopkins University Press, 1993).

CALL TO ACTION

To fulfill their mission, community colleges need equity-driven leaders. The blueprint for developing equity-driven leaders presented in this chapter serves as a launching point for collective action to support equity. Strategies that support the creation of an equity-driven community college include the following:

- Individuals taking responsibility for developing a transformative leadership identity:
    - Develop an equity mind-set through critical reflection, action, and giving voice.
    - Develop contextual competency by attending to people, places (or spaces on campus), events (both internal and external to the college), and the many systems embedded in and pressing upon the college.
    - Become an advocate for equity by taking action individually and by contributing to the collective work of moving equity to the heart of college work.
- Leaders assessing the level of organizational trust through humble inquiry, listening, and honestly identifying whether there is a low, medium, or high level of trust in the campus:
    - If your college has a high level of trust, maintain it through honest and transparent communications, consistent leadership, responding swiftly to crises and incidents on campus, and nurturing strong relationships with campus community members.
    - If your college has a medium level of trust, work to develop a high level of trust by engaging grassroots leaders and creating accountability groups, such as councils, committees, or task forces with wide representation from across the college that can then legitimize actions that drive change.
    - If your college has a low level of trust, work to develop a medium level of trust through humility and acknowledging past mistakes. Apologize for harm done. Build trust one person at a time until there is a small group of individuals who can move the college toward a medium level of trust.
- Creating and supporting a community of practice and collective energy to advance equity:
    - Identify and define shared goals that advance equity.
    - Attend to culture-sustaining practices that support collective action.
    - Use organizational learning practices to build collective critical consciousness.

  - Identify and address barriers to change.
  - Educate campus members to build shared responsibility for equity.
- Ensuring that each member of the campus community, regardless of title or position, plays a leadership role:
  - Make space for nontraditional leadership roles such as relationship builders and connectors.
  - Encourage and support the development of relationship-building and connector leaders.
  - Acknowledge the organizational complexity inherent in community colleges that requires individuals across roles to move past binary thinking.
  - Build a nomenclature around equity that is understood and recognized by all leaders, regardless of position.

MOVING FORWARD

Our blueprint for developing equity-driven leaders provides a tangible way to move beyond performative equity to achieve deep, pervasive change. Merely hiring a few people to do DEI work is not enough. Rather, equity-driven leaders in positions throughout the community college must work collectively for change. Building and expanding a community of practice focused on equity requires a foundation of trust that contributes to a sense of safety within the group, the emergence of collective critical consciousness, the establishment of a purpose and sense of shared responsibility, and an understanding that the community of practice exists within a social change ecosystem. This work is hard, especially in an environment where anti-DEI legislation runs rampant. Even in places where legislation does not pass, its mere proposal sends a threatening message. Additionally, when people are fearful and distrustful, it becomes hard to believe that working together will change anything. Yet hope exists. The ethos of the community college mission to support democracy, to address community needs, and to allow access to higher education remains at the core of the community college's institutional identity.

When leaders not in traditional leadership roles are recognized and valued, more can be done. The traditional roles of visionary, strategist, organizer, and change agent are still required, but adding the expanded roles of relationship builder and connector creates the web of networked leadership required for transformative change. Critically, no single person possesses all the leadership characteristics needed to leverage change. Change relies on the contributions of many, not a few, to leverage the possibilities of an equity-driven community of practice. Dedicated individuals are working tirelessly every day to support equity in community colleges. Imagine the power of the collective when those working now are joined by others from all across the campus.

APPENDIX A

National Surveys of Community College Leaders

2016 NATIONAL SURVEY OF COMMUNITY COLLEGE LEADERS

In 2016, we asked community college leaders to complete an online survey. Potential respondents were identified via website reviews of community colleges in each state. In this manner, up-to-date email addresses obtained via institutional or statewide community college associations' directories provided our potential survey population. This approach resulted in the distribution of a total of 9,217 surveys. After an initial email was sent requesting participation, three follow-up contacts via email were made by members of the research team. A total of 1,001 usable surveys comprise the data for this study (representing a response rate of 11 percent).

Presidents, vice presidents, deans, and directors from all functional areas (i.e., academic, administrative, and student affairs) responded to the survey. Seventeen percent of respondents were presidents; 26 percent were vice presidents; 28 percent were academic midlevel leaders; and 29 percent were administrative midlevel leaders. Fifty-three percent of respondents were women, and 47 percent were men. Less than 1 percent of respondents identified as a transgender man or transgender woman.

The 2016 survey instrument covered a variety of topics. First, questions about career background and pathway provided a backdrop. Second, participants supplied information about their educational background and past professional development. The third portion of the survey focused on how participants had learned to lead. Here, they responded to queries about what they felt most and least prepared for when assuming their leadership position. The fourth part of the survey asked about their access to development opportunities. The final portion of the survey focused on the American Association of Community Colleges leadership competencies. We collected demographic data to better understand how gender, race, and age influenced leadership options and choices.

2021 NATIONAL SURVEY OF COMMUNITY COLLEGE LEADERSHIP FOR SOCIAL JUSTICE

In 2021, we again asked community college leaders to complete an online survey. As with the 2016 survey, potential respondents were identified via website reviews of community colleges in each state. In this manner, up-to-date email addresses obtained via institutional or statewide community college associations' directories provided our potential survey population. This approach resulted in the distribution of a total of 8,555 surveys. After an initial email was sent requesting participation, three follow-up contacts via email were made by members of the research team. A total of 742 usable surveys comprise the data for this study (representing a response rate of 9 percent).

Presidents, chancellors, chief academic officers, vice presidents, deans, and directors from all functional areas (i.e., academic, administrative, and student affairs) responded to the survey. Fourteen percent of the respondents were presidents or chancellors; 30 percent were chief academic officers or vice presidents; 43 percent were academic or administrative deans; and 13 percent were in director-level roles. Fifty-six percent of respondents were women, and 42 percent were men. Less than 1 percent of respondents identified as transgender men (n = 2), and 1 percent of respondents chose not to provide their gender identity. Two-thirds of respondents were white (67 percent); 1 percent were Asian or Pacific Islander; 14 percent were Black or African American; 4 percent were Hispanic or Latino/a; 1 percent were Native American or American Indian; 4 percent were multiracial; and 9 percent chose not to indicate their race or ethnicity. Thirty-three percent of respondents were from southern states; 23 percent were from the Midwest; 21 percent were from western states; 15 percent were from the mid-Atlantic region of the country; and 9 percent were from the Northeast.

The first half of the survey asked for leaders' perspectives of social justice and equity efforts at their colleges such as whether respondents believed their college overall to be inclusive, diverse, and equitable. Questions also focused on perceptions of senior leaders and whether respondents believed senior leaders were focused on root causes of injustices and whether senior leaders provided safe spaces for dialogue.

The second half of the survey asked respondents to describe activities they had participated in at their college (i.e., whether they had examined or changed an unjust policy or practice, whether they had led a discussion on a social justice issue, whether they had confronted an individual who displayed offensive or discriminatory language or behaviors) or in their community (e.g., whether they had boycotted a product, service, or company because of a social justice issue, whether they had participated in a rally for a social justice issue) during the previous two years.

Each quantitative survey question was analyzed using descriptive statistics. Further, we ran cross-tabulations to examine differences based on position, gender, race and ethnicity, and region of the country. In a final open-ended question, leaders were asked to describe how they view themselves as leaders for social justice. Many leaders answered that they do see themselves as social justice leaders and shared their views, as well as examples of how they lead for social justice. These written responses are included throughout this book.

APPENDIX B

2022 In-Depth Interviews with Leaders for Social Justice

In 2022, we conducted twenty-five interviews with midlevel and senior leaders. Potential participants were identified through an open-ended question on the 2021 National Survey of Community College Leadership for Social Justice asking whether respondents were interested in participating in a phone interview. A total of 226 survey respondents indicated a willingness to participate in an interview. This list was further reduced by including only midlevel leaders and leaders of diversity, equity, and inclusion offices (ninety-five in total). Responses to the question, "Do you consider yourself a leader of social justice?" were used to identify individuals actively engaged in leading equity efforts on campus, which resulted in narrowing the list to fifty potential interviewees. All were invited to participate in an interview, with twenty-five agreeing to and participating in the interview.

Considerations in selecting interviewees were geographic region and other demographic variables, as well as ensuring a diverse representation of voices (i.e., people of color and both women and men). The final interviewees included sixteen men and nine women; twelve interviewees were people of color. Further, because of our interest in examining leadership contexts, we wanted to ensure that different parts of the United States were represented. Of the twenty-five leaders interviewed, six were from the East Coast, seven were from the West Coast, eight were from the South, and four were from the Midwest.

Each interview was conducted over Zoom (participants could opt not to turn on their camera if they preferred) and lasted about sixty to ninety minutes. The semistructured interview protocol included the following questions and follow-up prompts:

1. As a leader at your college, what does social justice mean to you? What does equity mean to you?
   a. How do you see social justice and equity informing your leadership?
   b. In what ways do you advocate for social justice and equity on your campus? Outside of your campus?
   c. As a leader, what activities have been most successful in implementing work on social justice?
2. How would you describe your institution's efforts associated with social justice and equity?
   a. In your opinion, how committed is your college to social justice and equity?
   b. In what ways are social justice and equity reflected in your college's mission statement? In its strategic plan?
   c. What barriers exist to efforts on campus?
3. Thinking about leadership development programs that are available to your faculty, staff, and leaders, what have you found the most valuable preparation?
   a. How are social justice and equity built into the programming?
   b. How is training done on how to use data to support social justice and equity?

While the interviews followed the protocol in most instances, the nature of the discussions were conversational, and interviewees were given ample opportunities to bring up topics, opinions, and perceptions of their campus culture.

We downloaded the interview transcripts from Zoom and uploaded them to Dedoose (cloud-based software for data analysis) for coding. One set of a priori codes centered on the role of advocacy (i.e., advocacy, activist, advocate, ally, equity champion) and definitions (i.e., of *equity* and *social justice*). Another set examined the role of context (i.e., contextual issues, challenges of context, contextual supports) and the influence of various roles (i.e., adult learning, faculty, leadership, role of others). The final set of codes involved change processes (i.e., organizational changes, equity-minded community of practice).

After being read and reread by the researchers, patterns and themes emerged that contributed to the development of our blueprint for developing equity-driven leaders. Our analysis of the interview data informed the data spotlights of voices from the field included throughout this book. The interview data also helped us triangulate the quantitative survey findings by expanding our understanding of differences in perspective based on position and region of the country. Giving voice to the various ways actions were occurring on campus to support equity initiatives and the challenges leaders were facing also corroborated existing literature. The leaders we interviewed cared passionately about the work they were doing and spoke of their commitment to students and the community. Their insights helped us understand which elements were critical to the development of a transformative leadership identity and how context influenced their actions.

Notes

Introduction

1. Linda L. Carli, "Women, Gender Equality and COVID-19," *Gender in Management: An International Journal* 35, nos. 7–8 (2020): 647–55; Lisa A. Cooper and David R. Williams, "Excess Deaths from COVID-19, Community Bereavement, and Restorative Justice for Communities of Color," *JAMA* 324, no. 15 (2020): 1491–92; Sang Yoon (Tim) Lee, Minsung Park, and Yongseok Shin, *Hit Harder, Recover Slower? Unequal Employment Effects of the COVID-19 Shock*, National Bureau of Economic Research Working Paper 28354 (Cambridge, MA: National Bureau of Economic Research, 2021), https://www.nber.org/papers/w28354.
2. *Fact Sheet: Anti-Asian Prejudice March 2020* (San Bernardino, CA: Center for the Study of Hate and Extremism, 2020), https://www.csusb.edu/sites/default/files/FACT%20SHEET-%20Anti-Asian%20Hate%202020%203.2.21.pdf.
3. Maurianne Adams and Lee Anne Bell, with Diane J. Goodman and Khyati Y. Joshi, *Teaching for Diversity and Social Justice*, 3rd ed. (New York: Routledge, 2016).
4. John Rawls, *A Theory of Justice* (Cambridge, MA: Harvard University Press, 1971); Victor Ray, "A Theory of Racialized Organizations," *American Sociological Review* 84, no. 1 (2019): 26–53, https://doi.org/10.1177/0003122418822335.
5. "Digest of Education Statistics," US Department of Education, Institute of Education Sciences, National Center for Education Statistics, 2023, https://nces.ed.gov/programs/digest/.
6. Arthur M. Cohen, Florence B. Brawer, and Carrie B. Kisker, *The American Community College*, 6th ed. (New York: Jossey-Bass, 2013).
7. George Frederick Zook, *Higher Education for American Democracy: A Report*, vols. 1–4 (Washington, DC: US Government Printing Office, 1947).
8. Cohen, Brawer, and Kisker, *The American Community College.*
9. Jan Jaro, "Turning Community Colleges Into Engines of Economic Mobility and Dynamism," Federation of American Scientists, October 31, 2023, https://fas.org/publication/community-colleges-economic-mobility/.
10. National Center for Education Statistics, *Characteristics of Postsecondary Students* (Washington, DC: US Department of Education, Institute of Education Sciences, 2023), https://nces.ed.gov/programs/coe/indicator/csb/postsecondary-students.
11. "Spotlight on Minority Serving Institutions," American Council on Education, accessed December 5, 2023, https://www.equityinhighered.org/indicators/spotlight-on-minority-serving-institutions/.
12. William H. Frey, *Diversity Explosion: How New Racial Demographics Are Remaking America* (Washington, DC: Brookings Institution Press, 2018).
13. "Postsecondary Faculty and Staff," American Council on Education, accessed April 25, 2023, https://www.equityinhighered.org/indicators/postsecondary-faculty-and-staff/race-and-ethnicity-of-higher-education-faculty/.

14. Megan Brenan, "Americans' Confidence in Higher Education Down Sharply," Gallup, July 11, 2023, https://news.gallup.com/poll/508352/americans-confidence-higher-education-down-sharply.aspx.
15. Katherine Brandon, "Investing in Education: The American Graduation Initiative," July 14, 2009, https://obamawhitehouse.archives.gov/blog/2009/07/14/investing-education-american-graduation-initiative.
16. "A Stronger Nation: Learning Beyond High School Builds American Talent," Lumina Foundation, accessed November 10, 2023, https://www.luminafoundation.org/stronger-nation/report/#/progress.
17. Jon Marcus, "Community Colleges Are Reeling. 'The Reckoning Is Here,'" *AP News*, April 4, 2023, https://apnews.com/article/community-college-enrollment-bb2e79222a4374f4869dc2e5359f2043.
18. Marcus, "Community Colleges are Reeling."
19. "DEI Legislation Tracker," *Chronicle of Higher Education*, accessed July 20, 2023, https://www.chronicle.com/article/here-are-the-states-where-lawmakers-are-seeking-to-ban-colleges-dei-efforts.
20. "Florida College System Presidents Reject 'Woke' Diversity, Equity and Inclusion (DEI), Critical Race Theory Ideologies and Embrace Academic Freedom," Florida Department of Education, January 18, 2023, https://www.fldoe.org/newsroom/latest-news/florida-college-system-presidents-reject-woke-diversity-equity-and-inclusion-dei-critical-race-theory-ideologies-and-embrace-academic-freedom-.stml.
21. Doug Shapiro et al., *Completing College: A National View of Student Attainment Rates by Race and Ethnicity–Fall 2010 Cohort*, Signature Report No. 12b (Herndon, VA: National Student Clearinghouse Research Center, 2017), https://nscresearchcenter.org/wp-content/uploads/Signature12-RaceEthnicity.pdf; Yuxin Lin, Maggie P. Fay, and John Fink, "Stratified Trajectories: Charting Equity Gaps in Program Pathways Among Community College Students," *Research in Higher Education* 64, no. 4 (2023): 547–73.
22. Rawls, *A Theory of Justice*.
23. "Leading for Community College Excellence: Curricular Resources," College Excellence Program, Aspen Institute, https://highered.aspeninstitute.org/curricular-resources/, accessed January 15, 2024.
24. Robert B. Barr and John Tagg, "From Teaching to Learning—A New Paradigm For Undergraduate Education," *Change: The Magazine of Higher Learning* 27, no. 6 (1995): 12–26, https://doi.org/10.1080/00091383.1995.10544672.
25. Burton R. Clark, "The 'Cooling-Out' Function in Higher Education," *American Journal of Sociology* 65, no. (1960): 559–76; Steven Brint and Jerome Karabel, *The Diverted Dream: Community Colleges and the Promise of Educational Opportunity in America, 1900–1985* (New York: Oxford University Press, 1991).

Chapter 1

1. Danielle Melidona et al., *The American College President: 2023 Edition* (Washington, DC: American Council on Education, 2023).
2. "Fast Facts: Postsecondary and Beyond," National Center for Education Statistics, accessed July 30, 2023, https://nces.ed.gov/fastfacts/index.asp?faq=FFOption4#faqFFOption4.
3. "Moving the Needle: Advancing Women in Higher Education Leadership," American Council on Education, accessed August 15, 2023, https://www.acenet.edu/Programs-Services/Pages/Communities/Moving-the-Needle.aspx.

4. Melidona et al., *The American College President.*
5. Melidona et al., *The American College President.*
6. Doug Lederman, "The Number of Colleges Continues to Shrink," *Inside Higher Education*, August 1, 2021, https://www.insidehighered.com/news/2021/08/02/number-colleges-shrinks-again-including-publics-and-private-nonprofits.
7. Victor Ray, "A Theory of Racialized Organizations," *American Sociological Review* 84, no. 1 (2019): 26–53, https://doi.org/10.1177/0003122418822335.
8. James MacGregor Burns, *Leadership* (New York: Harper & Row, 1978).
9. Pamela L. Eddy, Kim E. VanDerLinden, and Catherine Hartman, "Changing Definitions of Leadership or Same Old 'Hero' Leader?," *Community College Review* 51, no. 1 (2022): 30–51, https://doi.org/10.1177/00915521221125304.
10. Estela M. Bensimon, Anna Neumann, and Robert Birnbaum, *Making Sense of Administrative Leadership: The "L" Word in Higher Education*, ASHE-ERIC Higher Education Report 1 (Washington, DC: George Washington University, 1989); Pamela L. Eddy and Elizabeth Kirby, *Leading for Tomorrow: A Primer for Succeeding in Higher Education Leadership* (New Brunswick, NJ: Rutgers University Press, 2020); Adrianna Kezar, Rozana Carducci, and Melissa Contreras-McGavin, *Rethinking the "L" Word in Higher Education*, ASHE Higher Education Report 31, no. 6 (Hoboken, NJ: Wiley, 2006).
11. Ronald A. Heifetz, *Leadership Without Easy Answers* (Cambridge, MA: Harvard University Press, 1994).
12. Kezar et al., *Rethinking the "L" Word.*
13. Richard M. Cyert and James G. March, *A Behavioral Theory of the Firm* (Hoboken, NJ: Prentice-Hall, 1963).
14. Fred E. Fiedler, *A Theory of Leadership Effectiveness* (New York: McGraw-Hill, 1967).
15. Bruce J. Avolio, Bernard M. Bass, and Dong I. Jung, "Re-examining the Components of Transformational and Transactional Leadership Using the Multifactor Leadership," *Journal of Occupational and Organizational Psychology* 72, no. 4 (1999): 441–62.
16. Bernard M. Bass, "Two Decades of Research and Development in Transformational Leadership," *European Journal of Work and Organizational Psychology* 8, no. 1 (1999): 9–32.
17. Pamela L. Eddy et al., *Developing Tomorrow's Leaders: Context, Challenges, and Capabilities* (Lanham, MD: Rowman & Littlefield, 2015); Jean Lipman-Blumen, *Connective Leadership: Managing in a Changing World* (New York: Oxford University Press, 2000).
18. *Competencies for Community College Leaders*, 4th ed. (Washington, DC: American Association of Community Colleges, 2022).
19. "Leading for Community College Excellence: Curricular Resources," Aspen Institute, 2024, https://collegeexcellencecurriculum.aspeninstitute.org/.
20. Ashley L. Gray, *The Invisible Checklist: Ascension Implications for Women of Color Leaders* (Washington, DC: American Council on Education, 2023), https://www.acenet.edu/Documents/Invisible-Checklist.pdf.
21. Gray, *The Invisible Checklist.*
22. George Frederick Zook, *Higher Education for American Democracy: A Report*, vols. 1–4 (Washington, DC: US Government Printing Office, 1947).
23. George B. Vaughan, *The Community College Presidency* (Washington, DC: American Council on Education, 1986).
24. Terry O'Banion, *A Learning College for the 21st Century* (Lanham, MD: Rowman & Littlefield, 1997).

25. Christopher Shults, *The Critical Impact of Impending Retirements on Community College Leadership* (Washington, DC: American Association of Community Colleges, 2001).
26. Adrianna Kezar and Rozana Carducci, *Revolutionizing Leadership Development* (New York: Routledge, 2009).
27. Heather N. McCambly, "Community Colleges as Racialized Organizations: Outlining Opportunities for Equity," *Community College Review* 51, no. 4 (2023): 1–22, https://doi.org/10.1177/00915521231182121.
28. Laura L. Bierema, "Women's Leadership: Troubling Notions of the 'Ideal' (Male) Leader," *Advances in Developing Human Resources* 18, no. 2 (2016): 119–36.
29. Barbara K. Townsend and Susan B. Twombly, "Accidental Equity: The Status of Women in the Community College," *Equity & Excellence in Education* 40, no. 3 (2007): 208–17.
30. Pamela L. Eddy and Tehmina Khwaja, "What Happened to Re-visioning Community College Leadership? A 25-Year Retrospective," *Community College Review* 47, no. 1 (2019): 53–78, https://doi.org/10.1177/0091552118818742.
31. Melidona et al., *The American College President.*
32. Amy B. Diehl and Leanne M. Dzubinski, "An Overview of Gender-Based Leadership Barriers," in *Handbook of Research on Gender and Leadership*, ed. Susan R. Madsen (Cheltenham, UK: Edward Elgar, 2017), 271–86.
33. Crasha V. Townsend, "Identity Politics: Why African American Women Are Missing in Administrative Leadership in Public Higher Education," *Educational Management Administration & Leadership* 49, no. 4 (2021): 584–600, https://doi.org/10.1177/1741143220935455.
34. Adrianna J. Kezar and Elizabeth M. Holcombe, *Shared Leadership in Higher Education: Important Lessons from Research and Practice* (Washington, DC: American Council on Education, 2017).
35. Pamela L. Eddy, Catherine Hartman, and Eric Liu, "Gender Differences in Team Leadership," in *Team Leadership in Community Colleges*, ed. George R. Boggs and Christine Johnson McPhail (New York: Routledge, 2020), 19–40.
36. Regina Garza Mitchell and Marilyn J. Amey, "Editors' Notes," in "Midlevel Leadership," ed. Regina Garza Mitchell and Marilyn J. Amey, special issue, *New Directions for Community Colleges* 2020, no. 191 (2020): 7–10.
37. Marilyn J. Amey and Pamela L. Eddy, "Leading in the Middle," in *Understanding Community Colleges*, 2nd ed., ed. John S. Levin and Susan T. Kater (New York: Routledge, 2018), 203–26.
38. John Rawls, *A Theory of Justice* (Cambridge, MA: Harvard University Press, 1971).
39. Maurianne Adams and Lee Anne Bell, *Teaching for Diversity and Social Justice*, 3rd ed. (New York: Routledge, 2016).
40. Derald Wing Sue, Mikal N. Rasheed, and Janice Matthews Rasheed, *Multicultural Social Work Practice: A Competency-Based Approach to Diversity and Social Justice*, 2nd ed. (Hoboken, NJ: Wiley, 2016).
41. Eleanor Drago-Severson and Jessica Blum-DeStefano, "A Developmental Lens on Social Justice Leadership: Exploring the Connection Between Meaning Making and Practice," *Journal of Educational Leadership and Policy Studies* 3, no. 1 (2019).
42. Adrianna Kezar and Julie Posselt, eds., *Higher Education Administration for Social Justice and Equity: Critical Perspectives for Leadership* (New York: Routledge, 2020).
43. Luca E. Lewis, "Practitioner Reflection: Equity-Minded Leadership Perspectives for Community Colleges," in *Higher Education Administration for Social Justice and Equity: Critical*

Perspectives for Leadership, ed. Adriana Kezar and Julie Posselt (New York: Routledge, 2020), 251–64.

44. Adrianna Kezar et al., *Shared Equity Leadership: Making Equity Everyone's Work* (Washington, DC: American Council on Education, 2021).
45. Daniel Tarker, "Transformational Leadership and the Proliferation of Community College Leadership Frameworks: A Systematic Review of the Literature," *Community College Journal of Research and Practice* 43, no 3. (2019): 1–18.
46. Carolyn M. Shields, *Transformative Leadership in Education: Equitable and Socially Just Change in an Uncertain and Complex World*, 2nd ed. (New York: Routledge, 2017).
47. Shields, *Transformative Leadership.*
48. Shields, *Transformative Leadership.*
49. Elizabeth Ganga, Amy Mazzariello, and Nikki Edgecombe, *Developmental Education: An Introduction for Policymakers* (Denver, CO: Education Commission of the States, 2018).
50. Edward C. Bush et al., "Liberatory Community College Leadership: Education, Decolonization, and Emancipation," *New Directions for Community Colleges* 202 (2023): 206, https://doi.org/10.1002/cc.20579.
51. Adrianna Kezar et al., *Shared Equity Leadership*, 16.
52. Terrence MacTaggart, *The 21st-Century Presidency: A Call to Enterprise Leadership* (Washington, DC: Association of Governing Boards of Universities and Colleges, 2017), 1, https://agb.org/wp-content/uploads/2019/01/report_2017_21st_century_presidency.pdf.
53. *AACC Competencies for Community College Leaders*, 3rd ed. (Washington, DC: American Association of Community Colleges, 2018).
54. *AACC Competencies for Community College Leaders*, 3rd ed., 5.
55. *AACC Competencies for Community College Leaders*, 4th ed. (Washington, DC: American Association of Community Colleges, 2022), 8.
56. *AACC Competencies for Community College Leaders*, 4th ed.
57. *The Aspen Prize for Community College Excellence* (Washington, DC: Aspen Institute, 2011), https://www.aspeninstitute.org/wp-content/uploads/files/content/docs/pubs/AspenPrize021312.pdf.
58. *The 2023 Aspen Prize for Community College Excellence* (Washington, DC: Aspen Institute, 2023), https://highered.aspeninstitute.org/wp-content/uploads/2023/04/ASP010_AspenPrizePublication_vDigital.pdf.
59. "Leading for Community College Excellence: Curricular Resources."
60. "Defining Qualities of Transformational Leadership," Aspen Institute, accessed October 2, 2023, https://collegeexcellencecurriculum.aspeninstitute.org/module/defining-qualities-of-transformational-leadership/.
61. Danah Barazanji, "Teacher Social Justice Advocacy for Children: A Scale Development and Preliminary Validity Study" (PhD diss., University of Missouri-Kansas City, 2012), https://mospace.umsystem.edu/xmlui/bitstream/handle/10355/14241/BarazanjiTeaSocJus.pdf?sequence=1&isAllowed=y.
62. *2022 Educational Policy and Accreditation Standards for Baccalaureate and Master's Social Work Programs* (Alexandria, VA: Council on Social Work Education, 2022), https://www.cswe.org/getmedia/bb5d8afe-7680-42dc-a332-a6e6103f4998/2022-EPAS.pdf.
63. Janet L. Finn, *Just Practice: A Social Justice Approach to Social Work*, 4th ed. (New York: Oxford University Press, 2020).

64. Homer H. Johnson, "Mental Models and Transformative Learning: The Key to Leadership Development?," *Human Resource Development Quarterly* 19, no. 1 (2008): 85–89, https://doi.org/10.1002/hrdq.1227.

Chapter 2

1. Carolyn M. Shields, *Transformative Leadership in Education: Equitable and Socially Just Change in an Uncertain and Complex World*, 2nd ed. (New York: Routledge, 2017).
2. Adrianna Kezar, Tricia Bertram Gallant, and Jaime Lester, "Everyday People Making a Difference on College Campuses: The Tempered Grassroots Leadership Tactics of Faculty and Staff," *Studies in Higher Education* 36, no. 2 (2011): 129–51, https://doi.org/10.1080/03075070903532304.
3. David J. Teece, Margaret Peteraf, and Sohvi Leih, "Dynamic Capabilities and Organizational Agility: Risk, Uncertainty, and Strategy in the Innovation Economy," *California Management Review* 58, no. 4 (2016): 13–35, https://doi.org/10.1525/cmr.2016.58.4.13.
4. Daniel Lundqvist et al., "Leadership and Learning at Work: A Systematic Literature Review of Learning-Oriented Leadership," *Journal of Leadership & Organizational Studies* 30, no. 2 (2022): 205–38, https://doi.org/10.1177/15480518221133970.
5. Sharon B. Merriam and Lisa M. Baumgartner, *Learning in Adulthood: A Comprehensive Guide*, 4th ed. (New York: Jossey-Bass, 2020).
6. Lorna M. Earl and Helen Timperley, "Understanding How Evidence and Learning Conversations Work," in *Professional Learning Conversations: Challenges in Using Evidence for Improvement*, ed. Lorna M. Earl and Helen Timperley (Berlin: Springer, 2009), 9.
7. Chris Argyris, "Double Loop Learning in Organizations," *Business Review* 55 (1977): 115–25.
8. Christine Johnson McPhail and Kimberly Beatty, *Transformational Change in Community Colleges* (New York: Routledge, 2021).
9. Erin L. Castro, "Addressing the Conceptual Challenges of Equity Work: A Blueprint for Getting Started," in *Understanding Equity in Community College Practice*, New Directions for Community Colleges, no. 172, ed. Erin L. Castro (Hoboken, NJ: Wiley, 2015), 5–14.
10. Eric R. Felix et al., "Developing Agency for Equity-Minded Change," in *Understanding Equity in Community College Practice*, New Directions for Community Colleges, no. 172, ed. Erin L. Castro (Hoboken, NJ: Wiley, 2015), 28.
11. Mayra Puente et al., "Interrogating the Self En Route to Critical Consciousness: Cultivating Higher Education Leaders Through a Positionality-Centered, Doctoral-Level Course," *New Directions for Student Leadership* 177 (2023): 113, https://doi.org/10.1002/yd.20548.
12. Jennifer Perry Cheatham, Rodney Thomas, and Adam Parrott-Sheffer, *Entry Planning for Equity-Focused Leaders: Empowering Schools and Communities* (Cambridge, MA: Harvard Education Press, 2022), 18.
13. Chelse Lang Song, "'It's a Hot Queer Mess': Mental Health Providers' Experiences Counseling Survivors of Queer Intimate Partner Violence" (PhD diss., New Mexico State University, 2022).
14. Shardé M. Davis, "The Aftermath of #BlackGirlsRock vs. #WhiteGirlsRock: Considering the DisRespectability of a Black Women's Counterpublic," *Women's Studies in Communication* 41, no. 3 (2018): 274.
15. Kimberle Crenshaw, "Mapping the Margins: Intersectionality, Identity Politics, and Violence Against Women of Color," *Stanford Law Review* 43, no. 6 (1991): 1241–99.

16. Gareth Morgan, *Images of Organization* (Thousand Oaks, CA: Sage, 1997).
17. Diana Bilimoria and Kim Buch, "The Search Is On: Engendering Faculty Diversity Through More Effective Search and Recruitment," *Change: The Magazine of Higher Learning* 42, no. 4 (2010): 27–32, https://doi.org/10.1080/00091383.2010.489022.
18. Paulo Freire, *Pedagogy of the Oppressed* (New York: Penguin, 2017).
19. Sharon I. Radd and Bruce H. Kramer, "Dis Eased: Critical Consciousness in School Leadership for Social Justice," *Journal of School Leadership* 26, no. 4 (2016): 584.
20. Alexis Jemal, "Critical Consciousness: A Critique and Critical Analysis of the Literature," *Urban Review* 49, no. 4 (2017): 608.
21. Matthew A. Diemer et al., "Development and Validation of the Critical Consciousness Scale," *Youth & Society* 49, no. 4 (2017): 461–83.
22. Roderick J. Watts, Matthew A. Diemer, and Adam M. Voight, "Critical Consciousness: Current Status and Future Directions," *New Directions for Child and Adolescent Development* 134 (2011): 43–57.
23. Puente et al., "Interrogating the Self," 111–18.
24. Bradley P. Owens, Michael D. Johnson, and Terence R. Mitchell, "Expressed Humility in Organizations: Implications for Performance, Teams, and Leadership," *Organization Science* 24, no. 5 (2013): 1517–38.
25. Edgar H. Schein, *Humble Inquiry: The Gentle Art of Asking Instead of Telling* (San Francisco: Berrett-Koehler, 2013).
26. Joshua N. Hook et al., "Cultural Humility: Measuring Openness to Culturally Diverse Clients," *Journal of Counseling Psychology* 60, no. 3 (2013): 353–66, https://doi.org/10.1037/a0032595.
27. Melanie Tervalon and Jann Murray-Garcia, "Cultural Humility Versus Cultural Competence," *Journal of Health Care for the Poor and Underserved* 9, no. 2 (1998): 117–25.
28. Hook et al., "Cultural Humility."
29. Jean Watson, *Nursing: The Philosophy and Science of Caring* (Boulder: University Press of Colorado, 2008).
30. Darla J. Twale and Barbara M. De Luca, *Faculty Incivility: The Rise of the Academic Bully Culture and What to Do About It* (San Francisco: Wiley, 2008).
31. James R. Appleton, Channing M. Briggs, and James J. Rhatigan, *Pieces of Eight: The Rites, Roles, and Styles of the Dean* (Portland, OR: NASPA Institute of Research and Development, 1978).
32. "Caring Campus: Improving Student Retention and Success," Institute for Evidence-Based Change, accessed October 1, 2023, https://www.iebcnow.org/caring-campus/.
33. Elisabeth A. Barnett and Susan Bickerstaff, *Implementing Caring Campus with Nonacademic Staff* (New York: Columbia University, 2022).
34. Elisabeth A. Barnett and Selena Cho, *Caring Campus: Faculty Leadership in Student Success* (New York: Columbia University, 2023).
35. Barnett and Cho, *Caring Campus.*
36. Richard R. Valencia, ed., *The Evolution of Deficit Thinking: Educational Thought and Practice* (London: RoutledgeFalmer, 1997), xi.
37. Valencia, ed., *The Evolution of Deficit Thinking.*
38. Leon Festinger, *A Theory of Cognitive Dissonance* (Stanford, CA: Stanford University Press, 1957); Jack Mezirow, *Transformative Dimensions of Adult Learning* (San Francisco: Jossey-Bass, 1991).
39. Festinger, *A Theory of Cognitive Dissonance.*

40. Mary Rice-Booth, *Leading Within Systems of Inequity in Education: A Liberation Guide for Leaders of Color* (Arlington, VA: ACSD, 2023), 51.
41. Elizabeth L. McFalls and Deirdre Cobb-Roberts, "Reducing Resistance to Diversity Through Cognitive Dissonance Instruction: Implications for Teacher Education," *Journal of Teacher Education* 52, no. 2 (2001): 164–72.
42. Kenneth Jones and Tema Okun, "White Supremacy Culture," in *Dismantling Racism: A Workbook for Social Change Groups* (Durham, NC: ChangeWork, 2001), 28–35, accessed April 15, 2024, https://www.cwsworkshop.org/PARC_site_B/dr-culture.html.
43. Jones and Okun, "White Supremacy Culture."
44. Mezirow, *Transformative Dimensions of Adult Learning.*
45. Karl Weick, *Sensemaking in Organizations* (Thousand Oaks, CA: Sage, 1995).
46. Deborah Ancona, "Sensemaking: Framing and Acting in the Unknown," in *The Handbook for Teaching Leadership: Knowing, Doing, and Being*, ed. Scott Snook, Nitin Nohria, and Rakesh Khurana (Thousand Oaks, CA: Sage, 2012), 3–19.
47. Cheatham, Thomas, and Parrott-Sheffer, *Entry Planning for Equity-Focused Leaders*, 119.

Chapter 3

1. Paul LeBlanc, *Students First: Equity, Access, and Opportunity in Higher Education* (Cambridge, MA: Harvard Education Press, 2021).
2. Robert B. Schwartz et al., *America's Hidden Economic Engines: How Community Colleges Can Drive Shared Prosperity* (Cambridge, MA: Harvard Education Press, 2023).
3. "AACC Competencies for Community College Leaders," American Association of Community Colleges, accessed February 9, 2023, https://www.aacc.nche.edu/publications-news/aacc-competencies-for-community-college-leaders/.
4. Carolyn M. Shields, *Transformative Leadership in Education: Equitable and Socially Just Change in an Uncertain and Complex World*, 2nd ed. (New York: Routledge, 2017).
5. Danielle Melidona et al., *The American College President* (Washington, DC: American Council on Education, 2023); Jennifer Perry Cheatham, Rodney Thomas, and Adam Parrott-Sheffer, *Entry Planning for Equity-Focused Leaders: Empowering Schools and Communities* (Cambridge, MA: Harvard Education Press, 2022).
6. Edgar H. Schein, *Organizational Culture and Leadership*, 5th ed. (Hoboken, NJ: Wiley, 2016).
7. Cynthia J. Atman, Ken Yasuhara, and Deborah Kilgore, *Assessment Techniques for Contextual Competence*, CELT Technical Report 14-03 (Seattle, WA: Center for Engineering Learning & Teaching, University of Washington, 2014), 3.
8. Simon Marginson, "Higher Education and Public Good," *Higher Education Quarterly* 65, no. 4 (2011): 411–33, https://doi.org/10.1111/j.1468-2273.2011.00496.x; Lawrence Busch, *Knowledge for Sale: The Neoliberal Takeover of Higher Education* (Cambridge, MA: MIT Press, 2017).
9. Matt Hastings, "Neoliberalism and Education," Oxford Research Encyclopedia of Education, May 23, 2019, https://doi.org/10.1093/acrefore/9780190264093.013.404.
10. David F. Ayers, "Neoliberal Ideology in Community College Mission Statements: A Critical Discourse Analysis," *Review of Higher Education* 28, no. 4 (2005): 527–49, https://doi.org/10.1353/rhe.2005.0033.
11. Pamela L. Eddy et al., "A Call for Action to Strengthen the Commitment to Equitable Student Success: A Case Study of North Carolina Community College Strategic Plans,"

Community College Journal of Research and Practice 47, no. 4 (2023): 254, https://doi.org/10.1080/10668926.2021.1993380.

12. Ayers, "Neoliberal Ideology."
13. Christopher M. Mullin, *Doing More with Less: The Inequitable Funding of Community Colleges*, Policy Brief 2010-03PBL (Washington, DC: American Association of Community Colleges, 2010).
14. "Public Funding of Community Colleges," Community College Research Center, February 2022, https://ccrc.tc.columbia.edu/publications/public-funding-community-colleges.html.
15. Meredith S. Billings et al., "Financing Promise Programs: Where the Money Comes From and Where the Money Goes," *New Directions for Community Colleges* 196 (2021): 81–95, https://doi.org/10.1002/cc.20583.
16. Alicia C. Dowd and Branden D. Elmore, "Leadership for Equity-Minded Data Use Toward Racial Equity in Higher Education," in *Higher Education Administration for Social Justice and Equity*, ed. Adrianna Kezar and Julie Posselt (New York: Routledge, 2020), 159–75; Veronica Minaya and Judith Scott-Clayton, "Labor Market Trajectories for Community College Graduates: How Returns to Certificates and Associate's Degrees Evolve Over Time," *Education Finance and Policy* 17, no. 1 (2022): 53–80.
17. Megan Brenan, "Americans' Confidence in Higher Education Down Sharply," Gallup, July 11, 2023, https://news.gallup.com/poll/508352/americans-confidence-higher-education-down-sharply.aspx.
18. Brenan, "Americans' Confidence."
19. Rachel Fishman, Sophie Nguyen, and Louisa Woodhouse, *Varying Degrees 2022: New America's Sixth Annual Survey on Higher Education* (Washington, DC: New America, July 2022), https://d1y8sb8igg2f8e.cloudfront.net/Varying_Degrees_2022_2022-07-25_FINAL.pdf; Sophie Nguyen, Rachel Fishman, and Olivia Cheche, *Varying Degrees 2023: New America's Seventh Annual Survey on Higher Education* (Washington, DC: New America, August 2023), https://www.newamerica.org/education-policy/reports/varying-degrees-2023/.
20. Rachel Fishman, Manuela Ekowo, and Ernest Ezeugo, *Varying Degrees: New America's Annual Survey on Higher Education* (Washington, DC: New America, August 2017), https://na-production.s3.amazonaws.com/documents/Varying-Degrees.pdf; Alex Camardelle, Brian Kennedy II, and Justin Nalley, *The State of Black Students at Community Colleges* (Washington, DC: Joint Center for Political and Economic Studies, 2022).
21. Davis Jenkins, Taylor Myers, and Farzana Matin, *Whole-College Guided Pathways Reform Practices* (New York: Community College Research Center, 2023).
22. Ronald L. Heifetz, *Leadership Without Easy Answers* (Cambridge, MA: Harvard University Press, 1998).
23. Melidona et al., *The American College President.*
24. Michelle K. Ryan et al., "Getting on Top of the Glass Cliff: Reviewing a Decade of Evidence, Explanations, and Impact," *Leadership Quarterly* 27, no 3 (2016): 446–55, https://doi.org/10.1016/j.leaqua.2015.10.008.
25. Bryan J. Weiner, "A Theory of Organizational Readiness for Change," *Implementation Science* 4, no. 1 (2009): 1–9, https://doi.org/10.1186/1748-5908-4-67.
26. Jerel M. Ezell, " 'Trickle-Down' Racial Empathy in American Higher Education: Moving Beyond Performative Wokeness and Academic Panels to Spark Racial Equity," *Journal of Education* 203, no. 3 (2023): 718–25; Jal Mehta and Krista Galleberg, "Racial Equity

Work: Beyond Performative Change," Next Generation Learning Challenges, June 8, 2021, https://www.nextgenlearning.org/articles/racial-equity-work-beyond-performative-change.

27. John P. Kotter, *Leading Change* (Boston: Harvard Business Review Press, 2012).
28. Weiner, "A Theory of Organizational Readiness for Change"; Rune Lines et al., "The Production of Trust During Organizational Change," *Journal of Change Management* 5, no. 2 (2005): 221–45, https://doi.org/10.1080/14697010500143555.
29. Eric R. Felix and Ángel de Jesus González, *Mapping Organizational Support and Collective Action: Towards a Model for Advancing Racial Equity in Community College* (Berkeley, CA: University of California, Berkeley, Center for Studies in Higher Education, forthcoming).
30. Darren Osburn and Tammy M. Gocial, "Trust in Administrators Among Community College Faculty Members," *Community College Journal of Research and Practice* 44 (2020): 899–913, https://doi.org/10.1080/10668926.2019.1666064.
31. Osburn and Gocial, "Trust in Administrators."
32. Abigail Jean Winter, "The Human Cost of Change: Tales from the Campus About Personal Change Fatigue, Resistance, and Resilience" (PhD diss., Queensland University of Technology, 2013).
33. Jay R. Dee and LIudvika Leišytė, "Organizational Learning in Higher Education Institutions: Theories, Frameworks, and a Potential Research Agenda," in *Higher Education: Handbook of Theory and Research*, vol. 33, ed. Michael B. Paulsen (Cham, Switzerland: Springer, 2016), 275–348.
34. Heather N. McCambly et al., "Community Colleges as Racialized Organizations: Outlining Opportunities for Equity," *Community College Review* 51, no. 4 (2023): 658–79.
35. Erin E. Doran and Paul S. Hengesteg, "Advocating for Mexican American Studies in Whitestream Community Colleges: A Focus on Faculty Efforts," *Journal of Diversity in Higher Education* 14, no. 1 (2019): 84, https://doi.org/10.1037/dhe0000157.
36. Lily Zheng, *DEI Deconstructed: Your No-Nonsense Guide to Doing the Work and Doing It Right* (Oakland, CA: Berrett-Koehler, 2023).
37. "Equity Champions Leadership Development Program," accessed April 6, 2023, George Washington University, https://ccr.publichealth.gwu.edu/fostering-equity/champions.
38. Ezell, " 'Trickle-Down' Racial Empathy."
39. Arnold Madison Kee and James R. Mahoney, *Multicultural Strategies for Community Colleges: From Diversity to Synergy* (Washington, DC: American Association of Community Colleges, 1995).
40. Robert A. Rhoads and James R. Valadez, *Democracy, Multiculturalism, and the Community College: A Critical Perspective* (New York: Routledge, 1996).
41. Zelema M. Harris and Pauleen Kayes, "Multicultural and International Challenges to the Community College: A Model for College-Wide Proactive Response" (paper presented at the Annual Convention of the American Association of Community Colleges, Minneapolis, MN, April 22–25, 1995), https://files.eric.ed.gov/fulltext/ED387173.pdf.
42. Augustine P. Gallego, "Leading the Multicultural Community College," *Community College Journal of Research and Practice* 20, no. 1 (1996): 1–8.
43. Arthur E. Levine and Jeannette Cureton, "The Quiet Revolution: Eleven Facts About Multiculturalism and the Curriculum," *Change* 24 (1992): 25–29.
44. William E. Piland, Alexandria Piland, and Shelly Hess, "Status of Multicultural Education in the Curriculum," *New Directions for Community Colleges* 108 (1999): 81–88, https://doi.org/10.1002/cc.10808.

45. Robert Longley, "What Is Multiculturalism? Definition, Theories, and Examples," ThoughtCo, December 6, 2021, thoughtco.com/what-is-multiculturalism-4689285.
46. Patrick Sullivan, "Diversity, Leadership, and the Community College: A Case Study," *Community College Journal of Research and Practice* 30, nos. 5–6 (2006): 383–400, https://doi.org/10.1080/10668920500208096.
47. Martha M. Parham, *Diversity, Equity, and Inclusion: Framework for Action* (Washington, DC: American Association of Community Colleges, 2020), https://www.aacc.nche.edu/wp-content/uploads/2021/01/Diversity_Framework_for_Action_0121.pdf.
48. "Equity Toolkit," Achieving the Dream, accessed May 11, 2023, https://achievingthedream.org/areas-of-expertise/equity/.
49. Katie Hermann, "4 Key Components of a Strong Higher Ed DEI Plan," EAB, December 2, 2020, https://eab.com/insights/expert-insight/academic-affairs/components-of-a-strong-dei-plan/.
50. Zheng, *DEI Deconstructed*.
51. Terrell Strayhorn, "Workplace Belonging in Higher Education," *Higher Education Digest*, April 13, 2023, https://www.highereducationdigest.com/workplace-belonging-in-higher-education/.
52. Strayhorn, "Workplace Belonging."
53. Eric Kelderman, "Why College Presidents Don't Speak Their Minds," *Chronicle of Higher Education*, July 26, 2022.
54. "Diversity, Equity, Inclusion, and Accessibility (DEIA)," California Community Colleges, 2024, https://www.cccco.edu/About-Us/diversity-equity-inclusion#:~:text=These%20initiatives%20promote%20diversity%20in,students%20reach%20their%20end%20goals.
55. Sara Weissman, "California Community College Professors Sue Over DEI Rules," *Inside Higher Education*, October 3, 2023.
56. Michael Poliakoff, "Do Campus Diversity Offices (DEI) Help or Harm Diversity?," *Forbes*, March 29, 2023, https://www.forbes.com/sites/michaelpoliakoff/2023/03/29/do-campus-diversity-offices-dei-help-or-harm-diversity/?sh=3da01b7571a5.
57. Janice Gassam Asare, "Is DEI Officially Dead?," *Forbes*, July 16, 2023, https://www.forbes.com/sites/janicegassam/2023/07/16/is-diversity-equity-and-inclusion-officially-dead/?sh=62c2703d49e1.
58. Ariana González Stokas, "Higher Ed's DEI Lip Service: On My Disillusioning Experience as a Chief Diversity Officer," *Chronicle of Higher Education*, May 4, 2023, https://www.chronicle.com/article/higher-eds-dei-lip-service?sra=true; Adrianna Kezar, "Higher Education DEI Efforts Are in Trouble. Here's How We Change That," *Diverse: Issues in Higher Education*, March 14, 2023, https://www.diverseeducation.com/opinion/article/15352470/higher-education-dei-efforts-are-in-trouble-heres-how-we-change-that.
59. Frank Dobbin and Alexandra Kalev, "Why Diversity Programs Fail: And What Works Better," *Harvard Business Review* 94, no. 7 (2016), https://hbr.org/2016/07/why-diversity-programs-fail.
60. "DEI Legislation Tracker," accessed January 15, 2024, *Chronicle of Higher Education*, https://www.chronicle.com/article/here-are-the-states-where-lawmakers-are-seeking-to-ban-colleges-dei-efforts.
61. Zachary Bleemer, "Affirmative Action, Mismatch, and Economic Mobility After California's Proposition 209," *Quarterly Journal of Economics* 137, no. 1 (2022): 115–60.
62. Felicia Toliver, "Ready: An Exploration of the Factors Impacting Readiness of Former Highest-Ranking Diversity Officers in the Kentucky Community and Technical Colleges System" (PhD diss., Northern Kentucky University, 2022).

63. Zheng, *DEI Deconstructed.*
64. *A Framework for Advancing Anti-Racism Strategy on Campus* (Fort Lauderdale, FL: National Association of Diversity Officers in Higher Education, 2021), https://nadohe.memberclicks.net/assets/2021/Framework/National%20Association%20of%20Diversity%20Officers%20in%20Higher%20Education%20-%20Framework%20for%20Advancing%20Ant-Racism%20on%20Campus%20-%20first%20edition.pdf.

Chapter 4

1. Carolyn M. Shields, *Transformative Leadership in Education: Equitable and Socially Just Change in an Uncertain and Complex World*, 2nd ed. (New York: Routledge, 2017).
2. Lily Zheng, *DEI Deconstructed: Your No-Nonsense Guide to Doing the Work and Doing It Right* (Oakland, CA: Berrett-Koehler, 2023).
3. Allan Bukusi, "What Transformative Leaders Do: Emerging Perspectives in the 21st Century," *International Journal of Sociology and Anthropology* 12, no. 4 (2020): 85–93; Shields, *Transformative Leadership.*
4. Shields, *Transformative Leadership.*
5. Eric Kelderman, "The Plan to Dismantle DEI," *Chronicle of Higher Education*, January 20, 2023.
6. Jesse J. Tauriac et al., "Utilizing Affinity Groups to Enhance Intergroup Dialogue Workshops for Racially and Ethnically Diverse Students," *Journal for Specialists in Group Work* 38, no. 3 (2013): 241–60, https://doi.org/10.1080/01933922.2013.800176.
7. Emiko J. Muraki et al., "Affinity and Allyship Groups to Advance Inclusion in Postsecondary Institutions: A Systematic Scoping Review," *Journal of Diversity in Higher Education* (forthcoming), https://doi.org/10.1037/dhe0000543.
8. Muraki et al., "Affinity and Allyship Groups."
9. Muraki et al., "Affinity and Allyship Groups."
10. Belle Rose Ragins and Kathy E. Kram, *The Handbook of Mentoring at Work: Theory, Research, and Practice* (Thousand Oaks, CA: Sage, 2007).
11. Carol A. Mullen and Cindy C. Klimaitis, "Defining Mentoring: A Literature Review of Issues, Types, and Applications," *Annals of the New York Academy of Sciences* 1483, no. 1 (2021): 19–35.
12. Gayle E. Barrett, "Exploring the Role of Mentoring Networks in the Career Development of Women Community College Leaders," *Journal of Applied Research in the Community College* 27, no. 2 (2020): 37–50; Jorge Burmicky, "Advancing Presidential Careers: Operationalizing Sponsorship in Higher Education," *Journal of Higher Education* (2024), https://doi.org/10.1080/00221546.2024.2301916; Ruth A. Hopkins and Elizabeth Grigoriu, "Mentoring Community College Faculty and Staff: Balancing Contradictions of Informal Program Components and Formal Program Structure," *Community College Review* 32, no. 4 (2005): 40–59; Natalie A. Tran, "The Role of Mentoring in the Success of Women Leaders of Color in Higher Education," *Mentoring & Tutoring: Partnership in Learning* 22, no. 4 (2014): 302–15.
13. Danielle Melidona et al., *The American College President* (Washington, DC: American Council on Education, 2023).
14. Jamie Washington and Nancy J. Evans, "Becoming an Ally," in *Beyond Tolerance*, ed. Nancy J. Evans and Vernon M. Wall (Alexandria, VA: American College Personnel Association), 195–204.
15. Lori D. Patton and Stephanie Bondi, "Nice White Men or Social Justice Allies? Using Critical Race Theory to Examine How White Male Faculty and Administrators Engage in Ally

Work," *Race Ethnicity and Education* 18, no. 4 (2015): 488–514, https://doi.org/10.1080/13613324.2014.1000289.

16. Marc Brenman and Thomas W. Sanchez, "Social Activism," in *Encyclopedia of Quality of Life and Well-Being Research*, ed. Alex C. Michalos (Dordrecht, Netherlands: Springer, 2014), https://doi.org/10.1007/978-94-007-0753-5_2729.
17. Bill Moyer et al., *Doing Democracy: The MAP Model for Organizing Social Movements* (Gabriola Island, BC: New Society, 2001).
18. Shields, *Transformative Leadership.*
19. Izhak Berkovich, "A Socio-ecological Framework of Social Justice Leadership in Education," *Journal of Educational Administration* 52, no. 3 (2014): 282–309, https://doi.org/10.1108/JEA-12-2012-0131.
20. Mavis Sanders and Adia Harvey, "Beyond the School Walls: A Case Study of Principal Leadership for School-Community Collaboration," *Teachers College Record* 104, no. 7 (2002): 1345–68, https://doi.org/10.1111/1467-9620.00206.
21. "Leadership Through Civic Engagement Award," Alfred State College of Technology, accessed November 16, 2023, https://www.alfredstate.edu/center-for-civic-engagement/celebrate/leadership-through-civic-engagement-award.
22. Isis Artze-Vega et al., *The Norton Guide to Equity-Minded Teaching* (New York: Norton, 2023).
23. J. Luke Wood and Frank Harris III, "Equity-Minded Educators: Identifying Differences in Student Services Practices That Benefit Students of Color," *Journal of Applied Research in the Community College* 27, no. 2 (2020): 25–36.
24. Gloria Ladson-Billings, "Culturally Relevant Pedagogy 2.0: A.K.A. the Remix," *Harvard Educational Review* 84, no. 1 (2014): 74–84, https://doi.org/10.17763/haer.84.1.p2rj131485484751.
25. Ladson-Billings, "Culturally Relevant Pedagogy 2.0."
26. Erin E. Doran, "What Does Culturally Relevant Pedagogy Mean in the Community College Context?," *New Directions for Community Colleges* 2021, no. 195 (2021): 81–90, https://doi.org/10.1002/cc.20468.
27. Laura I. Rendon, "Validating Culturally Diverse Students: Toward a New Model of Learning and Student Development," *Innovative Higher Education* 19 (1994): 33–51, https://doi.org/10.1007/BF01191156.
28. Claude M. Steele and Joshua Aronson, "Stereotype Threat and the Intellectual Test Performance of African Americans," *Journal of Personality and Social Psychology* 69, no. 5 (1995): 797, https://doi.org/10.1037/0022-3514.69.5.
29. Scientist Spotlights Initiative (website), accessed October 5, 2023, https://scientistspotlights.org/.
30. Andrea E. Goering et al., "Diversity by Design: Broadening Participation Through Inclusive Teaching," *New Directions for Community Colleges* 2022, no. 199 (2022): 77–91.
31. Goering et al., "Diversity by Design."
32. "About Universal Design for Learning," CAST, accessed October 5, 2023, https://www.cast.org/impact/universal-design-for-learning-udl.
33. "About Universal Design for Learning."
34. Asao B. Inoue, *Labor-Based Grading Contracts: Building Equity and Inclusion in the Compassionate Writing Classroom*, 2nd ed. (Denver: University Press of Colorado, 2022), https://doi.org/10.37514/PER-B.2022.1824.
35. Kristin O'Connell et al., "Faculty Change Agent Model: Cultivating Faculty to Catalyze Change," *Change: The Magazine of Higher Learning* 54, no. 3 (2022): 11–18.

36. "Ally Training and Education," Coast Community College District, accessed November 11, 2023, https://www.cccd.edu/employees/hr/equity/ate.html.
37. Zheng, *DEI Deconstructed*, 19.
38. Janine Graziano and Gabrielle Kahn, "Sustained Faculty Development in Learning Communities," *Learning Communities: Research & Practice* 1, no. 2 (2013): 5.
39. O'Connell et al., "Faculty Change Agent Model."
40. Seth H. Miller et al., "Faculty-Led Professional Development: Designing Effective Workshops to Facilitate Change," *New Directions for Community Colleges* 2022, no. 199 (2022): 149–61.
41. Frank Dobbin and Alexandra Kalev, "Why Diversity Programs Fail," *Harvard Business Review* 94, no. 7 (2016).
42. Dobbin and Kalev, "Why Diversity Programs Fail."
43. Kathleen M. Brown and Haim Shaked, *Preparing Future Leaders for Social Justice: Bridging Theory and Practice Through a Transformative Andragogy*, 2nd ed. (Lanham, MD: Rowman & Littlefield, 2018), 83.
44. Jack Mezirow, *Transformative Dimensions of Adult Learning* (San Francisco: Jossey-Bass, 1991).
45. Mezirow, *Transformative Dimensions of Adult Learning*, 198.
46. Derald Wing Sue and Lisa Spanierman, *Microaggressions in Everyday Life*, 2nd ed. (Hoboken, NJ: Wiley, 2020).
47. Sue and Spanierman, *Microaggressions in Everyday Life*.
48. Sue and Spanierman, *Microaggressions in Everyday Life*.
49. Jennifer Y. Kim and Alyson Meister, "Microaggressions, Interrupted: The Experience and Effects of Gender Microaggressions for Women in STEM," *Journal of Business Ethics* 185, no. 3 (2022): 513–31, https://doi.org/10.1007/s10551-022-05203-0.
50. Arathi Krishna and Devi Soumyaja, "Exploring the Escalation Process of Academic Bullying," *Journal of Higher Education Theory and Practice* 22, no. 11 (2022): 79–88.
51. Leah P. Hollis, "Spirit Murdering and Mobbing Working Strategies for Underrepresented Minority Faculty Survivors of Academic Workplace Bullying," *Taboo: The Journal of Culture & Education* 22, no. 3 (2023): 6–20.
52. Josh Moody, "Connecticut College President Resigns Under Pressure," *Inside Higher Education*, March 26, 2023, https://www.insidehighered.com/news/2023/03/27/connecticut-college-president-resigns-under-pressure.
53. Sara Weissman, "Administrator's Suicide Leaves Campus Reeling with 'Despair' and 'Disappointment,'" *Insider Higher Ed*, January 12, 2024, https://www.insidehighered.com/news/governance/executive-leadership/2024/01/12/lincoln-university-administrators-suicide-roils.
54. "Anti-bullying Policy," Highland Community College, April 18, 2022, https://highland.edu/cougar-corner/anti-bullying-policy/.
55. Magdalena Martinez and Deanna Cooper, "Practitioner Reflection: Equity-Minded Leadership Perspectives for Community Colleges," in *Higher Education Administration for Social Justice and Equity*, ed. Adrianna Kezar and Julie Posselt (New York: Routledge, 2020), 240.
56. Martinez and Cooper, "Practitioner Reflection."
57. Gail T. Fairhurst, *The Power of Framing: Creating the Language of Leadership* (San Francisco: Jossey-Bass, 2011).
58. Peter I. De Costa, Lee Her, and Vashti Lee, "Weaponizing and De-weaponizing Antiracist Discourse: Some Things for Language Educators to Consider," *International Journal of Literacy, Culture, and Language Education* 2 (2022): 98–107, https://doi.org/10.14434/ijlcle.v2iMay.34393.

Chapter 5

1. Xueli Wang et al., "Stated Value, Renewed Commitment? Community and Technical Colleges' Response to Racial (In)equities During COVID-19," *Journal of Higher Education* (2023): 1–25, https://doi.org/10.1080/00221546.2023.2251865.
2. Victor Ray, "A Theory of Racialized Organizations," *American Sociological Review* 84, no. 1 (2019): 26–53, https://doi.org/10.1177/0003122418822335; Heather N. McCambly et al., "Community Colleges as Racialized Organizations: Outlining Opportunities for Equity," *Community College Review* 51, no. 4 (2023): 658–79.
3. James M. Kouzes and Barry Z. Posner, *The Leadership Challenge*, 6th ed. (Hoboken, NJ: Wiley, 2017).
4. Edgar H. Schein, *Humble Inquiry: The Gentle Art of Asking Instead of Telling* (Oakland, CA: Berrett-Koehler, 2013).
5. Lily Zheng, *DEI Deconstructed: Your No-Nonsense Guide to Doing the Work and Doing It Right* (Oakland, CA: Berrett-Koehler, 2023).
6. Zheng, *DEI Deconstructed*, 206.
7. Zheng, *DEI Deconstructed*, 215.
8. Zheng, *DEI Deconstructed*, 223.
9. John P. Kotter, *Leading Change* (Boston, MA: Harvard Business Review Press, 2012).
10. Kotter, *Leading Change.*
11. "Center for Equity & Social Justice," Housatonic Community College, accessed October 1, 2023, https://housatonic.edu/equity-center.
12. Etienne Wenger-Trayner and Beverly Wenger-Trayner, *Learning to Make a Difference: Value Creation in Social Learning Spaces* (Cambridge: Cambridge University Press, 2020).
13. Adrianna Kezar, Sean Gehrke, and Samantha Bernstein-Sierra, "Designing for Success in STEM Communities of Practice: Philosophy and Personal Interactions," *Review of Higher Education* 40, no. 2 (2017): 217–44, https://doi.org/10.1353/rhe.2017.0002; Wenger-Trayner and Wenger-Trayner, *Learning to Make a Difference.*
14. Iris Marion Young, *Responsibility for Justice* (New York: Oxford University Press, 2011), 105.
15. Young, *Responsibility for Justice*, 52.
16. Daniel Coyle, *The Culture Code: The Secrets of Highly Successful Groups* (New York: Bantam, 2018).
17. Marwa El Zein, Bahador Bahrami, and Ralph Hertwig, "Shared Responsibility in Collective Decisions," *Nature Human Behaviour* 3, no. 6 (2019): 554–59.
18. Urie Bronfenbrenner, *The Ecology of Human Development* (Cambridge, MA: Harvard University Press, 1979).
19. Deepa Iyer, *Social Change Now: A Guide for Reflection and Connection* (Washington, DC: Thick, 2022).
20. Iyer, *Social Change Now*; Zheng, *DEI Deconstructed*; Estela Mara Bensimon and Anna Neumann, *Redesigning Collegiate Leadership: Teams and Teamwork in Higher Education* (Baltimore, MD: Johns Hopkins University Press, 1993).
21. Zheng, *DEI Deconstructed*, 174.
22. Debra E. Meyerson and Maureen A. Scully, "Tempered Radicalism and the Politics of Ambivalence and Change," *Organization Science* 6, no. 5 (1995): 585–600, https://doi.org/10.1287/orsc.6.5.585.
23. Debra E. Meyerson, "The Tempered Radicals," *Stanford Social Innovation Review* 2, no. 2 (2004): 17.
24. Meyerson, "The Tempered Radicals," 17.

Acknowledgments

The process of writing a book has its ebbs and flows. The genesis of this book started with a conversation that Pam had with Jayne Fargnoli from Harvard Education Press at an American Educational Research Association meeting in Toronto in 2019. The conversation revolved around the idea of how to bring the voices of community college leaders into the center of a story that highlighted the complexity of the work occurring on these campuses across the nation. The many crises of 2020 solidified the idea of centering this narrative on equity and social justice. The book you hold in your hands tells a story of how to think about developing equity-driven community college leaders, and we are grateful to Jayne for opening a pathway for us to highlight this work and to Molly Cerrone for her editorial feedback and guidance.

We recognize that as white women, our positionality provides a certain window into equity work, and we strove to remind ourselves of the influence of our assumptions and experiences in how we interpreted our data and how we heard the stories leaders shared in their survey responses and interviews. We drew on the research of community college equity scholars to ground our perspectives. Eboni Zamani-Gallaher, Lorenzo Baber, Eric Felix, Ángel de Jesus González, and Erin Doran have provided profound foundational scholarship in the field of equity and social justice, which we found invaluable in our own work. Read them, cite them.

The Belk Center for Community College Leadership and Research team of Roshaunda Breeden, Micara Lewis-Sessoms, and Jorge Burmicky were conducting equity case studies on rural community colleges with Pam during the writing of this book, and this research helped expand our thinking about how to create a blueprint to develop community college leaders to do the work of equity on campuses. Seeing firsthand what leaders face in advancing equity on campus—what works, where challenges emerge, and how campus members work together—provided valuable insights that informed our thinking.

We recognize the foundation that Marilyn Amey provided to us during our graduate program at Michigan State University. Learning from her how to think about leadership and organizations, especially community colleges, established our writing careers in this area. Using survey data Marilyn collected, we wrote our first coauthored article on community colleges in 2006 in the *Community College Review* ("Emerging Definitions of Leadership in Higher Education: New Visions of Leadership or Same Old 'Hero' Leader?"). Marilyn has been figuratively sitting on our shoulders during our writing time over the past year, and we owe her a debt of gratitude.

An early conversation with Julie White, the district chancellor and CEO of Pierce College, helped us in designing our survey and compiling questions for our interviews with midlevel leaders and leaders of diversity, equity, and inclusion centers. Likewise, our thanks go to Catherine Hartman, who collaborated with us extensively throughout our work on this book. She helped with survey design, coauthored publications emerging from the 2016 National Survey of Community College Leaders, and served as a valued thought partner in writing this volume.

Finally, we give thanks to the William & Mary graduate students Sharice Adkins, Samantha Easby, and Melissa Allen, who gathered email addresses for the surveys, conducted interviews, and provided sundry other forms of support over the past three years. A special shout-out goes to Melissa Allen for her help turning handwritten drawings into many of the models presented in this book.

About the Authors

Pamela L. Eddy is the associate provost of Faculty Affairs and Faculty Development and a professor of higher education in Educational Policy, Planning, and Leadership at William & Mary. Her research interests include community college leadership and development, organizational change and educational partnerships, gender roles in higher education, and faculty development.

Dr. Eddy serves as a consultant for campuses, system offices, and on funded grants regarding strategies to support community college student success and to promote leadership development. Dr. Eddy has authored six books and edited seven others. Her most recent book, with Betty Kirby, is titled *Leading for Tomorrow: A Primer for Succeeding in Higher Education Leadership* (2020). She is the editor-in-chief of *New Directions for Community Colleges* and serves on the editorial boards of the *Community College Journal of Research and Practice*, the *Journal of Women and Gender in Higher Education*, and *Innovative Higher Education*. She received the 2006 Emerging Scholar Award and the 2013 Senior Scholar Award from the Council for the Study of Community Colleges. Dr. Eddy was recognized with a 2021 Outstanding Faculty Award from the State Council of Higher Education for Virginia and the 2023 Association for the Study of Higher Education Mentoring Award. Dr. Eddy also received the 2011 Plumeri Award for Faculty Excellence at William & Mary. She was a Fulbright Scholar in Dublin, Ireland, in 2009 and continues her research on partnerships there.

Dr. Eddy received her PhD in Higher, Adult, and Lifelong Education from Michigan State University, her MS from Cornell University, and her BS in economics from Allegheny College.

Kim E. VanDerLinden is the director of Interdisciplinary Social Sciences Programs at the University at Buffalo (SUNY). She also serves as an adjunct instructor in the Educational Policy, Planning, and Leadership Department at William & Mary.

Her scholarship focuses on assessment strategies and organizational processes that support student success, as well as administrative leadership in community colleges and how data-driven leadership can transform higher education.

Dr. VanDerLinden has held faculty positions at St. John Fisher University in the Executive Leadership Program and at Northern Arizona University in the Educational Leadership Department. She has also held administrative positions in assessment and institutional research at the University of Utah and at the College of DuPage in Glen Ellyn, Illinois.

Dr. VanDerLinden has presented at more than one hundred conferences and regularly conducts on-campus workshops on assessment in higher education and program evaluation. She has published in *Research in Higher Education*, the *Community College Review*, and the *Community College Journal of Research and Practice*.

She holds a PhD in Higher, Adult, and Lifelong Education from Michigan State University, an MEd from Pennsylvania State University, and a BA from Nazareth College.

Index